Let the Nations be Glad!

The supremacy of God in missions

John Piper

Inter-Varsity Press

INTER-VARSITY PRESS
38 De Montfort Street, Leicester LE1 7GP, England

First British edition 1994

British Library Cataloguing in Publication Data
A catalogue record for this book is available from the British Library.

ISBN 0-85110-990-X

Typeset in Great Britain by Parker Typesetting Service
Printed in Great Britain by Cox & Wyman Ltd, Reading

Inter-Varsity Press is the book-publishing division of the Universities and Colleges Christian Fellowship (formerly the Inter-Varsity Fellowship), a student movement linking Christian Unions in universities and colleges throughout the United Kingdom and the Republic of Ireland, and a member movement of the International Fellowship of Evangelical Students. For information about local and national activities write to UCCF, 38 De Montfort Street, Leicester LE1 7GP.

Let the Nations be Glad!

Other IVP books by John Piper

Desiring God: Meditations of a Christian Hedonist
The Supremacy of God in Preaching

Contents

Dedicated to
Tom Steller
in the precious partnership of
worship, prayer, and suffering
for the supremacy of God

Preface

This book is a partial payment of a debt I owe to the nations. The apostle Paul is not alone in saying, "I am a debtor to the Greeks and to the Barbarians, to the wise and to the foolish" (Romans 1:14). To those culturally near me and those culturally far I am a debtor. Not because they gave me anything that I must pay back, but because God gave me what can't be paid back. He gave me the all-satisfying pleasure of knowing him and being loved by him through his Son Jesus Christ.

What makes a debt a debt is that if you don't pay it, you lose a possession. They take back your house or your car. And the more precious the possession, the more urgent the payment of the debt. If I don't do my utmost to show the nations "the light of the knowledge of the glory of God in the face of Christ," I will in effect be saying, "It is not infinitely valuable. It is not absolutely necessary for eternal life. It is not great enough to satisfy the deepest needs in every culture on earth. And its beauty has not freed me to be a man for others." But if I say this, then I do not believe in "the surpassing worth of knowing Christ Jesus my Lord". And if I do not believe, I lose everything. Therefore I am a debtor. For I would rather lose anything and anyone on earth, than to lose Christ.

But the debt is not onerous. It requires living in the light and singing in the night. "I will give thanks to you, O LORD, among the peoples; I will *sing* praises to you among the nations" (Psalm 57:9). It is not onerous to live in the love of God and sing his glory among the nations. It may be dangerous. But it is not onerous. It may cost us our lives, but it will not cost us our joy. We may lose all the world, but we will not lose Christ.

So it is a debt to the nations that I discharge with joy. If this book inspires missionaries to go and sing of God among the nations, I will be glad. Believing that my life counts for this, is one of the main ways God keeps me going in the pastorate in America. It is not easy to stay in a metropolitan area where there may be more churches than there are missionaries in the world working among 1.7 billion Hindus, Buddhists and Muslims who do not believe in Christ.

I have said to the missionaries of our church, "Your devotion has a tremendous power in my life. Your leaving is a means of my staying. Your strengths make up for my weaknesses. Your absence empowers my presence. So I thank God for you. May God make the reciprocity of our motivation more and more effective in the years to come."

But this book is not just for missionaries. It's for pastors who (like me) want to connect their fragile, momentary, local labors to God's invincible, eternal, global purposes. It's for lay people who want a bigger motivation for being world Christians than they get from statistics. It's for college and seminary classes on the theology of missions that really want to be *theo*logical as well as anthropological, methodological and technological. And it's for leaders who need the flickering wick of their vocation fanned into flame again with a focus on *the supremacy of God in missions*.

Thanks to Carol Steinbach (again!) for good editorial suggestions and for the text and person indexes. The superfluous notes of encouragement in the margins meant more than you know. Thanks to Maria denBoer at Baker for shepherding the book through the press. Thanks to my wife Noël for two meticulous readings, and for being a single parent for the month of May. You have said yes to every dream. Thanks to Bethlehem Baptist Church for a writing leave to finish the book, and for going hard after God in missions.

And, finally, a word to Tom Steller, my associate for 13 years. God has knit our souls together in profound ways. Your engagement with God in worship has brought me in when I was languishing. Your fervor in prayer has breathed fire into my smoldering flax. Your patience in suffering has brought strength out of weakness. "Owe no one anything except to love one another", says the apostle. I will then gladly be your debtor as long as we live – to make the nations glad in the glory of God.

Part one

Making God supreme in missions

The purpose, the power, and the price

1
The supremacy of God in missions through worship

Missions is not the ultimate goal of the church. Worship is. Missions exists because worship doesn't. Worship is ultimate, not missions, because God is ultimate, not man. When this age is over, and the countless millions of the redeemed fall on their faces before the throne of God, missions will be no more. It is a temporary necessity. But worship abides forever.

Worship, therefore, is the fuel and goal in missions. It's the goal of missions because in missions we simply aim to bring the nations into the white-hot enjoyment of God's glory. The goal of missions is the gladness of the peoples in the greatness of God. "The LORD reigns; let the earth *rejoice*; let the many coastlands *be glad*!" (Psalm 97:1). "Let the peoples praise thee, O God; let all the peoples praise thee! Let the nations *be glad and sing for joy*!" (Psalm 67:3–4).

But worship is also the fuel of missions. Passion for God in worship precedes the offer of God in preaching. You can't commend what you don't cherish. Missionaries will never call out, "Let the nations *be glad*!", who cannot say from the heart, "*I rejoice* in the LORD . . . *I will be glad and exult in thee*, I will sing praise to thy name, O Most High" (Psalm 104:34; 9:2). Missions begins and ends in worship.

If the pursuit of *God*'s glory is not ordered above the pursuit of *man*'s good in the affections of the heart and the priorities of the church, *man* will not be well served and *God* will not be duly honored. I am not pleading for a diminishing of missions but for a magnifying of God. When the flame of worship burns with the heat of God's true worth, the light of missions will shine to the most remote peoples on earth. And I long for that day to come!

Where passion for God is weak, zeal for missions will be weak. Churches that are not centered on the exaltation of the majesty and beauty of God will scarcely kindle a fervent desire to "declare *his glory* among the nations" (Psalm 96:3). Even outsiders feel the disparity between the boldness of our claim upon the nations and the blandness of our engagement with God.

Albert Einstein's indictment

For example, Charles Misner, a scientific specialist in general relativity theory, expressed Albert Einstein's skepticism over the church with words that should waken us to the shallowness of our experience with God in worship:

> The design of the universe ... is very magnificent and shouldn't be taken for granted. In fact, I believe that is why Einstein had so little use for organized religion, although he strikes me as a basically very religious man. *He must have looked at what the preachers said about God and felt that they were blaspheming. He had seen much more majesty than they had ever imagined, and they were just not talking about the real thing.* My guess is that he simply felt that religions he'd run across did not have proper respect ... for the author of the universe.[1]

The charge of blasphemy is loaded. The point is to pack a wallop behind the charge that in our worship services God simply doesn't come through for who he is. He is unwittingly belittled. For those who are stunned by the indescribable magnitude of what God has made, not to mention the infinite greatness of the One who made it, the steady diet on Sunday morning of practical "how to's" and psychological soothing and relational therapy and tactical planning seem dramatically out of touch with Reality – the God of overwhelming greatness.

It is possible to be distracted from God in trying to serve God. Martha-like, we neglect the one thing needful, and soon begin to present God as busy and fretful. A. W. Tozer warned us about this: "We commonly represent God as a busy, eager, somewhat frustrated Father hurrying about seeking help to carry out His benevolent plan to bring peace and salvation to the world. . . . Too many missionary appeals are based upon this fancied frustration of Almighty God."[2]

Scientists know that light travels at the speed of 5.87

trillion miles a year. They also know that the galaxy of which our solar system is a part is about 100,000 light-years in diameter – about five hundred and eighty-seven thousand trillion miles. It is one of about a million such galaxies in the optical range of our most powerful telescopes. In our galaxy there are about 100 billion stars. The sun is one of them, a modest star burning at about 6,000 degrees Centigrade on the surface, and traveling in an orbit at 155 miles per second, which means it will take about 200 million years to complete a revolution around the galaxy.

Scientists know these things and are awed by them. And they say, "If there is a personal God, as the Christians say, who spoke this universe into being, then there is a certain respect and reverence and wonder and dread that would have to come through when we talk about him and when we worship him."

We who believe the Bible know this even better than the scientists because we have heard something even more amazing.

> "To whom then will you compare me, that I should be like him?" says the Holy One. Lift up your eyes on high and see: who created these [stars]? He who brings out their host by number, calling them all by name; by the greatness of his might, and because he is strong in power not one is missing. (Isaiah 40:25–26)

Every one of the billions of stars in the universe is there by God's specific appointment. He knows their number. And, most astonishing of all, he knows them by name. They do his bidding as his personal agents. When we feel the weight of this grandeur in the heavens, we have only touched the hem of his garment. "Lo, these are but the outskirts of his ways! And how small a whisper do we hear of him" (Job 26:14). That is why we cry, "Be exalted, O God, *above* the heavens!" (Psalm 57:5). God is the absolute reality that everyone in the universe must come to terms with. Everything depends utterly on his will. All other realities compare to him like a raindrop compares to the ocean, or like an anthill compares to Mount Everest. To ignore him or belittle him is unintelligible and suicidal folly. How shall one ever be the emissary of this great God who has not trembled before him with joyful wonder?

The second greatest activity in the world

The most crucial issue in missions is the centrality of God in the life of the church. Where people are not stunned by the greatness of God, how can they be sent with the ringing message, "*Great* is the LORD and *greatly* to be praised; he is to be feared above all gods!" (Psalm 96:4)? Missions is not first and ultimate: God is. And these are not just words. This truth is the lifeblood of missionary inspiration and endurance. William Carey, the father of modern missions, who set sail for India from England in 1793, expressed the connection:

> When I left England, my hope of India's conversion was very strong; but amongst so many obstacles, it would die, unless upheld by God. Well, I have God, and His Word is true. Though the superstitions of the heathen were a thousand times stronger than they are, and the example of the Europeans a thousand times worse; though I were deserted by all and persecuted by all, yet my faith, fixed on the sure Word, would rise above all obstructions and overcome every trial. God's cause will triumph.[3]

Carey and thousands like him have been moved by the vision of a great and triumphant God. That vision must come first. Savoring it in worship precedes spreading it in missions. All of history is moving toward one great goal, the white-hot worship of God and his Son among all the peoples of the earth. Missions is not that goal. It is the means. And for that reason it is the second greatest human activity in the world.

God's passion for God is the foundation for ours

One of the things God uses to make this truth take hold of a person and a church is the stunning realization that it is also true for God himself. Missions is not *God's* ultimate goal, worship is. And when this sinks into a person's heart everything changes. The world is often turned on its head. And everything looks different – including the missionary enterprise.

The ultimate foundation for our passion to see God glorified is his own passion to be glorified. God is central and supreme in his own affections. There are no rivals for the supremacy of God's glory in his own heart. God is not an idolater. He does not disobey the first and great commandment. With all his heart and soul and strength and mind he delights in the glory of his manifold perfections.[4] The most passionate heart for God in all the universe is God's heart.

This truth, more than any other I know, seals the conviction that worship is the fuel and goal of missions. The deepest reason why our passion for God should *fuel* missions is that God's passion for God fuels missions. Missions is the overflow of our delight in God because missions is the overflow of God's delight in being God. And the deepest reason why worship is the *goal* in missions is that worship is God's goal. We are confirmed in this goal by the Biblical record of God's relentless pursuit of praise among the nations. "Praise the LORD, all nations! Extol him, all peoples!" (Psalm 117:1). If it is God's goal it must be our goal.

The chief end of God is to glorify God and enjoy himself for ever

All my years of preaching and teaching on the supremacy of God in the heart of God have proved that this truth hits most people like a truck laden with unknown fruit. If they survive the impact, they discover that it is the most luscious fruit on the planet. I have unpacked this truth with lengthy arguments in other places.[5] So here I will just give a brief overview of the Biblical basis. What I am claiming is that the answer to the first question of the Westminster Catechism is the same when asked concerning God as it is when asked concerning man. Question: "What is the chief end of man?" Answer: "The chief end of man is to glorify God and enjoy him for ever." Question: "What is the chief end of God?" Answer: "The chief end of God is to glorify God and enjoy himself for ever."

Another way to say it is simply, God is righteous. The opposite of righteousness is to value and enjoy what is not truly valuable or rewarding. This is why people are called

15

unrighteous in Romans 1:18. They suppress the truth of God's value and exchange God for created things. So they belittle God and discredit his worth. Righteousness is the opposite. It means recognizing true value for what it is and esteeming it and enjoying it in proportion to its true worth. The unrighteous in 2 Thessalonians 2:10 perish because they refuse to *love* the truth. The righteous, then, are those who welcome a *love* for the truth. Righteousness is recognizing and welcoming and loving and upholding what is truly valuable.

God is righteous. This means that he recognizes, welcomes, loves and upholds with infinite jealousy and energy what is inifinitely valuable, namely, the worth of God. God's righteous passion and delight is to display and uphold his infinitely valuable glory. This is not a vague theological conjecture. It flows inevitably from dozens of Biblical texts that show God in the relentless pursuit of praise and honor from creation to consummation.

Probably no text in the Bible reveals the passion of God for his own glory more clearly and bluntly than Isaiah 48:9–11 where God says,

> *For my name's sake* I defer my anger, *for the sake of my praise* I restrain it for you, that I may not cut you off. Behold, I have refined you, but not like silver, I have tried you in the furnace of affliction. *For my own sake, for my own sake*, I do it, for *how should my name be profaned? My glory I will not give to another*.

I have found that for many people these words come like six hammer blows to a man-centred way of looking at the world:

> For *my* name's sake!
> For the sake of *my* praise!
> For *my* own sake!
> For *my* own sake!
> How should *my* name be profaned!
> *My* glory I will not give to another!

What this text hammers home to us is the centrality of God in his own affections. The most passionate heart for the glorification of God is God's heart. God's ultimate goal is to uphold and display the glory of his name.

Biblical texts to show God's zeal for his own glory

God chose his people for his glory:

> He chose us in him before the foundation of the world that we should be holy and blameless before him. He destined us in love to be his sons through Jesus Christ according to the purpose of his will *unto the praise of the glory of his grace.* (Ephesians 1:4–6; cf. vv. 12, 14)

God created us for his glory:

> Bring my sons from afar and my daughters from the end of the earth, every one who is called by my name, *whom I created for my glory.* (Isaiah 43:6–7)

God called Israel for his glory:

> You are my servant, Israel, in whom *I will be glorified.* (Isaiah 49:3)

> I made the whole house of Israel and the whole house of Judah cling to me, says the LORD, *that they might be for me a people, a name, a praise, and a glory.* (Jeremiah 13:11)

God rescued Israel from Egypt for his glory:

> Our fathers when they were in Egypt did not consider thy wonderful works . . . but rebelled against the Most High at the Red Sea. Yet he saved them *for his name's sake that he might make known his mighty power.* (Psalm 106:7–8)

God raised Pharaoh up to show his own power and glorify his own name:

> For the scripture says to Pharaoh, "I have raised you up for this very purpose of showing my power in you, so that my name may be proclaimed in all the earth." (Romans 9:17)

God defeated Pharaoh at the Red Sea to show his glory:

> And I will harden Pharaoh's heart, and he will pursue them and *I will get glory over Pharaoh* and all his host; and the Egyptians *shall know that I am the LORD.* . . . And *the Egyptians shall know that I am the LORD, when I have gotten glory* over

Pharaoh, his chariots, and his horsemen. (Exodus 14:4; cf. vv. 17, 18)

God spared Israel in the wilderness for the glory of his name:

> *I acted for the sake of my name, that it should not be profaned* in the sight of the nations in whose sight I had brought them out. (Ezekiel 20:14)

God gave Israel victory in Canaan for the glory of his name:

> What other nation on earth is like thy people Israel, whom God went to redeem to be his people, *making himself a name*, and doing for them great and terrible things, by driving out before his people a nation and its gods? (2 Samuel 7:23)

God did not cast away his people for the glory of his name:

> Fear not, you have done all this evil, yet do not turn aside from following the Lord ... For the LORD will not cast away his people *for his great name's sake*. (1 Samuel 12:20–22)

God saved Jerusalem from attack for the glory of his name:

> For I will defend this city to save it, *for my own sake* and for the sake of my servant David. (2 Kings 19:34; cf. 20:6)

God restored Israel from exile for the glory of his name:

> Thus says the LORD God, It is not for your sake, O house of Israel, that I am about to act, but *for the sake of my holy name* ... and the nations will know that I am the LORD. (Ezekiel 36:22–23, 32)

Jesus sought the glory of his Father in all he did:

> He who speaks on his own authority seeks his own glory; but *he who seeks the glory of him who sent him* is true, and in him there is no falsehood. (John 7:18)

Jesus told us to do good works so that God gets glory:

> Let your light so shine before men, that they may see your

good works and *give glory to your Father who is in heaven.*
(Matthew 5:16; cf. 1 Peter 2:12)

Jesus warned that not seeking God's glory makes faith impossible:

How can you believe who seek glory from one another and do not *seek the glory that comes from the only God?* (John 5:44)

Jesus said that he answers prayer so that God would be glorified:

Whatever you ask in my name, I will do it *that the Father may be glorified in the Son.* (John 14:13)

Jesus endured his final hours of suffering for God's glory:

"Now is my soul troubled. And what shall I say? 'Father, save me from this hour?' No, *for this purpose I have come to this hour. Father, glorify thy name.*" Then a voice came from heaven, "*I have glorified it, and I will glorify it again.*" (John 12:27, 28)

Father, the hour has come; *glorify thy Son that the Son may glorify thee.* (John 17:1; cf. 13:31–32)

God gave his Son to vindicate the glory of his righteousness:

God put Christ forward as a propitiation by his blood . . . *to demonstrate God's righteousness* . . . It was *to prove at the present time that he himself is righteous.* (Romans 3:25–26)

God forgives our sins for his own sake:

I, I am he who blots out your transgressions *for my own sake*, and I will not remember your sins. (Isaiah 43:25)

For *thy name's sake*, O Lᴏʀᴅ, pardon my guilt, for it is great. (Psalm 25:11)

Jesus receives us into his fellowship for the glory of God:

Welcome one another, therefore, as Christ has welcomed you, *for the glory of God.* (Romans 15:7)

The ministry of the Holy Spirit is to glorify the Son of God:

He will glorify me, for he will take what is mine and declare it to you. (John 16:14)

God instructs us to do everything for his glory:

> So whether you eat or drink, or whatever you do, *do all to the glory of God*. (1 Corinthians 10:31; cf. 6:20)

God tells us to serve in a way that will glorify him:

> Whoever renders service [let him do it] as one who renders it by the strength which God supplies; *in order that in everything God may be glorified* through Jesus Christ. To him belong glory and dominion forever and ever. Amen. (1 Peter 4:11)

Jesus will fill us with fruits of righteousness for God's glory:

> It is my prayer ... that you be filled with the fruits of righteousness which come through Jesus Christ *to the glory and praise of God*. (Philippians 1:11)

All are under judgment for dishonoring God's glory:

> They became fools and *exchanged the glory of the immortal God for images*. (Romans 1:23).

> For *all have fallen short of the glory of God*. (Romans 3:23)

Herod is struck dead because he did not give glory to God:

> Immediately an angel of the Lord smote him because *he did not give glory to God*. (Acts 12:23)

Jesus is coming again for the glory of God:

> Those who do not obey the gospel will suffer the punishment of eternal destruction and exclusion from the presence of the Lord and from the glory of his might, when he comes on that day *to be glorified in his saints and to be marveled at in all who have believed*. (2 Thessalonians 1:9–10)

Jesus' ultimate aim for us is that we see and enjoy his glory:

> Father, I desire that they also, whom thou hast given me, may be with me where I am, *to behold my glory*, which thou hast given me in thy love for me before the foundation of the world. (John 17:24)

Even in wrath God's aim is to make known the wealth of his glory:

> Desiring to show his wrath and make known his power, he

endured with much patience the vessels of wrath prepared for destruction, *in order to make known the riches of his glory* for the vessels of mercy which he prepared beforehand for glory. (Romans 9:22–23)

God's plan is to fill the earth with the knowledge of his glory:

For the earth will be filled with *the knowledge of the glory of the Lord* as the waters cover the sea. (Habakkuk 2:14)

Everything that happens will redound to God's glory:

From him, to him and through him are all things. *To him be glory for ever*. Amen. (Romans 11:36)

In the New Jerusalem the glory of God replaces the sun:

And the city has no need of sun or moon to shine upon it, for *the glory of God is its light*, and its lamp is the lamb. (Revelation 21:23)

God's passion for God is unmistakable. God struck me with this most powerfully when I first read Jonathan Edwards' book entitled *A Dissertation Concerning the End for Which God Created the World*. There he piles reason upon reason and scripture on scripture to show this truth: "The great end of God's works, which is so variously expressed in Scripture, is indeed but ONE; and this *one* end is most properly and comprehensively called, THE GLORY OF GOD."[6] In other words, the chief end of God is to glorify God, and enjoy himself for ever.

The belittling of God's glory, and the horrors of hell

The condition of the human heart throws God's God-centeredness into stark relief. Man by nature does not have a heart to glorify God. "All have sinned and *fall short of God's glory*" (Romans 3:23). In our wickedness we suppress the truth that God is our Sovereign and worthy of all our allegiance and affection. By nature we exchange the glory of the immortal God for dim images of it in creation (Romans 1:18, 23). We forsake the fountain of living waters and hew out for ourselves broken cisterns that can hold no water (Jeremiah 2:13).

The nations "are darkened in their understanding, alienated from the life of God because of the ignorance that is in them, due to their hardness of heart" (Ephesians 4:18). By nature we were all once dead in trespasses and sins following the slave master Satan, and therefore children of wrath (Ephesians 2:1–3). Our end was "eternal punishment" (Matthew 25:46), and "exclusion from the presence of the Lord's glory" (2 Thessalonians 1:9), and endless torments in "the second death which is the lake of fire" (Revelation 14:11; 20:10; 21:8).[7]

The infinite horrors of hell are intended by God to be a vivid demonstration of the infinite value of the glory of God. The Biblical assumption of the justice of hell is a clear testimony to the infiniteness of the sin of failing to glorify God. All of us have failed. All the nations have failed. Therefore the weight of infinite guilt rests on every human head because of our failure to cherish the glory of God. The Biblical vision of God, then, is that he is supremely committed, with infinite passion, to uphold and display the glory of his name. And the Biblical vision of man without grace is that he suppresses this truth and by nature finds more joy in his own glory than he does in God's. God exists to be worshipped, but man worships the work of his own hands. This two-fold reality creates the critical need for missions. And the very God-centeredness of God, which creates the crisis, also creates the solution.

How can self-exaltation be love?

For over twenty years I have tried to present to Christians in various places this central Biblical truth of God's passion for the glory of God. The major objection has been that it seems to make God unloving. The merciful, kind, loving heart of God seems to disappear in the passions of an overweening ego. Doesn't the Bible say, "Love seeks not its own" (1 Corinthians 13:5)? How then can God be loving and seek his own glory? It's a good question. And in answering it we will see how the supremacy of God in the heart of God is the spring of mercy and kindness and love – which means the spring of missions.

There are two ways to see harmony between God's

passion for his own glory and Paul's statement, "Love seeks not its own." One is to say that Paul doesn't mean that *every* way of seeking your own is wrong. Some ways are and some ways aren't. The other is to say that God is unique, and that Paul's statement does not apply to him the way it does to us. I think both of these are true.

Love seeks its own joy in the joy of others

First, "Love seeks not its own" was not meant by Paul to condemn every possible way of "seeking your own". He did not mean, for example, that if doing good for someone happens to make you happy it ceases to be love. In other words, he did not mean that seeking your own happiness in loving others is loveless. We know this because in Acts 20:35 Paul told the elders of the church of Ephesus to "*remember*" the word of the Lord Jesus: "It is more blessed to give than to receive." If it were unloving to be motivated by the blessedness of loving, then Paul would not have told the elders to "*remember*" this word, that is, to keep it in their mind where it could function as a conscious motive. If seeking your own blessing in giving to others ruined the act, Paul would not have told us to keep this blessing in mind.

Those who have thought most deeply about motivation realize this and have interpreted Paul's words in 1 Corinthians 13:5 with great wisdom. For example, Jonathan Edwards pointed out that what Paul is opposing in the words, "Love seeks not its own" is not

> the degree in which [a person] loves his own happiness, but in his placing his happiness where he ought not, and in limiting and confining his love. Some, although they love their own happiness, do not place that happiness in their own confined good, or in that good which is limited to themselves, but more in the common good – in that which is the good of others, or in the good to be enjoyed in and by others . . . And when it is said that *Charity seeketh not her own*, we are to understand it of her own private good – good limited to herself.[8]

In other words, Paul did not mean to condemn every possible way of seeking your own. He had in mind the selfish

23

attitude that finds its happiness not in helping others but in using others or ignoring others for personal gain. He did not have in mind the attitude that *seeks its own* joy precisely in doing good to others. In fact he appeals to that motive two verses earlier when he says, "If I give away all I have, and deliver my body to be burned, and have not love, *I gain nothing*" (1 Corinthians 13:3). He is saying, "Surely you do not want to 'gain nothing', do you? Well then, be sure that you love. Then you will gain much." So he actually appeals to the very motive that some say he is denouncing. But he is not appealing to low, selfish, materialistic motives. He is calling for the radical transformation of heart that finds its joy *in* the act of love and all the goodness that comes from it.

So the way is opened perhaps for God to "seek his own" and still be loving. But I said there are two ways to see harmony between God's passion for his own glory and Paul's statement, "Love seeks not its own." We've seen one: namely, that Paul is not opposing "seeking one's own" if "one's own" is really the good of others.

The sin of imitating God

Now the other way to see this harmony is to say that God is unique and that Paul's statement does not apply to him the way it does to us. This is true. Things are forbidden to us that are not forbidden to God precisely because we are not God and he is. The reason we are not to exalt our own glory, but God's, is because he is God and we are not. For God to be faithful to this same principle means that he too would exalt not our glory, but his. The unifying principle is not: don't exalt your own glory. The unifying principle is: exalt the glory of what is infinitely glorious. For us that means exalt God. And for God that means exalt God. For us it means *don't* seek your own glory. For God it means *do* seek your own glory.

This can be very slippery. Satan saw this and used it in the garden of Eden. He came with the temptation to Adam and Eve: If you eat from the forbidden tree, "you will be like God, knowing good and evil" (Genesis 3:5). Now what Adam and Eve should have said was, "We are already like

God. We have been created *in his image*" (Genesis 1:27). But instead of putting this truth against Satan's temptation, they allowed the truth to make error look plausible: "If we are in the image of God, then it can't be wrong to want to be like God. So the suggestion of the serpent that we will be like God can't be bad." So they ate.

But the problem is that it is *not* right for humans to try to be like God in every way. God's goodness makes some things right for him to do that are not right for us to do. In Adam and Eve's case it is God's right to decide for them what is good and what is evil, what is helpful and what is harmful. They are finite and do not have the wisdom to know all the factors to take into account in order to live a happy life. Only God knows all that needs to be known. Therefore humans have no right to be independent of God. Independent judgment about what is helpful and harmful is folly and rebellion. That was the temptation. And that was the essence of their disobedience.

The point is simply to illustrate that even though we are created in the image of God, and even though in some ways we are to "be imitators of God" (Ephesians 5:1), nevertheless it's a mistake to think that God does not have some rights that we do not have. A father wants his child to imitate his manners and courtesies and integrity, but does not want the child to imitate his authority, neither toward his parents nor toward his brothers and sisters.

Thus I conclude that it is right for God to do some things that we are forbidden to do. And one of those things is to exalt his own glory. He would be unrighteous not to do so since he would not be prizing what is infinitely valuable. He would be, in fact, an idolator if he esteemed as his infinite treasure something less precious than his own glory.

God is most glorified in us when we are most satisfied in him

But is it loving for God to exalt his own glory? Yes it is. And there are several ways to see this truth clearly. One way is to ponder this sentence: *God is most glorified in us when we are most satisfied in him*. This is perhaps the most important sentence in my theology. If it is true, then it becomes plain why God is loving when he seeks to exalt his glory in my life. For that would mean that he would seek to maximize my satisfaction in him, since he is most glorified in me when I am most satisfied in him. Therefore God's pursuit of his own glory is not at odds with my joy, and that means it is not unkind or unmerciful or unloving of him to seek his glory. In fact it means that the more passionate God is for his own glory the more passionate he is for my satisfaction in that glory. And therefore God's God-centeredness and God's love soar together.

Duty or delight in a hospital room?

To illustrate the truth that God is most glorified in us when we are most satisfied in him, consider what I might say on a pastoral visit when entering the hospital room of one of my people. They look up from their bed with a smile and say, "O, Pastor John, how good of you to come. What an encouragement." And suppose I lift my hand, as if to deflect the words, and say matter-of-factly, "Don't mention it. It's my duty as a pastor." Now what is wrong here? Why do we cringe at such a thoughtless pastoral statement? It *is* my duty. And duty is a good thing. So why does that statement do so much damage?

It damages because it does not honor the sick person. Why? Because delight confers more honor than duty does. Doing hospital visitation out of mere duty honors duty. Doing it out of delight honors the patients. And they feel that. The right pastoral response to the patient's greeting would have been: "It's a pleasure to be here. I'm glad I could come." Do you see the paradox here? Those two sentences would show that I am "seeking my own". "It's *my* pleasure to be here. *I'm* glad I could come." And yet the reason these statements are not selfish is that they confer honor on the patient, not on the pastor. When someone delights in you, you feel honored. When someone finds happiness in being around you, you feel treasured, appreciated, glorified. It is a loving thing to visit the sick because it makes you glad to be there.

This then is the answer to why God is not unloving to magnify his glory. God is glorified precisely when we are satisfied in him – when we delight in his presence, when we like to be around him, when we treasure his fellowship. This is an utterly life-changing discovery. It frees us to pursue our joy in God and God to pursue his glory in us. Because they are not two different pursuits. God is most glorified in us when we are most satisfied in him.

God's self-exaltation: signpost to human satisfaction

Therefore when we read hundreds of texts in the Bible that show God passionately exalting his own glory, we no longer hear them as the passions of an overweening, uncaring ego. We hear them as the rightful exaltation of One who is infinitely exalted, and we hear them as God's pursuit of our deepest satisfaction in him. God is utterly unique. He is the only being in the universe worthy of worship. Therefore when he exalts himself he thus directs people to true and lasting joy. "In your presence is fullness of joy; at your right hand are pleasures for evermore" (Psalm 16:11). But when we exalt ourselves we are distracting people from what will bring true and lasting joy. So for us to be loving we must exalt God, and for God to be loving he must exalt God. Love is helping people toward the greatest beauty and the highest value and the deepest satisfaction and the most lasting joy and the biggest reward and the most wonderful friendship and the most overwhelming worship – love is helping people toward God. We do this by pointing to the greatness of God. And God does it by pointing to the greatness of God.

God exalts himself in mercy

There is another way to see how God's passion for his own glory is loving. And here the connection between the supremacy of God and the cause of missions becomes explicit. The connection between missions and the supremacy of God is found in this sentence: The glory God seeks to magnify is supremely the glory of his mercy. The key text is Romans 15:8–9:

> I tell you that Christ became a servant to the circumcised [Jewish people] to show God's truthfulness, in order to

confirm the promises given to the patriarchs, and *in order that the nations might glorify God for his mercy*.

Notice three interlocking truths in these great missionary verses.

1. *Zeal for the glory of God motivates world missions*. Paul gives three reasons that Christ humbled himself as a servant and came into the world on that first great missionary journey from heaven to earth. First, "Christ became a servant . . . *to show God's truthfulness*." Second, he came "in order *to confirm [God's] promises*". Third, he came "in order that the nations *might glorify God* for his mercy".

In other words Christ was on a mission to magnify God. He came to show that *God* is truthful. He came to show that *God* is a promise-keeper. And he came to show that *God* is glorious. Jesus came into the world *for God's sake* – to certify *God*'s integrity; to vindicate *God*'s word; to magnify *God*'s glory. Since God sent his Son to do all this, it is plain that the primary motive of the first great mission to unreached peoples – the mission of Jesus from heaven – was God's zeal for the glory of God. That's the first truth from Romans 15:8–9: zeal for the glory of God motivates world missions.

2. *A servant spirit and a heart of mercy motivate world missions*. "Christ became a *servant* . . . in order that the nations might glorify God for his *mercy*." Christ became a servant . . . and Christ brought mercy. He was a servant not only in that he humbled himself to do what the Father wanted him to do at great cost to himself. He was also a servant in that he lived his life for the sake of extending mercy to the nations. During his lifetime he showed the connection between compassion and missions. We see this, for example, in Matthew 9:36–38:

> When Jesus saw the crowds, he had compassion for them, because they were harassed and helpless, like sheep without a shepherd. Then he said to his disciples, "The harvest is plentiful, but the laborers are few; pray therefore the Lord of the harvest to send out laborers into his harvest."

Jesus' compassion came to expression in the call to pray for more missionaries. From first to last mercy was moving missions in the life of Jesus.

And not only in his life, but also in his death. "You were *slain* and by your *blood* you ransomed men for God from every tribe and tongue and people and nation" (Revelation 5:9). Mercy was the very heart of Jesus' mission. No one deserved his mission. It was all mercy and all servanthood. That's the second truth from Romans 15:8–9: a servant spirit and a heart of mercy motivate world missions.

3. *The third truth is that the first and second truth are one truth.* Zeal for the glory of God and a servant heart of mercy for the nations are one. This is plain from the wording of verse 9: Christ came "in order that the nations might glorify God . . ." Yes! That was the passion of Christ, and it should be our passion – that the nations might love the glory of God and praise the glory of God. But the verse goes on: Christ came "that the nations might glorify God *for his mercy*". The motive of mercy and the motive of God's glory are not two different motives because the glory we want to see exalted among the nations is supremely the glory of God's mercy.

Mercy is the apex of God's glory the way the overflow of a fountain is the apex of the fountain's fullness. God is free to be merciful because he is full and utterly self-sufficient in himself. He has no deficiencies or needs or defects. He relies totally on himself for all that he is. He never had a beginning, nor underwent any process of improvement through some influence outside himself. The glory of his all-sufficiency overflows in the freedom of his mercy to the nations. Therefore extending God's mercy and exalting God's glory are one.[9]

A heart for the glory of God and a heart of mercy for the nations make a Christ-like missionary. These must be kept together. If we have no zeal for the glory of God our mercy becomes superficial, man-centered human improvement with no eternal significance. And if our zeal for the glory of God is not a revelling in his mercy, then our so-called zeal, in spite of all its protests, is out of touch with God and hypocritical (cf. Matthew 9:13).

He does everything for the praise of the glory of his grace

This wonderful agreement between God's passion to be glorified and his passion to be gracious is also strikingly evident in the first chapter of Ephesians. Three times Paul says that God is doing all his saving work "to the praise of his glory". And verse 6 makes clear that his glory is "the glory of his *grace*". Election, predestination, adoption, redemption, sealing by the Spirit, working all things according to the counsel of his will – God does all this to elicit praise for the glory of his grace. Verses 5–6: "He destined us in love to be his sons through Jesus Christ . . . *to the praise of the glory of his grace*." Verses 11–12: "We who first hoped in Christ have been destined and appointed to live *for the praise of his glory*." Verse 14: "You were sealed with the promised Holy Spirit which is the guarantee of our inheritance until we acquire possession of it, *to the praise of his glory*."

This is just what we saw in Romans 15:9. There the nations glorify God for his mercy. Here they praise God for his grace. In both cases God gets the glory and humans get the joy. So the more passionate God is for his glory the more passionate he is for meeting our need as sinners. Grace is our only hope, and the only hope of the nations. Therefore the more zealous God is for his grace to be glorified the more hope there is that missions will succeed.

In summary: the power of missions is worship

What we have been showing is that God's supremacy in his own heart is not unloving. It is, in fact, the fountain of love. God's full delight in his own perfections overflows in his merciful will to share that delight with the nations. We may reaffirm then the earlier truth that worship is the fuel and goal that drives us in missions, because it is the fuel and goal that drives God in missions. Missions flows from the fullness of God's passion for God and it aims at the participation of the nations in the very passion that he has for himself (cf. John 15:11; 17:13, 26; Matthew 25:21, 23). The power of the missionary enterprise is to be caught up into God's fuel and God's goal. And that means being caught up in worship.

Only one God works for people who wait for him

This remarkable vision of God as one who "exalts himself to show mercy" (Isaiah 30:18) impels world missions in more ways than one. One way we have not pondered is the sheer uniqueness of this God among all the gods of the nations. Isaiah realizes this and says, "From of old no one has heard or perceived by the ear, no eye has seen a God besides thee, who works for those who wait for him" (Isaiah 64:4). In other words, Isaiah is stunned that the greatness of God has the paradoxical effect that he does not need people to work for him, but rather magnifies himself by working for them, if they will renounce self-reliance and "wait for him".

Isaiah anticipated the words of Paul in Acts 17:25, "God is not served by human hands as though he needed anything, since he himself gives to all men life and breath and everything." The uniqueness at the heart of Christianity is the glory of God manifest in the freedom of grace. God is glorious because he does not need the nations to work for him. He is free to work for them. "The Son of man came not to be served but to serve and to give his life a ransom for many" (Mark 10:45). Missions is not a recruitment project for God's labor force. It is a liberation project from the heavy burdens and hard yokes of other gods (Matthew 11:28–30).

Isaiah says that such a God has not been seen or heard anywhere in the world. "From of old no one has heard or perceived by the ear, no eye has seen a God besides thee." What Isaiah sees everywhere he looks are gods who have to *be served* rather than serve. For example, the Babylonian gods Bel and Nebo:

> Bel bows down, Nebo stoops, their idols are on beasts and cattle; these things you carry are loaded as burdens on weary beasts. They stoop, they bow down together, they cannot save the burden, but themselves go into captivity. "Hearken to me, O house of Jacob, all the remnant of the house of Israel, who have been borne by me from your birth, carried from the womb; even to your old age I am he, and to gray hairs I will carry you. I have made, and I will bear; I will carry and will save." (Isaiah 46:1–4; cf. Jeremiah 10:5)

The difference between the true God and the gods of the nations is that the true God carries and the other gods must be carried. God serves, they must be served. God glorifies his might by showing mercy. They glorify theirs by gathering slaves. So the vision of God as one whose passion for his glory moves him to mercy impels missions because he is utterly unique among all the gods.

The most shareable message in the world

There is yet another way that such a God motivates the missionary enterprise. The gospel demand that flows from such a God to the nations is an eminently shareable, do-able demand, namely to rejoice and be glad in God. "The LORD reigns; let the earth *rejoice*; let the many coastlands *be glad*!" (Psalm 97:1). "Let the peoples praise thee, O God; let all the peoples praise thee! Let the nations *be glad and sing for joy*!" (Psalm 67:3–4). "Let the oppressed see it and *be glad*; you who seek God, *let your hearts revive*" (Psalm 69:32). "Let all who seek thee *rejoice and be glad in thee*! May those who love thy salvation say evermore, God is great!" (Psalm 70:4). What message would missionaries rather take than the message: Be glad in God! Rejoice in God! Sing for joy in God! For God is most glorified in you when you are most satisfied in him! God loves to exalt himself by showing mercy to sinners.

The liberating fact is that the message we take to the frontiers is that people everywhere should seek their own best interest. We are summoning people to God. And those who come say, "In your presence is fullness of joy and at your right hand are pleasures for evermore" (Psalm 16:11). God glorifies himself among the nations with the command, "Delight yourself in the LORD!" (Psalm 37:4). His first and great requirement of all men everywhere is that they repent from seeking their joy in other things and begin to seek it only in him. A God who cannot be served[10] is a God who can only be enjoyed. The great sin of the world is not that the human race has failed to work for God so as to *increase* his glory, but that we have failed to delight in God so as to *reflect* his glory. For God's glory is most reflected in us when we are most delighted in him.

The most exhilarating thought in the world is that God's inexorable purpose to display his glory in the mission of the church is virtually the same as his purpose to give his people infinite delight. The glory of a mountain spring is seen in how many people (and how many different peoples!) find satisfaction and life in its overflowing streams. Therefore God is committed to the holy joy of the redeemed, gathered from every tribe and tongue and people and nation, with the same zeal that moves him to seek his own glory in all that he does. The supremacy of God in the heart of God is the driving force of his mercy and the missionary movement of his church.

Biblical expressions of the supremacy of God in missions

Against the background we have developed so far we may now be able to feel the full force of those Biblical texts that emphasize the supremacy of God in the missionary impulse of the church. The motives we see will confirm the centrality of God in the missionary vision of the Bible.

We have seen some of the Old Testament texts which make the glory of God the centerpiece of missionary proclamation: "Declare *his glory* among the nations, *his marvelous works* among all the peoples!" (Psalm 96:3). "Proclaim that *his name is exalted*!" (Isaiah 12:4). There are many others.[11] But we have not yet seen the straightforward statements of Jesus and Paul and John that say the same thing.

Leaving family and possessions for the sake of the name

When Jesus turned the rich young ruler away because he was not willing to leave his wealth to follow Jesus, the Lord said, "It will be hard for a rich man to enter the kingdom of heaven" (Matthew 19:23). The apostles were amazed and said, "Who then can be saved?" (v. 25). Jesus answered, "With men this is impossible, but with God all things are possible" (v. 26). Then Peter, speaking as a kind of missionary who had left his home and business to follow Jesus, said, "Lo, we have left everything and followed you. What shall we have?" (v. 27). Jesus answered with a mild rebuke of Peter's sense of sacrifice: "Everyone who has left houses or brothers or sisters or father or mother or children or lands, *for my name's sake*, will receive a hundredfold and inherit eternal life" (v. 29).

The one point of focus for us here is the phrase, "for my

name's sake". The motive that Jesus virtually takes for granted when a missionary leaves home and family and possessions is that it is *for the sake of the name of Jesus*. That means for the sake of Jesus' reputation. God's goal is that his Son's name be exalted and honored among all the peoples of the world. For when the Son is honored, the Father is honored (Mark 9:37). When every knee bows at the name of Jesus, it will be "to the glory of God the Father" (Philippians 2:10–11). Therefore God-centered missions exists for the sake of the name of Jesus.

A missionary prayer for God's name to be hallowed

The first two petitions of the Lord's Prayer are perhaps the clearest statement of all in the teachings of Jesus that missions is driven by the passion of God to be glorified among the nations. "Hallowed be thy name. Thy kingdom come" (Matthew 6:9–10). Here Jesus teaches us to ask God to hallow his name and to make his kingdom come. This is a missionary prayer. Its aim is to engage the passion of God for his name among those who forget or revile the name of God (Psalm 9:17; 74:18). To hallow God's name means to put it in a class by itself and to cherish and honor it above every claim to our allegiance or affection. Jesus' primary concern – the very first petition of the prayer he teaches – is that more and more people, and more and more peoples, come to hallow God's name. This is the reason the universe exists. Missions exists because this hallowing doesn't.

How much he must suffer for the name

When Paul was converted on the Damascus road, Jesus Christ became the supreme treasure and joy of his life. "I count everything as loss because of the surpassing worth of knowing Christ Jesus my Lord" (Philippians 3:8). It was a costly allegiance. What Paul learned there in Damascus was not only the joy of sins forgiven and fellowship with the King of the universe, but also how much he would have to suffer. Jesus sent Ananias to him with this message: "I will show him how much he must suffer *for the sake of my name*" (Acts 9:16). Paul's missionary sufferings were "for the sake of the name". When he came near the end of his life and was warned not to go to Jerusalem, he answered, "What are you doing, weeping and breaking my heart? For I am ready not only to be imprisoned but even to die at Jerusalem *for the name of the Lord Jesus*" (Acts 21:13). For Paul, the glory of the name of Jesus and his reputation in the world were more important than life.

"For the sake of his name among all the nations"

Paul makes crystal clear in Romans 1:5 that his mission and calling are for the name of Christ among all the nations: "We have received grace and apostleship to bring about the obedience of faith *for the sake of his name among all the nations*."

The apostle John described the motive of early Christian missionaries in the same way. He wrote to tell one of his churches that they should send out Christian brothers in a manner "worthy of God". And the reason he gives is that "they have gone out *for the sake of the name*, taking nothing from the Gentiles" (3 John 6–7).

John Stott comments on these two texts (Romans 1:5; 3 John 7): "They knew that God had superexalted Jesus, enthroning him at his right hand and bestowing upon him the highest rank, in order that every tongue should confess his lordship. They longed that Jesus should receive the honor due to his name."[12] This longing is not a dream but a certainty. At the bottom of all our hope, when everything else has given way, we stand on this great reality: the everlasting, all-sufficient God is infinitely, unwaveringly, and eternally committed to the glory of his great and holy name. For the sake of his fame among the nations he will act. His name will not be profaned for ever. The mission of the church will be victorious. He will vindicate his people and his cause in all the earth.

May the blessed redeemer see the travail of his soul!

David Brainerd, the missionary to the Indians in New Jersey in the 1740s, was sustained by this confidence to his death at age 29. Seven days before he died in 1747 he spoke of his longing for the glory of God in the world.

These are the last words he had the strength to write with his own hand:

> Friday, October 2. My soul was this day, at turns, sweetly set on God: I longed to be "with him" that I might "behold his glory" . . . Oh, that his kingdom might come in the world; that they might all love and glorify him for what he is in himself; and that the blessed Redeemer might "see of the travail of his soul, and be satisfied." Oh, "come, Lord Jesus, come quickly! Amen."[13]

The absence of Brainerd's passion for God is the great cause of missionary weakness in the churches. This was Andrew Murray's judgment a hundred years ago:

> As we seek to find out why, with such millions of Christians, the real army of God that is fighting the hosts of darkness is so small, the only answer is – lack of heart. The enthusiasm of the kingdom is missing. And that is because there is so little enthusiasm for *the King*.[14]

This is still true today. Peter Beyerhaus also sees it clearly and calls us to put the glory of God at the center of our life and mission.

> We are called and sent to glorify the reign of God and to manifest His saving work before the whole world . . . Today it is extremely important to emphasize the priority of this doxological aim before all other aims of mission. Our one-sided concern with man and his society threatens to pervert mission and make it a secular or even a quasi-atheistic undertaking. We are living in an age of apostasy where man arrogantly makes himself the measuring rod of all things. Therefore, it is a part of our missionary task courageously to confess before all enemies of the cross that the earth belongs to God and to His anointed . . . Our task in mission is to uphold the banner of the risen Lord before the whole world, because it is his own.[15]

The zeal of the church for the glory of her King will not rise until pastors and mission leaders and seminary teachers make much more of the King. When the glory of God himself saturates our preaching and teaching and conversation and writings, and when he predominates above our talk of methods and strategies and psychological buzz words and cultural trends, then the people might begin to feel that he is the central reality of their lives and that the spread of his glory is more important than all their possessions and all their plans.

The power of missions when love for the lost is weak

Compassion for the lost is a high and beautiful motive for missionary labor. Without it we lose the sweet humility of sharing a treasure we have freely received. But we have seen that compassion for people must not be detached from passion for the glory of God. John Dawson, a leader in Youth With a Mission, gives an additional reason why this is so. He points out that a strong feeling of love for "the lost" or "the world" is a very difficult experience to sustain and is not always recognizable when it comes.

> Have you ever wondered what it feels like to have a love for the lost? This is a term we use as part of our Christian jargon. Many believers search their hearts in condemnation, looking for the arrival of some feeling of benevolence that will propel them into bold evangelism. It will never happen. It is impossible to love "the lost". You can't feel deeply for an abstraction or a concept. You would find it impossible to love deeply an unfamiliar individual portrayed in a photograph, let alone a nation or a race or something as vague as "all lost people".
>
> Don't wait for a feeling of love in order to share Christ with a stranger. You already love your heavenly Father, and you know that this stranger is created by Him, but separated from Him, so take those first steps in evangelism because you love God. It is not primarily out of compassion for humanity that we share our faith or pray for the lost; it is first of all, love for God. The Bible says in Ephesians 6:7–8: "With good will doing service, as to the Lord, and not to men, knowing that whatever good anyone does, he will receive the same from the Lord, whether he is a slave or free."
>
> Humanity does not deserve the love of God any more than you or I do. We should never be Christian humanists, taking Jesus to poor sinful people, reducing Jesus to some kind of product that will better their lot. People deserve to be damned but Jesus, the suffering Lamb of God, deserves the reward of his suffering.[16]

37

The miracle of love

Dawson's words are a wise and encouraging warning not to limit our mission engagement to the level of compassion we feel for people we do not know. However, I don't want to minimize what the Lord is able to do in giving people a supernatural burden of love for distant peoples. For example, Wesley Duewel of OMS International tells the story of his mother's remarkable burden for China and India:

> My mother for years carried a hunger for the people of China and India. For many years practically every day as she prayed during family prayer for these two nations she would break down and weep before she finished praying. Her love was deep and constant, and she will be rewarded eternally for her years of love-burden for those lands. This is the love of Jesus reaching out and mediated through Christians by the Holy Spirit.[17]

I emphasize again that the motive of compassion and the motive of zeal for the glory of God are not separate. The weeping of compassion is the weeping of joy in God impeded in the extension of itself to another.

The call of God

God is calling us above all else to be the kind of people whose theme and passion are the supremacy of God in all of life. No one will be able to rise to the magnificence of the missionary cause who does not feel the magnificence of Christ. There will be no big world vision without a big God. There will be no passion to draw others into our worship where there is no passion for worship.

God is pursuing with omnipotent passion a worldwide purpose of gathering joyful worshipers for himself from every tribe and tongue and people and nation. He has an inexhaustible enthusiasm for the supremacy of his name among the nations. Therefore let us bring our affections into line with his, and, for the sake of his name, let us renounce the quest for worldly comforts, and join his global purpose. If we do this, God's omnipotent commitment to his name will be over us like a banner, and we will not lose, in spite of many tribulations (Acts 9:16; Romans

8:35–39). Missions is not the ultimate goal of the church. Worship is. Missions exists because worship doesn't. The Great Commission is first to delight yourself in the Lord (Psalm 37:4). And then to declare, "Let the nations *be glad and sing for joy!*" (Psalm 67:4). In this way God will be glorified from beginning to end and worship will empower the missionary enterprise till the coming of the Lord.

> Great and wonderful are your deeds,
> O Lord God the Almighty!
> Just and true are your ways,
> O King of the ages!
> Who shall not fear and glorify your name, O Lord?
> For you alone are holy.
> All nations shall come and worship you,
> for your judgments have been revealed.
>
> (Revelation 15:3–4)

Notes

1. Quoted in *First Things*, Dec. 1991, No. 18, p. 63 (italics added).
2. Quoted in Tom Wells, *A Vision for Missions* (Carlisle, Pennsylvania: Banner of Truth Trust, 1985), p. 35.
3. Quoted in Iain Murray, *The Puritan Hope* (Edinburgh: Banner of Truth Trust, 1971), p. 140.
4. I have tried to unfold this wonderful truth of the Father's delight in himself, that is, his Son, in *The Pleasures of God: Meditations on God's Delight in Being God* (Portland: Multnomah Press, 1991), chapter one, "The Pleasure of God in His Son".
5. See especially "Appendix One: The Goal of God in Redemptive History", in *Desiring God: Meditations of a Christian Hedonist* (Leicester: IVP, 1989), pp. 227–238; and the entirety of *The Pleasures of God*.
6. Jonathan Edwards, *A Dissertation Concerning the End for Which God Created the World, The Works of Jonathan Edwards*, Vol. 1, ed. by Sereno Dwight (Edinburgh: Banner of Truth Trust, 1974), p. 119.
7. In defense of the reality of eternal conscious torment in hell for those who reject the truth of God see chapter four.
8. Jonathan Edwards, *Charity and Its Fruits* (Edinburgh: Banner of Truth Trust, 1969, originally 1852), p. 164.
9. For a more extended treatment of how God's God-centeredness is the ground of his mercy see *The Pleasures of God*, pp. 107–112.

10. I am aware that the Bible is replete with pictures of God's people serving him. I have dealt in some detail with the way service can be conceived Biblically so as not to put God in the category of an employer who depends on wage earners. See *Desiring God: Meditations of a Christian Hedonist*, pp. 138–143.

11. See an extensive list of these texts in chapter five.

12. John Stott, "The Bible in World Evangelization", in Ralph D. Winter and Steven C. Hawthorne, eds., *Perspectives on the World Christian Movement* (Pasadena: William Carey Library, 1981), p. 4.

13. Jonathan Edwards, *The Life of David Brainerd*, ed. Norman Pettit, *The Works of Jonathan Edwards*, Vol. 7 (New Haven: Yale University Press, 1985), p. 474.

14. Andrew Murray, *Key to the Missionary Problem* (Fort Washington, Pennsylvania: Christian Literature Crusade, 1979), p. 133.

15. Peter Beyerhaus, *Shaken Foundations: Theological Foundations for Missions* (Grand Rapids: Zondervan Publishing House, 1972), pp. 41–42.

16. John Dawson, *Taking Our Cities for God* (Lake Mary, Florida: Creation House, 1989), pp. 208–209.

17. Wesley Duewel, *Ablaze for God* (Grand Rapids: Francis Asbury Press of Zondervan Publishing House, 1989), pp. 115–116.

2

The supremacy of God in missions through prayer

We cannot know what prayer is for until we know that life is war

Life is war. That's not all it is. But it is always that. Our weakness in prayer is owing largely to our neglect of this truth. Prayer is primarily a wartime walkie-talkie for the mission of the church as it advances against the powers of darkness and unbelief. It is not surprising that prayer malfunctions when we try to make it a domestic intercom to call upstairs for more comforts in the den. God has given us prayer as a wartime walkie-talkie so that we can call headquarters for everything we need as the kingdom of Christ advances in the world. Prayer gives *us* the significance of front-line forces, and gives *God* the glory of a limitless Provider. The one who gives the power gets the glory. Thus prayer safeguards the supremacy of God in missions while linking us with endless grace for every need.

Life is war

When Paul came to the end of his life, he said in 2 Timothy 4:7, "I have fought *the good fight*, I have finished the race, I have kept the faith." In 1 Timothy 6:12 he tells Timothy, "*Fight the good fight* of faith; lay hold on eternal life to which you were called." For Paul all of life was war. Yes, he used other images as well – farming, athletics, family, building, shepherding and so on. And yes, he was a man who loved peace. But the pervasiveness of war is seen precisely in the fact that one of the weapons of war is the gospel of peace (Ephesians 6:15)! Yes, he was a man of tremendous joy. But this joy was usually a "rejoicing in the tribulations" of his embattled mission (Romans 5:3; 12:12; 2 Corinthians 6:10; Philippians 2:17; Colossians 1:24; cf. 1 Peter 1:6; 4:13).

Life is war because the maintenance of our faith and the

41

laying hold on eternal life is a constant fight. Paul makes clear in 1 Thessalonians 3:5 that Satan targets our faith for destruction: "I sent that I might know of your *faith*, for fear that somehow the *tempter* had tempted you and that *our labor would be in vain*." Satan's attack in Thessalonica was against the Christians' faith. His aim was to make Paul's work there "vain" – empty, destroyed.

It's true that Paul believed in the eternal security of the elect ("Those whom [God] justified he also glorified", Romans 8:30). But the only people who are eternally secure are those who "confirm their calling and election" by "fighting the good fight of faith, and laying hold on eternal life" (2 Peter 1:10; 1 Timothy 6:12). Jesus said, "He who endures to the end will be saved" (Mark 13:13). And Satan is fighting always to bring us to ruin by destroying our faith.

The word for "fight" in 1 Timothy (*agōnizomai* from which we get "agonize") is used repeatedly in describing the Christian life. Jesus said, "*Strive* to enter by the narrow door; for many, I tell you, will seek to enter and will not be able" (Luke 13:24). Hebrews 4:11 says, "Let us therefore *strive* to enter that rest, that no one fall by the same sort of disobedience." Paul compares the Christian life to a race and says, "Every athlete *strives* and uses self-control in all things. They do it to obtain a perishable crown, but we do it to obtain an imperishable one" (1 Corinthians 9:25). He describes his ministry of proclamation and teaching in these terms: "For this I toil, *striving* with all the energy which he mightily inspires within me" (Colossians 1:29). And he says that prayer is part of this fight: "Epaphras, a servant of Christ and one of your own, greets you, always *striving* on your behalf in *prayers*" (Colossians 4:12). "*Strive* with me in your *prayers* on my behalf to God" (Romans 15:30). It's the same word each time: the word for "fight".

Paul is even more graphic at times with other warfare language. Concerning his own life of warfare he said, "I do not *run* aimlessly, I do not *box* as one beating the air; but *I pommel my body and subdue it*, lest after preaching to others I myself should be disqualified" (1 Corinthians 9:26–27). He runs a race, he fights a boxing match and he strives against the forces of his own body. Concerning his ministry he said, "Though we live in the world we are not carrying on a worldly *war*, for the *weapons of our warfare* are not worldly but have divine power to destroy strongholds. We destroy arguments and every proud obstacle to the knowledge of God, and take every thought captive to obey Christ" (2 Corinthians 10:3–5).

Paul encouraged Timothy to see his whole ministry as war: "This charge I commit to you, Timothy, my son, that in accordance with the prophetic utterances which pointed to you, that inspired by them you may *wage the good warfare*" (1 Timothy 1:18). "No *soldier on service* gets entangled in civilian pursuits" (2 Timothy 2:4). In other words, missions and ministry are war.

Probably the most familiar passage on the warfare we live in daily is Ephesians 6:12–18 where Paul lists the pieces of the "whole armor of God". We must not miss the forest for the trees here. The simple assumption of this familiar passage is this: life is war. Paul simply assumes this, and then tells us what kind of war it is: "not against flesh and blood, but against the principalities, against the powers, against the world rulers of this present darkness, against the spiritual hosts of wickedness in the heavenly places. Therefore take the whole armor of God" (vv. 12–13).

Then all the precious blessings of life could be thought of in other contexts besides war are drafted for the battle. If we know *truth*, it is for a belt in the armor. If we have *righteousness*, we must wear it as a breastplate. If we cherish *the gospel of peace*, it must become a soldier's footwear. If we love *resting* in the promises of God, that faith must be fastened on our left arm as a shield against flaming arrows. If we delight in our *salvation*, we must fit it securely on our head as a helmet. If we love *the word of God* as sweeter than honey, we must make the honey a sword. Virtually every "civilian" blessing in the Christian life is conscripted for the war. There is not a warfare part of life and a non-warfare part. Life is war.[1]

The absence of austerity

But most people do not believe this in their heart. Most people show by their priorities and their casual approach to spiritual things that they believe we are in peacetime not wartime.

In wartime the newspapers carry headlines about how the troops are doing. In wartime families talk about the sons and daughters on the front lines and write to them and pray for them with heart-wrenching concern for their safety. In wartime we are on the alert. We are armed. We are vigilant. In wartime we spend money differently – there is austerity, not for its own sake, but because there are more strategic ways to spend money than on new tires at home. The war effort touches everybody. We all cut back. The luxury liner becomes a troop carrier.

Very few people think that we are in a war that is greater than World War II, or any imaginable nuclear war. Few reckon that Satan is a much worse enemy than any earthly foe, or realize that the conflict is not restricted to any one global theater, but is in every town and city in the world. Who considers that the casualties of this war do not merely lose an arm or an eye or an earthly life, but lose everything, even their own soul and enter a hell of everlasting torment?

Prayer is for wielding the word

Until we feel the force of this, we will not pray as we ought. We will not even know what prayer is. In Ephesians 6:17–18 Paul makes the connection between the life of war and the work of prayer. Verse 17: "Take the helmet of salvation, and the sword of the Spirit, which is the word of God." Verse 18: *"Pray at all times in the Spirit with all prayer and supplication. To that end keep alert with all perseverance making supplication for all the saints."* In the original Greek, verse 18 does not begin a new sentence. It connects with verse 17 like this: "Take the sword of the Spirit, which is the word of God, *praying through all prayer and supplication on every occasion . . .*" Take the sword . . . praying! This is how we are to wield the word – by prayer.

Prayer is the communication with headquarters by which the weapons of warfare are deployed according to the will of God. That's the connection between the weapons and prayer in Ephesians 6. Prayer is for war.

44

Missions is given as a field for prayer

This connection between prayer and missions can be seen in a passage that doesn't use warfare words but deals with the same reality, namely, John 15:16. Jesus said,

> You did not choose me, but I chose you and appointed you that you should go and bear fruit and that your fruit should abide; *so that* whatever you ask the Father in my name, he may give it to you.

The logic of this sentence is crucial. Why is the Father going to give the disciples what they ask in Jesus' name? Answer: Because they have been sent to bear fruit. The reason the Father gives the disciples the instrument of prayer is because Jesus has given them a mission. In fact, the grammar of John 15:16 implies that the reason Jesus gives them their mission is so that they will be able to use the power of prayer. "I send you to bear fruit ... *so that* whatever you ask the Father in my name, he may give you." This is just another way of saying that prayer is a wartime walkie-talkie. God designed it and gave it to us for use on a mission. You can say the mission is to "bear fruit" or you can say the mission is to "set the captives free". The point stays the same: prayer is designed to extend the kingdom into fruitless enemy territory.

Why prayer malfunctions

Probably the number one reason why prayer malfunctions in the hands of believers is that we try to turn a wartime walkie-talkie into a domestic intercom. Until you know that life is war, you cannot know what prayer is for. Prayer is for the accomplishment of a wartime mission. It is as though the field commander (Jesus) called in the troops, gave them a crucial mission (go and bear fruit), handed each of them a personal transmitter coded to the frequency of the General's headquarters, and said, "Comrades, the General has a mission for you. He aims to see it accomplished. And to that end he has authorized me to give each of you personal access to him through these transmitters. If you stay true to his mission and seek his victory first, he will always be as close as your transmitter, to give tactical advice and to send air cover when you need it."

But what have millions of Christians done? We have stopped believing that we are in a war. No urgency, no watching, no vigilance. No strategic planning. Just easy peace and prosperity. And what did we do with the walkie-talkie? We tried to rig it up as an intercom in our houses and cabins and boats and cars – not to call in fire power for conflict with a mortal enemy, but to ask for more comforts in the den.

Times of great distress

In Luke 21:34–36 Jesus warned his disciples that times of great distress and opposition were coming. Then he said, "But watch at all times, *praying* that you may have strength to escape all these things that will take place, and to stand before the Son of man." In other words, if we follow Jesus it will lead us into severe conflict with evil. It will mean war. Evil will surround us and attack us and threaten to destroy our faith. But God has given us a transmitter. If we go to sleep it will do us no good. But if we are alert, as Jesus says, and call for help in the conflict, the help will come and the Commander will not let his faithful soldiers be denied their crown of victory before the Son of man. Thus repeatedly we see the same truth: we cannot know what prayer is for until we know that life is war.

Praying for peace is part of the war

But 1 Timothy 2:1–4 looks like it might conflict with this battlefield image of prayer. Paul says that he wants us to pray for kings and for all who are in high positions "that we may lead a quiet and peaceable life, godly and respectful in every way" (v. 2). Now that sounds very domestic and civilian and peaceful.

But read on. The reason for praying this way is highly strategic. Verses 3–4 say, "This [praying for peace] is good, and acceptable in the sight of God our Savior, who desires all men to be saved and to come to the knowledge of the truth." God aims to save people from every tribe and tongue and people and nation. But one of the great obstacles to victory is when people are swept up into social and political and militaristic conflicts that draw away their attention and time and energy and creativity from the real battle of the universe.

Satan's aim is that nobody be saved and come to a knowledge of the truth. And one of his key strategies is to start battles in the world which draw our attention away from the real battle for the salvation of the lost and the perseverance of the saints. He knows that the real battle, as Paul says, is not against flesh and blood. So the more wars and conflicts and revolutions of "flesh and blood" he can start, the better, as far as he is concerned.

So when Paul tells us to pray for peace precisely because God desires all men to be saved and to come to a knowledge of the truth, he is not picturing prayer as a kind of harmless domestic intercom for increasing our civilian conveniences. He is picturing it as a strategic appeal to headquarters to ask that the enemy not be allowed to draw away any fire power onto decoy conflicts of flesh and blood.

The crying need of the hour

So the truth is reaffirmed: God has given us prayer because Jesus has given us a mission. We are on this earth to press back the forces of darkness, and we are given access to headquarters by prayer to advance this cause. When we try to turn it into a civilian intercom to increase our conveniences, it stops working, and our faith begins to falter. We have so domesticated prayer that for many of us it is no longer what it was designed to be – a wartime walkie-talkie for the accomplishment of Christ's mission.

We simply must seek for ourselves and for our people a wartime mentality. Otherwise the Biblical teaching about the urgency of prayer, and the vigilance of prayer, and the watching in prayer and the perseverance of prayer, and the danger of abandoning prayer will make no sense and find no resonance in our hearts. Until we feel the desperation of a bombing raid, or the thrill of a new strategic offensive for the gospel, we will not pray in the spirit of Jesus.

The crying need of the hour is to put the churches on a

47

wartime footing. Mission leaders are crying out, "Where is the church's concept of militancy, of a mighty army willing to suffer, moving ahead with exultant determination to take the world by storm? Where is the risk-taking, the launching out on God alone?"[2] The answer is that it has been swallowed up in a peace-time mentality.

We are a "third soil century". In the parable of the soils Jesus says that the seed is the word. He sows his urgent word of kingdom power. But instead of taking it up as our sword (or bearing fruit) we "are those who hear the word, but the *cares of the world and the delight in riches and the desire for other things* enter and choke the word and it proves unfruitful" (Mark 4:18–19).

This is why Paul says that *all* of life is war – every moment. Before we can even engage in the mission of the church we have to fight against "the delight in riches" and "desire for other things". We must fight to cherish the kingdom above all "other things" – that is our first and most constant battle. That is the "fight of faith". Then, when we have some experience in that basic battle we join the fight to commend the kingdom to all the nations.

God will win the war

Now into this warfare God asserts himself for the triumph of his cause. He does this in an unmistakable way so that the victory will redound to his glory. His purpose in all of history is to uphold and display his glory for the enjoyment of his redeemed people from all the nations. Therefore God engages in the battle so that the triumphs are manifestly his. As we saw in chapter one, the chief end of God is to glorify God and enjoy his excellence for ever. This is what guarantees the victory of his cause. In order to magnify his glory he will exert his sovereign power and complete the mission he has commanded.

Power of the Puritan hope

This confidence in the sovereignty of God and the triumph of his cause is essential in the prayers of God's people and the mission of the church. It has proven to be a powerful force in the history of missions. The first missionary endeavor of the Protestants in England burst forth from the soil of Puritan hope. The Puritans were those pastors and teachers in England (and then New England), roughly between the years 1560 and 1660, who wanted to purify the Church of England and bring it into theological and practical alignment with the teachings of the Reformation.

They had a view of God's sovereignty that produced an undaunted hope in the victory of God over all the world. They were deeply stirred by a passion for the coming of God's kingdom over all the nations. Their hearts really believed the truth of the promises that Christ's cause would triumph. "I will build my church and the gates of hell shall not prevail against it" (Matthew 16:18). "This gospel of the kingdom will be preached throughout the whole world as a testimony to *all the nations*, and the end will come" (Matthew 24:14). "*All the nations* thou hast made shall come and bow down before thee, O LORD, and shall glorify thy name" (Psalm 86:9). "In thee shall *all the families* of the earth be blessed" (Genesis 12:3). "I shall give thee *the nations* for thine inheritance" (Psalm 2:8). "*All the ends of the world* shall remember and turn unto the Lord: and all the families of the nations shall worship before thee" (Psalm 22:27). "All the earth shall worship thee, and shall sing unto thee; they shall sing to thy name" (Psalm 66:4). "To him shall be the obedience of the peoples" (Genesis 49:10).[3]

This tremendous confidence that Christ would one day conquer hearts in every nation and be glorified by every people on earth gave birth to the first Protestant missionary endeavor in the English-speaking world, and it happened 150 years before the modern missionary movement began with William Carey in 1793.

Between 1627 and 1640, 15,000 people emigrated from England to America, most of them Puritans, carrying this great confidence in the worldwide reign of Christ. In fact, the seal of the colonists of Massachusetts Bay had on it a North American Indian with these words coming out of his mouth: "Come over into Macedonia and help us," which was taken from Acts 16:9. What this shows is that in general the Puritans saw their emigration to America as part of God's missionary strategy to extend his kingdom among the nations.

The prayers and pains of John Eliot

One of those hope-filled Puritans who crossed the Atlantic in 1631 was John Eliot. He was 27 years old and a year later became the pastor of a new church in Roxbury, Massachusetts, about a mile from Boston. But something happened that made him much more than a pastor.

According to Cotton Mather, there were twenty tribes of Indians in that vicinity. John Eliot could not avoid the practical implications of his theology: if the infallible Scriptures promise that all nations will one day bow down to Christ, and if Christ is sovereign and able by his Spirit through prayer to subdue all opposition to his promised reign, then there is good hope that a person who goes as an ambassador of Christ to one of these nations will be the chosen instrument of God to open the eyes of the blind and set up an outpost of the kingdom of Christ.

And so when he was slightly over 40 (not 20! but 40!) years old Eliot set himself to study Algonquin. He deciphered the vocabulary and grammar and syntax and eventually translated the entire Bible as well as books that he valued like Richard Baxter's *Call to the Unconverted*. By the time Eliot was 84 years old, there were numerous Indian churches, some with their own Indian pastors. It is an amazing story of a man who once said, "Prayers and pains through faith in Christ Jesus will do any thing!"[4]

The reason I tell this story is to highlight the tremendous importance of solid Biblical *hope* on the basis of which we pray in the cause of world missions. God has promised and God is sovereign: "*All the nations* ... shall come and bow down before thee, O LORD, and shall glorify thy name" (Psalm 86:9).

That is what gripped the Puritan mind and eventually gave birth to the modern missionary movement in 1793. William Carey was nourished on this tradition, as were David Brainerd and Adoniram Judson, Alexander Duff and David Livingston, John Paton and a host of others who gave their lives to reach the unreached peoples of the world. The modern missionary movement did not arise in a theological vacuum. It grew out of a great Reformation tradition that put the sovereignty of God square in the center of human life. In the warfare of world missions God bares his arm and triumphs for his own glory.[5]

Missions is supremely the work of God

It is even more important to see this from Scripture than in the faith of great missionaries. The New Testament makes clear that God has not left his Great Commission to the uncertainties of the human will. The Lord said from the beginning, "I will build my church" (Matthew 16:18). World missions is supremely the work of the risen Lord Jesus.

"I have other sheep ... I must bring them also"

In the Gospel of John, Jesus put it like this: "I have other sheep, that are not of this fold; I must bring them also, and they will heed my voice" (John 10:16). This is the great missionary text in the Gospel of John. It is full of hope and power. It means that Christ has people besides those already converted. "I have *other sheep* that are not of this fold." This is a reference to the doctrine of election.[6] God chooses who will belong to his sheep and they are already his before Jesus calls them. "All that the Father gives me *will* come to me; and him who comes to me I *will* not cast out" (John 6:37; cf. 6:44–45; 8:47; 10:26–27; 17:6; 18:37). These sovereign "wills" of the Lord Jesus guarantee his invincible engagement in world missions.

There will always be people who argue that the doctrine of election makes missions unnecessary. But they are wrong. It does not make missions unnecessary; it makes missions hopeful. John Alexander, a former president of InterVarsity Christian Fellowship, said in a message at Urbana '67 (a decisive event in my own life), "At the beginning of my missionary career I said that if predestination were true I could not be a missionary. Now after 20-some years of struggling with the hardness of the human heart, I say I could never be a missionary *unless I believed in the doctrine of predestination*."[7] It gives hope that

51

Christ most certainly has "other sheep" among the nations.[8]

When Jesus says, "I must bring them also", he does not mean that he will do it without missionaries. That's plain from the fact that salvation comes through faith (John 1:12; 3:16; 6:35), and faith comes through the word of his disciples (John 17:20). Jesus brings his sheep into the fold through the preaching of those whom he sends, just as the Father sent him (John 20:21). So it is just as true today as in that day, "My sheep hear my voice, and I know them, and they follow me" (John 10:27). In the gospel it is *Christ* who calls. In world missions, *Christ* gathers his sheep. That is why there is complete assurance that they will come.

Clothed with power for missions

When Jesus ascended to heaven he told the disciples, "All authority in heaven and earth has been given to me ... I will be with you to the end of the age" (Matthew 28:18, 20). That's the authority with which he calls his sheep.

Then to make it plain that it would be *his* authority and *his* presence that would give success to the mission, he told his disciples to wait in Jerusalem until they were clothed with his power from on high (Luke 24:49). He said that the coming of that power through the Holy Spirit would enable them to be his witnesses "in Jerusalem and in all Judea and Samaria and to the end of the earth" (Acts 1:8). When the Spirit comes it is the Lord himself fulfilling the promise to build his church. Accordingly Luke says, "*The Lord* added to their number day by day those who were being saved" (Acts 2:47). The Lord did it. And he continued to do it by converting the greatest missionary of all time (Acts 26:16–18) and directing the missionaries in their travels (Acts 8:26, 29; 16:7, 10) and giving them the words that they needed (Mark 13:11; Acts 6:10).

"Not I, but the grace of God which is with me"

Paul was deeply aware that the success of his mission was the Lord's work and not his own. He said, "I will not venture to speak of anything except *what Christ has wrought through me* to win obedience from the Gentiles by word and deed, by the power of signs and wonders, *by the power of the Holy Spirit*" (Romans 15:18–19). Paul's passion, as always, was to focus all glory on the supremacy of Christ in the mission of the church. *The Lord* was building his church.

How did Paul then speak of his own labors? He said, "By the grace of God I am what I am, and his grace toward me was not in vain. On the contrary, I worked harder than any of them, *though it was not I, but the grace of God which is with me*" (1 Corinthians 15:10). Paul worked. Paul fought the fight and ran the race. But he did so, as he said in Philippians 2:13, because beneath and within his willing, God was at work to will and to do his good pleasure. Using a farming image, Paul put it like this: "I planted, Apollos watered, but *God* gave the growth. So neither he who plants nor he who waters is anything, but only God who gives the growth" (1 Corinthians 3:6–7). Paul was jealous to uphold the supremacy of God in the mission of the church.

This jealousy for the glory of God in the mission of the church drove the apostles to minister in a way that would always magnify God and not themselves. For example, Peter taught the young churches, "Let him who serves serve in the strength which God supplies *in order that in everything God may be glorified through Jesus Christ*" (1 Peter 4:11; cf. Hebrews 13:20–21). The one who gives the strength gets the glory. So Peter drove home the absolute necessity of serving in the strength that God supplies and not our own. If God did not build his church, he would not get the glory, and all would be in vain, no matter how "successful" the work may look to the world.

New covenant confidence in the sovereignty of God

The apostles knew that what was happening in their mission was the fulfillment of the promises of the new covenant. "God has made us competent to be ministers of a new covenant" (2 Corinthians 3:6). And the new covenant promises were that God would overcome hardness of heart and make people new on the inside. "A new heart I will give you, and a new Spirit I will put within you, and I

53

will take out of your flesh the heart of stone and give you a heart of flesh. And I will put my Spirit within you and cause you to walk in my statutes" (Ezekiel 36:26–27).

So as Luke tells how the Christian movement spread, he repeatedly records God's sovereign initiative in the growth of the church. When Cornelius and his household are converted it is described as God's doing. "Then to the Gentiles also *God has granted repentance* unto life" (Acts 11:18). "*God visited the Gentiles* to take out of them a people for his name" (Acts 15:14). When the gospel broke loose on European soil in Philippi beginning with Lydia, it was God who did it: "*The Lord opened her heart* to give heed to what was said by Paul" (Acts 16:14).

In all these ways the supremacy of God in the mission of the church comes through. God does not put his gospel and his people in the world and leave them to wage war on their own. He is the main combatant. And the battle is to be fought in a way that gives him the glory.

Prayer proves the supremacy of God in missions

That is why God has ordained prayer to have such a crucial place in the mission of the church. The purpose of prayer is to make clear to all the participants in this war that the victory belongs to the Lord. Prayer is God's appointed means of bringing grace to us and glory to himself. This is crystal clear in Psalm 50:15. God says, "Call on me in the day of trouble and I will deliver you, and *you shall glorify me*." Charles Spurgeon makes the point unavoidable:

> God and the praying man take shares . . . First, here is your share: "Call upon me in the day of trouble." Secondly, here is God's share: "I will deliver thee." Again, you take a share – for you shall be delivered. And then again it is the Lord's turn – "Thou shalt glorify me." Here is a compact, a covenant that God enters into with you who pray to Him, and whom He helps. He says, "You shall have the deliverance, but I must have the glory . . ." Here is a delightful partnership: we obtain that which we so greatly need, and all that God getteth is the glory which is due unto His name.[9]

Prayer puts God in the place of the all-sufficient Benefactor and puts us in the place of the needy beneficiaries.

So when the mission of the church moves forward by prayer the supremacy of God is manifest and the needs of the Christian troops are met.

Prayer is for the glory of the Father

Jesus had taught this to his disciples before he left. He had told them, "Whatever you ask in my name, I will do it, *that the Father may be glorified in the Son*" (John 14:13). In other words, the ultimate purpose of prayer is that the Father be glorified. The other side of the purpose comes out in John 16:24. Jesus says, "Till now you have asked nothing in my name; ask, and you will receive *that your joy may be full.*" The purpose of prayer is that our joy may be full. The unity of these two goals – the glory of God and the joy of his people – is preserved in the act of prayer.

The zeal that the apostles had for the exaltation of God's supreme influence in all their missionary work was built into them by Jesus. In John 15:5 Jesus says, "I am the vine, you are the branches. He who abides in me and I in him, he it is that bears much fruit, *for apart from me you can do nothing.*" So we really are totally ineffective as missionaries in ourselves. We may have many human strategies and plans and efforts. But the spiritual effect for the glory of Christ will be nothing. According to John 15:5, God does not intend for us to be fruitless but to "bear much fruit". So he promises to do for us and through us what we can't do in and of ourselves.

How then do we glorify him? Jesus gives the answer in John 15:7: "If you abide in me, and my words abide in you, *ask* whatever you will and it shall be done for you." We *pray*. We *ask* God to do for us through Christ what we can't do for ourselves – bear fruit. Then verse 8 gives the result: "*By this is my Father glorified*, that you bear much fruit." So how is God glorified by prayer? Prayer is the open admission that without Christ we can do nothing. And prayer is the turning away from ourselves to God in the confidence that he will provide the help we need. Prayer humbles *us* as needy and exalts *God* as all-sufficient.

This is why the missionary enterprise advances by prayer. The chief end of God is to glorify God. He will do this in the sovereign triumph of his missionary purpose that the nations worship him. He will secure this triumph by entering into the warfare and becoming the main combatant. And he will make that engagement plain to all the participants *through prayer*. Because prayer shows that the power is from the Lord. The range of his powerful engagement in the warfare of missions becomes evident from the range of things which the church prays for in her missionary enterprise. Consider the amazing scope of prayer in the vibrant missionary life of the early church. How greatly was God glorified in the breadth of his provision!

God was sought in everything

They called on God to exalt his name in the world:

> Pray then like this: Our Father who art in heaven, Hallowed be thy name. (Matthew 6:9)

They called on God to extend his kingdom in the world:

> Thy kingdom come. Thy will be done, On earth as it is in heaven. (Matthew 6:10)

They called on God that the gospel would run and triumph:

> Finally, brethren, pray for us, that the word of the Lord may speed on and triumph, as it did among you. (2 Thessalonians 3:1)

They called on God for the fullness of the Holy Spirit:

> If you then, who are evil, know how to give good gifts to your children, how much more will the heavenly Father give the Holy Spirit to those who ask him! (Luke 11:13; cf. Ephesians 3:19)

They called on God to vindicate his people in their cause:

> And will not God vindicate his elect, who cry to him day and night? Will he delay long over them? (Luke 18:7)

They called on God to save unbelievers:

> Brethren, my heart's desire and prayer to God for them is that they may be saved. (Romans 10:1)

They called on God to direct the use of the sword:

> Take the sword of the Spirit, which is the word of God, praying through all prayer and supplication on every occasion . . . (Ephesians 6:17–18)

They called on God for boldness in proclamation:

> Pray at all times in the Spirit . . . and also for me, that utterance may be given me in opening my mouth boldly to proclaim the mystery of the gospel. (Ephesians 6:18–19)

> And now, Lord, look upon their threats, and grant to thy servants to speak thy word with all boldness. (Acts 4:29)

They called on God for signs and wonders:

> And now, Lord . . . grant your servants to speak thy word with boldness . . . while you stretch out your hand to heal, and signs and wonders are performed through the name of your holy servant Jesus. (Acts 4:30)

> Elijah was a man of like nature with ourselves and he prayed fervently that it might not rain, and for three years and six months it did not rain on the earth. Then he prayed again and the heaven gave rain, and the earth brought forth its fruit. (James 5:17–18)

They called on God for the healing of wounded comrades:

> Let them pray over him, anointing him with oil in the name of the Lord, and the prayer of faith will save the sick man and the Lord will raise him up. (James 5:14–15)

They called on God for the healing of unbelievers:

> It happened that the father of Publius lay sick with fever and dysentery; and Paul visited him and prayed, and putting his hands on him healed him. (Acts 28:8)

They called on God for the casting out of demons:

> And he said to them, "This kind cannot be driven out by anything but prayer." (Mark 9:29)

They called on God for miraculous deliverances:

> So Peter was kept in prison; but earnest prayer for him was

made to God by the church ... When he realized [he had been freed], he went to the house of Mary, the mother of John whose other name was Mark, where many were gathered together and were praying. (Acts 12:5, 12)

But about midnight Paul and Silas were praying and singing hymns to God, and the prisoners were listening to them, and suddenly there was a great earthquake. (Acts 16:25–26)

They called on God for the raising of the dead:

But Peter put them all outside and knelt down and prayed; then turning to the body he said, "Tabitha, rise." And she opened her eyes, and when she saw Peter she sat up. (Acts 9:40)

They called on God to supply his troops with necessities:

Give us this day our daily bread. (Matthew 6:11)

They called on God for strategic wisdom:

If any of you lacks wisdom, let him ask God, who gives to all men generously and without reproaching, and it will be given him. (James 1:5)

They called on God to establish leadership in the outposts:

And when they had appointed elders for them in every church, with prayer and fasting they committed them to the Lord in whom they believed. (Acts 14:23)

They called on God to send out reinforcements:

Pray therefore the Lord of the harvest to send out laborers into his harvest. (Matthew 9:38)

While they were worshiping the Lord and fasting, the Holy Spirit said, "Set apart for me Barnabas and Saul for the work to which I have called them." Then after fasting and praying they laid their hands on them and sent them off. (Acts 13:2–3)

They called on God for the success of other missionaries:

I appeal to you, brethren, by our Lord Jesus Christ and by the love of the Spirit, to strive together with me in your prayers to God on my behalf, that I may be delivered from the unbelievers in Judea, and that my service for Jerusalem may be acceptable to the saints. (Romans 15:30–31)

They called on God for unity and harmony in the ranks:

I do not pray for these only, but also for those who believe in me through their word, that they may all be one; even as thou, Father, art in me, and I in thee, that they also may be in us, so that the world may believe that thou hast sent me. (John 17:20–21)

They called on God for the encouragement of togetherness:

[We are] praying earnestly night and day that we may see you face to face and supply what is lacking in your faith? (1 Thessalonians 3:10)

They called on God for a mind of discernment:

And it is my prayer that your love may abound more and more in knowledge and all discernment, so that you may approve what is excellent, and may be pure and blameless for the day of Christ. (Philippians 1:9–10)

They called on God for a knowledge of his will:

And so, from the day we heard of it, we have not ceased to pray for you, asking that you may be filled with the knowledge of his will in all spiritual wisdom and understanding. (Colossians 1:9)

They called on God to know him better:

[We have not ceased to pray for you to be] increasing in the knowledge of God. (Colossians 1:10; cf. Ephesians 1:17)

They called on God for power to comprehend the love of Christ:

I bow my knees before the Father ... that you may have power to comprehend with all the saints what is the breadth and length and height and depth and to know the love of Christ which surpasses knowledge. (Ephesians 3:14, 18)

They called on God for a deeper sense of assured hope:

I do not cease to give thanks for you, remembering you in my prayers ... that you may know what is the hope to which he has called you, what are the riches of his glorious inheritance in the saints. (Ephesians 1:16, 18)

They called on God for strength and endurance:

[We have not ceased to pray for you to be] strengthened with all power, according to his glorious might, for all endurance and patience with joy. (Colossians 1:11; cf. Ephesians 3:16)

They called on God for deeper sense of his power within them:

I do not cease to give thanks for you, remembering you in my prayers ... that you may know ... what is the immeasurable greatness of his power toward us who believe. (Ephesians 1:16, 19)

They called on God that their faith not be destroyed:

I have prayed for you that your faith may not fail; and when you have turned again, strengthen your brethren. (Luke 22:32)

Watch at all times, praying that you may have strength to escape all these things that will take place, and to stand before the Son of man. (Luke 21:36)

They called on God for greater faith:

Immediately the father of the child cried out and said, "I believe; help my unbelief!" (Mark 9:24; cf. Ephesians 3:17)

They called on God that they might not fall into temptation:

Lead us not into temptation. (Matthew 6:13)

Watch and pray that you may not enter into temptation; the spirit indeed is willing, but the flesh is weak. (Matthew 26:41)

They called on God that he would complete their resolves:

To this end we always pray for you, that our God may make you worthy of his call, and may fulfil every good resolve and work of faith by his power. (2 Thessalonians 1:11)

They called on God that they would do good works:

[We have not ceased to pray for you that you] lead a life worthy of the Lord, fully pleasing to him, bearing fruit in every good work. (Colossians 1:10)

They called on God for forgiveness of their sins:

Forgive us our debts as we forgive our debtors. (Matthew 6:12)

They called on God for protection from the evil one:

Deliver us from evil. (Matthew 6:13)

Since the Giver gets the glory, what all this prayer shows is that the early church meant to make God supreme in the mission of the church. She would not live on her own strength or her own wisdom or even her own faith. She would live on God. God would be the one who would give the power and the wisdom and the faith. And therefore God would get the glory.

God's ultimate goal will come only through prayer

This crucial place of prayer reaffirms the great goal of God to uphold and display his glory for the enjoyment of the redeemed from all the nations. God has made it the ground of his oath: "The earth shall be filled with the glory of the LORD" just as surely as that the Lord lives (Numbers 14:21). The missionary purpose of God is as invincible as the fact that he is God. He will achieve this purpose by creating white-hot worshipers from every people tongue and tribe and nation (Revelation 5:9; 7:9). And he will be engaged to do it through prayer.

But *the* work of missions is not prayer

Therefore it is almost impossible to overemphasize the awesome place of prayer in the purposes of God for the world. But a caution is needed here. I sense the danger of overstating the role of prayer in relation to the word of God and the preaching of the gospel. I am not comfortable, for example, with calling prayer "*the* work of missions". I believe wholeheartedly that it is the proclamation of the gospel that is *the* work of missions. I do not say this from a desire to minimize the place of prayer, or to jeopardize its awesome indispensability. Rather I say it out of zeal for the place of the word of God in missions. Prayer is the power that wields the weapon of the word, and the word is the weapon by which the nations will be brought to faith and obedience.

The front-line work of missions is the preaching of the word of God, the gospel. If this public act is displaced by prayer, the supremacy of Christ in the mission of the church will be compromised. Jesus said, "When the Spirit of truth comes . . . he will glorify me" (John 16:13–14). This is why the Spirit becomes active to save people precisely where the gospel of Jesus is preached. His mission is to glorify Jesus. Where Jesus and his saving work are not proclaimed, there is no truth for the Holy Spirit to empower and no knowledge of Christ for him to exalt. Therefore it is vain to pray that the hearts of people will be opened where there is no gospel portrait of Christ to see.

> Everyone who calls upon the name of the Lord will be saved. But how are they to call upon him in whom they have not believed? And how are they to believe in him of whom they have never *heard* and how are they to *hear* without a *preacher*? . . . Faith comes by *hearing* and hearing by the word of Christ. (Romans 10:13–17)

God has ordained that saving faith come by hearing the word of Christ because faith is a response to Christ. If Christ is to be glorified in the mission of the church he must be heard and known.[10] This happens only through the word. No prayer can replace it. Prayer can only empower it. The New Testament pattern is: "Take the sword of the Spirit, which is the word of God, *praying* . . ." (Ephesians 6:17–18). "When they had *prayed* . . . they were filled with the Holy Spirit and *spoke the word of God with boldness*" (Acts 4:31).

Prayer releases the power of the gospel

But even the power that comes from the Holy Spirit through prayer is in some sense the unique power of the word of God itself: "*The gospel is the power of God* unto salvation" (Romans 1:16). Perhaps we should speak of prayer as God's instrument to *release* the power of the gospel. For it is clear that the word of God is the immediate regenerating instrument of the Spirit: "You have been born anew not of perishable seed, but of imperishable, through the living and abiding *word of God*" (1 Peter 1:23). "[God] brought us forth by the *word of truth* that we should be a kind of first fruits of his creatures" (James 1:18).

The central promise of world missions in the teaching of Jesus concerns the spreading of the *word*: "This *gospel of the kingdom* will be *preached* throughout the whole world, as a *testimony* to all nations; and then the end will come" (Matthew 24:14). In his parable about sowing, Jesus said, "The seed is *the word of God*" (Luke 8:11). When he prayed for the future mission of his disciples he said, "I do not pray for these only, but also for those who will believe on me *through their word*" (John 17:20). And after his resurrection, in his risen lordship over the mission of his church he continued to exalt the word: "The Lord bore witness to *the word of his grace*, granting signs and wonders to be done by [the apostles'] hands" (Acts 14:3).

When the Christian movement spread in the book of Acts, Luke repeatedly described its growth as the growth of the word of God. "And *the word of God* increased and the number of disciples multiplied greatly in Jerusalem" (Acts 6:7). "*The word of God* grew and multiplied" (Acts 12:24). "*The word of the Lord* spread through all that region" (Acts 13:49). "*The word of the Lord grew* and prevailed mightily" (Acts 19:20).

This is why I am jealous to say that the proclamation of the gospel is "*the* work of missions". It is the weapon that God designed to use in penetrating the kingdom of darkness and gathering the children of light from all the nations (Acts 26:16–18). His whole redemptive plan for the universe hangs on the success of his word. If the proclamation of the word aborts, the purposes of God fail.

63

The word of God cannot fail

But that cannot happen,

> For as the rain and the snow come down from heaven, and return not thither but water the earth, making it bring forth and sprout, giving seed to the sower and bread to the eater, *so shall my word be that goes forth from my mouth*; it shall not return to me empty, but it shall accomplish that which I purpose, and prosper in the thing for which I sent it. (Isaiah 55:10–11)

God is sovereign. Yes, he has made all his plans hang on the success of his word proclaimed by frail and sinful men and women; nevertheless his purposes cannot fail. This is the essence of the new covenant oath: "I will put my Spirit within you and cause you to walk in my statutes" (Ezekiel 36:27). "The LORD your God will circumcise your heart and the heart of your offspring so that you will love the LORD your God with all your heart and with all your soul" (Deuteronomy 30:6). The Lord will work in his church "to will and to do his good pleasure" (Philippians 2:13). A generation may be passed over in their disobedience, but none can undermine the plan of God. Job learned this long ago: "I know that thou canst do all things, and that no purpose of yours can be thwarted" (Job 42:1). Whenever God wills, his word stands and none can stay his hand.[11]

Victory even from inside the tomb

It will often look as though Christ is defeated. That's the way it looked on Good Friday. He *let* himself be libeled and harassed and scorned and shoved around and killed. But in it all he was in control. "No one takes [my life] from me" (John 10:18). So it will always be. If China was closed for 40 years to the western missionaries, it was not as though Jesus accidentally slipped and fell into the tomb. He *stepped* in. And when it was sealed over, he saved 50 million Chinese from inside – without western missionaries. And when it was time, he pushed the stone away so we could see what he had done.

When it looks like he is buried for good, Jesus is doing something awesome in the dark. "The kingdom of God is like a man who scattered seed on the ground. He sleeps and rises, night and day, and the seed sprouts and grows, but he knows not how" (Mark 4:26–27). The world thinks Jesus is done for – out of the way. They think his word is buried and his plans have failed.

But Jesus is at work in the dark places: "Unless a grain of wheat falls into the ground and dies, it remains alone; but if it dies, it bears much fruit" (John 12:24). He lets himself be buried, and he comes out in power when and where he pleases. And his hands are full of fruit made in the dark. "God loosed him from the pangs of death because *it was not possible for him to be held by it*" (Acts 2:24). Jesus goes about his invincible missionary plan "by the power of an *indestructible life*" (Hebrews 7:16).

For twenty centuries the world has given it their best shot to hold him in. They can't bury him. They can't hold him in. They can't silence him or limit him. Jesus is alive and utterly free to go and come wherever he pleases. "All authority in heaven" is his. All things were made through him and for him, and he is absolutely supreme over all other powers (Colossians 1:16–17). He upholds the universe by the word of his power (Hebrews 1:3). And the preaching of his word is *the* work of missions that cannot fail.

The truly awesome place of prayer in the purpose of God

Now we can say and again, safely and stunningly, what the awesome place of prayer is in the purpose of God to fill the earth with his glory. Not only has God made the accomplishment of his purposes hang on the preaching of the word; but has also made the success of that preaching hang on prayer. God's goal to be glorified will not succeed without the powerful proclamation of the gospel. And that gospel will not be proclaimed in power to all the nations without the prevailing, earnest, faith-filled prayers of God's people. This is the awesome place of prayer in the purpose of God for the world. That purpose won't happen without prayer.

This accounts for Paul's repeated call for prayer in support of the word. "Finally, brethren, *pray* for us, that the

65

word of the Lord may run and be glorified" (2 Thessalonians 3:1). "*Pray* also for me, that *utterance* may be given me in opening my mouth boldly to proclaim the mystery of the *gospel*" (Ephesians 6:19). "*Pray* for us also, that God may open to us a door for the *word*" (Colossians 4:3). "[God] will deliver us [to go on preaching the word], if you help us by *prayer*" (2 Corinthians 1:11; cf. Philippians 1:19).

Prayer is the walkie-talkie of the church on the battlefield of the world in the service of the word. It is not a domestic intercom to increase the temporal comforts of the saints. It malfunctions in the hands of soldiers who have gone AWOL. It is for those on active duty. And in their hands it proves the supremacy of God in the pursuit of the nations. When missions moves forward by prayer it magnifies the power of God. When it moves by human management it magnifies man.

The return to prayer in our day

The return to prayer at the end of the twentieth century is a remarkable work of God. It is full of hope for the awakening of the church and the finishing of the Great Commission. Looking back on the way God aroused and honored seasons of prayer in the past should enlarge our expectation that wonderful works of power are on the horizon. A hundred years ago, A. T. Pierson made this point exactly the way I would like to make it, namely, by highlighting the connection between prayer and the supremacy of God. He said,

> Every new Pentecost has had its preparatory period of supplication ... God has compelled his saints to seek Him at the throne of grace, so that every new advance might be so plainly due to His power that even the unbeliever might be constrained to confess: "Surely this is the finger of God!"[12]

More recently there have been movements in our own century that kindle expectation of significant breakthroughs in missions today. Thousands of us have been stirred deeply by the missionary credo of Jim Elliot: "He is no fool who gives what he cannot keep to gain what he cannot lose." But not as many of us know the atmosphere of prayer from which the missionary passions in the late 1940's and 1950's came. David Howard, the General Director of the World Evangelical Fellowship, was in that atmosphere and tells part of the story of what God was doing to magnify himself in the prayers of students in those days.

I still have a small, faded World Evangelism Decision Card dated 1946, with my signature. Unfortunately, I did not record the day, but it is quite possible that I signed this card at the close of the first student missionary convention at the University of Toronto.

The card used to be green. I can tell by the small green circle where a thumb tack used to hold this card above my desk throughout the rest of my college days. It served as a daily prayer reminder that I had committed myself to serve God overseas unless he were clearly to direct otherwise. The fact that I had 15 years of exciting service in Latin America is attributable in large measure to prayer – much of it stimulated by that little card.

Upon returning to college after the Toronto convention students began to meet regularly to pray for missions. My closest friend in college was Jim Elliot. Jim was only to live for a few years beyond college, but in that short life he would leave a mark for eternity on my life and the lives of hundreds of others. Exactly 10 years to the week when the Toronto convention ended, Jim and his four companions were speared to death by the Auca Indians on the Curaray River in Ecuador. In his death he would speak to multiplied thousands, although we did not know that in our college days. Jim encouraged a small group of us to meet every day at 6:30 a.m. to pray for ourselves and our fellow students on behalf of missions. This became a regular part of my college life.

Jim Elliot also organized a round-the-clock cycle, asking students to sign up for a 15 minute slot each day when he or she would promise to pray for missions and for mission recruitment on our campus. The entire 24 hours were filled in this way. Thus, every 15 minutes throughout the day and night at least one student was on his knees interceding for missions at Wheaton College.

Art Wiens was a war veteran who had served in Italy and planned to return as a missionary. He decided to pray systematically through the college directory, praying for 10 students by name every day. Art followed this faithfully through his college years.

I did not see Art again until we met in 1974 at the Lausanne Congress on World Evangelization in Switzerland. As we renewed fellowship and reminisced about old times, he said, "Dave, do you remember those prayer meetings we used to have at Wheaton?" "I certainly do," I replied.

Then Art said, "You know, Dave, I am still praying for 500 of our college contemporaries who are now on the mission field." "How do you know that many are overseas?" I asked. "I kept in touch with the alumni office and found out who was going as a missionary, and I still pray for them."

Astounded, I asked Art if I could see his prayer list. The next day he brought it to me, a battered old notebook he had started in college days with the names of hundreds of our classmates and fellow students.[13]

When I first read that account of prevailing prayer and the remarkable fruit that has come of it to the glory of Christ through the lives of radical, Spirit-empowered missionaries, I felt a surge of longing to set my hand to the plow and never take it off. I long to be like George Müller in the tenacity of prayer and missions. Müller wrote in his autobiography,

> I am now, in 1864, waiting upon God for certain blessings, for which I have daily besought Him for 19 years and 6 months, without one day's intermission. Still the full answer is not yet given concerning the conversion of certain individuals. In the meantime, I have received many thousands of answers to prayer. I have also prayed daily, without intermission, for the conversion of other individuals about ten years, for others six or seven years, for others four, three, and two years, for others about eighteen months; and still the answer is not yet granted, concerning these persons [whom I have prayed for nineteen years and six months] . . . Yet I am daily continuing in prayer and expecting the answer . . . Be encouraged, dear Christian reader, with fresh earnestness to give yourself to prayer, if you can only be sure that you ask for things which are for the glory of God.[14]

The call of Jesus is for prevailing prayer: "Always pray and do not lose heart" (Luke 18:1). By this his Father will be glorified (John 14:13). The supremacy of God in the mission of the church is proved and prized in prevailing prayer. I believe Christ's word to his church at the end of the twentieth century is a question:

> Will not God vindicate his elect, who cry to him day and night? Will he delay long over them? I tell you, he will vindicate them speedily. (Luke 18:7–8)

Do you ever cry out to the Lord, "How long, O Lord, how long till you vindicate your cause in the earth? How long till you rend the heavens and come down with power on your church? How long till you bring forth victory among all the peoples of the world?"

Is not his answer plain: "When my people cry to me *day and night*, I will vindicate them, and my cause will prosper among the nations." The war will be won by God. He will win it through the gospel of Jesus Christ. This gospel will run and triumph through prevailing prayer – so that in everything God might be glorified through Jesus Christ.

Notes

1. There are other texts we could look at besides those cited, for example, Revelation 6:2; 12:17; 17:14.
2. James Reapsome, "What's Holding up World Evangelization?", *Evangelical Missions Quarterly*, Vol. 24, No. 2, April, 1988, p. 118.
3. For additional texts concerning the promise of Christ's victory over the nations and their eventual turning to him see chapter five, pp. 185–188.
4. Cotton Mather, *The Great Works of Christ in America*, Vol. 1 (Edinburgh: Banner of Truth Trust, 1979, originally 1702), p. 562.
5. Whether one is a post-millennialist, as were most of the Puritans (though not all, e.g. William Twisse, Thomas Goodwin, William Bridge and Jeremiah Burroughs, who were all premillennial Westminster divines in the seventeenth century), or whether one is pre- or a-millennial, my point remains the same. Hope for the unstoppable success of Christ's mission (whether you see it as a golden age of gospel sway on earth, or as an ingathering of the elect from every people group on earth) is a crucial element in motivation and power for missions. Iain Murray's book, *The Puritan Hope* (Edinburgh: Banner of Truth Trust, 1971), is an inspiring and compelling account of this truth. Its thesis is: "We believe it can be conclusively shown that the inspiration which gave

rise to the first missionary societies of the modern era was nothing other than the doctrine and outlook which, revitalized by the eighteenth-century revival, had come down from the Puritans" (p. 135).

6. I have given an extensive Biblical defense of this truth in "The Pleasure of God in Election", in: *The Pleasures of God* (Portland: Multnomah Press, 1991), pp. 123–160.

7. This is a paraphrase of a sentence that is emblazoned on my memory because of the effect it had on my life at the time.

8. It was precisely this truth that encouraged the apostle Paul when he was downcast in Corinth. "And the Lord said to Paul one night in a vision, 'Do not be afraid, but speak and do not be silent; for I am with you, and no man shall attack you to harm you; *for I have many people in this city*'" (Acts 18:9–10). In other words, there are sheep here, and Jesus will call them through you, and they *will* come. Take heart.

9. Charles Spurgeon, *Twelve Sermons on Prayer* (Grand Rapids: Baker Book House, 1971), p. 105.

10. This is what I argue for in chapter four.

11. I have tried to argue extensively for the sovereignty of God in this irresistible sense in "The Pleasure of God in All that He Does", in *The Pleasures of God*, pp. 47–78.

12. A. T. Pierson, *The New Acts of the Apostles* (New York: 1894), pp. 352ff.

13. David Howard, "The Road to Urbana and Beyond", *Evangelical Missions Quarterly*, 21/1, January, 1985, pp. 115–116.

14. George Müller, *Autobiography*, compiled by G. Fred Bergin (London: J. Nisbet & Co. Ltd., 1906), p. 296.

3

The supremacy of God in missions through suffering

We measure the worth of a hidden treasure by what we will gladly sell to buy it. If we will sell all, then we measure the worth as supreme. If we will not, what we have is treasured more. "The kingdom of heaven is like a treasure hidden in a field, which a man found and covered up; then *in his joy* he goes and sells *all that he has* and buys that field" (Matthew 13:44). The extent of his *sacrifice* and the depth of his *joy* display the worth he puts on the treasure of God. Loss and suffering, joyfully accepted for the kingdom of God, show the supremacy of God's worth more clearly in the world than all worship and prayer.

This is why the stories of missionaries who gladly gave their all have made God more real and precious to many of us. The life of Henry Martyn has had this remarkable effect for almost 200 years.

Henry Martyn submits to God

He was born in England, February 18, 1781. His father was well-to-do and sent his son to a fine grammar school, and then to Cambridge in 1797, when he was 16. Four years later he took highest honors in mathematics, and the year after that first prize in Latin prose composition.

He had turned his back on God as a youth and during these days of academic achievement he became disillusioned with his dream. "I obtained my highest wishes, but was surprised to find that I had grasped a shadow." The treasure of the world rusted in his hands. The death of his father, the prayers of his sister, the counsel of a godly minister and the diary of David Brainerd brought him to his knees in submission to God. In 1802 he resolved to forsake a life of academic prestige and ease, and become a missionary. That was the first measure of the kingdom's worth in his life.

He became the assistant of Charles Simeon, the great evangelical preacher at Trinity Church in Cambridge, until his departure to India on July 17, 1805. His ministry was to be a chaplain with the East India Company. He arrived in Calcutta May 16, 1806, and the first day ashore found William Carey.

Martyn was an evangelical Anglican; Carey was a Baptist. And there was some tension over the use of liturgy. But Carey wrote that year, "A young clergyman, Mr. Martyn, is lately arrived, who is possessed of a truly missionary spirit . . . We take sweet counsel together, and go to the house of God as friends."

Alongside his chaplain's duties Martyn's main work was translation. Within two years, by March, 1808, he had translated part of the Book of Common Prayer, a commentary on the parables, and the entire New Testament into "Hindostanee".

He was then assigned to supervise the Persian version of the New Testament. It was not so well received as the other, and his health gave way in the process. So he decided to return to England for recovery, but to go by land through Persia in the hope of revising his translation on the way.

But he became so sick that he could barely press on. He died among strangers in the city of Tocat in Asiatic Turkey October 16, 1812. He was 31 years old.

Martyn's hidden pain

What you can't see in this overview of Martyn's life is the inner flights and plunges of spirit that make his achievement so real and so helpful to real people. I'm persuaded that the reason David Brainerd's *Life and Diary* and Henry Martyn's *Journal and Letters* have such abiding and deep power for the cause of mission is that they portray the life of the missionary as a life of constant warfare in the soul, not a life of uninterrupted calm. The suffering and struggle make us feel the supremacy of God in their lives all the more.

Listen to him on the boat on the way to India:

> I found it hard to realize divine things. I was more tried with desires after the world, than for two years past . . . The

seasickness, and the smell of the ship, made me feel very miserable, and the prospect of leaving all the comforts and communion of saints in England, to go forth to an unknown land, to endure such illness and misery with ungodly men for so many months, weighed heavy on my spirits. My heart was almost ready to break.

On top of this there is a love story to tell. Martyn was in love with Lydia Grenfell. He didn't feel right taking her along without going before her and proving his own reliance on God alone. But two months after he arrived in India on July 30, 1806 he wrote and proposed and asked her to come.

He waited 15 months (!) for the reply. His journal entry on October 24, 1807 reads:

An unhappy day; received at last a letter from Lydia, in which she refuses to come, because her mother will not consent to it. Grief and disappointment threw my soul into confusion at first; but gradually, as my disorder subsided, my eyes were opened, and reason resumed its office. I could not but agree with her, that it would not be for the glory of God, nor could we expect his blessing, if she acted in disobedience to her mother.

He took up his pen and wrote her that same day:

Though my heart is bursting with grief and disappointment, I write not to blame you. The rectitude of all your conduct secures you from censure ... Alas my rebellious heart – what a tempest agitates me! I knew not that I had made so little progress in a spirit of resignation to the Divine will.

For five years he held out hope that things might change. A steady stream of letters covered the thousands of miles between India and England. The last known letter that he wrote two months before his death (August 28, 1812) was addressed as usual to "My dearest Lydia". It closed:

Soon we shall have occasion for pen and ink no more; but I trust I shall shortly see thee face to face. Love to all the saints.
Believe me to be yours ever,
most faithfully and affectionately,
H. Martyn

Martyn never saw her again on this earth. But dying was not what he feared most, nor seeing Lydia what he desired most. His passion was to make known the supremacy of Christ in all of life. Near the very end he wrote, "Whether life or death be mine, may Christ be magnified in me! If he has work for me to do, I cannot die." Christ's work for Martyn was done. And he had done it well. His losses and pain made the supremacy of God in his life powerful for all time.[1]

"He bids him come and die"

Some suffering is the calling of every believer, but especially of those God calls to bear the gospel to the unreached. Dietrich Bonhoeffer's famous lines are absolutely Biblical: "The cross is not the terrible end to an otherwise God-fearing and happy life, but it meets us at the beginning of our communion with Christ. When Christ calls a man, he bids him come and die."[2] This is simply a paraphrase of Mark 8:34, "If any man would come after me, let him deny himself and *take up his cross* and follow me." To take up a cross and follow Jesus means to join Jesus on the Calvary road with a resolve to suffer and die with him. The cross is not a burden to bear, it is an instrument of pain and execution. It would be like saying, "Pick up your electric chair and follow me to the execution room." Or: "Pick up this sword and carry it to the place of beheading." Or: "Take up this rope and carry it to the gallows."

The domestication of cross-bearing into coughs and cranky spouses takes the radical thrust out of Christ's call. He is calling every believer to "renounce everything that he has," and to "hate his own life" (Luke 14:33, 26), and to take the road of obedience joyfully, no matter the loss on this earth. Following Jesus means that wherever obedience requires it, we will accept betrayal and rejection and beating and mockery and crucifixion and death. Jesus gives us the assurance that if we will follow him to Golgotha during all the Good Fridays of this life, we will also rise with him on the last Easter day of the resurrection. "Whoever loses his life for my sake and the gospel's will save it" (Mark

74

8:35). "He who hates his life in this world will keep it for eternal life" (John 12:25).

Do we need martyr models?

One of the most stunning and sobering words spoken at the second Lausanne Congress of World Evangelization in Manila in 1989 was spoken by George Otis concerning the call to martyrdom. He asked, "Is our failure to thrive in Muslim countries owing to the absence of martyrs? Can a covert church grow in strength? Does a young church need martyr models?" Many places in the world today feel the words of Jesus with all their radical impact: to choose Christ is to choose death, or the very high risk of death. David Barrett estimates that in 1993 about 150,000 Christians died as martyrs. He foresees that annual number moving to 200,000 by the year 2000.[3]

"I am crucified with Christ"

It's true that taking up our cross involves a spiritual transaction by which our "old nature" or "the flesh" dies with Christ and a "new creature" comes into being. This is one way the apostle applies the call of Jesus to take up our cross. "Those who belong to Christ Jesus *have crucified the flesh* with its passions and desires" (Galatians 5:24). "*I am crucified with Christ*. It is no longer I who live but Christ who lives in me. And the life I now live in the flesh I live by faith in the Son of God who loved me and gave himself for me" (Galatians 2:20). "Our old self *was crucified with him* so that the sinful body might be destroyed, and we might no longer be enslaved to sin" (Romans 6:6). "Set your minds on things that are above, not on things that are on the earth. For *you have died* and your life is hid with Christ in God" (Colossians 3:2–3).

But the point of this spiritual death is not that it takes the place of a real practical application of Jesus' teaching to physical suffering and death, but that it makes that application possible. Precisely because our old selfish, worldly, unloving, fearful, proud selves have died with Christ, and a new trusting, loving, heaven-bent, hope-filled self has come into being – precisely because of this inner death and new life, we are able to take risks, and suffer the pain, and even die without despair but full of hope.

"If they persecuted me, they will persecute you"

So we must not water down the call to suffer. We must not domesticate all the New Testament teaching on affliction and persecution just because our lives are so smooth. It may be that we have not chosen to live in all the radical ways of love that God wants us to. It may be that our time of suffering is just around the corner. But it will not do to take our own comfortable lives and make them the measure of what we allow the Bible to mean.

Jesus came into the world to give his life as a ransom for many (Mark 10:45). There was a divine necessity upon him to suffer: "The Son of man *must* suffer many things" (Mark 8:31; cf. Luke 17:25). Because this was his vocation, suffering also becomes the vocation of those who follow him. It is implied in the words, "As the Father has sent me, even so send I you" (John 20:21). And Jesus made it explicit when he said, "Remember the word that I said to you, 'A servant is not greater than his master.' If they persecuted me, they will persecute you" (John 15:20). "If they have called the master of the house Beelzebul, how much more will they malign those of his household" (Matthew 10:25).

Does his suffering for us mean we escape suffering?

It would be easy to make a superficial mistake about the death of Christ as a substitutionary atonement. The mistake would be to say that, since Christ died for me, I don't need to die for others. Since he suffered for me, I don't need to suffer for others. In other words, if his death is really substitutionary shouldn't I escape what he bore for me? How can his death be a call for my death, if his death took the place of my death?

The answer is that Christ died for us so that we would not have to die for sin, *not* so that we would not have to die for others. Christ bore the punishment of our sin so that our death and suffering is never a punishment from God. The call to suffer with Christ is not a call to bear our sins the way he bore them but to love the way he loved. The

76

death of Christ for the sin of my selfishness is not meant to help me escape the suffering of love but to enable it. Because he took my guilt and my punishment and reconciled me to God as my Father, I do not need to cling any longer to the comforts of earth in order to be content. I am free to let things go for the sake of making the supremacy of God's worth known.

Christ's death: substitution and pattern

Peter shows us the connection between the death of Christ as a substitution to be received and a pattern to be followed. He speaks to Christian slaves who may be mistreated by their unbelieving masters:

> For what credit is it, if when you do wrong and are beaten for it you take it patiently? But if when you do right and suffer for it you take it patiently, you have God's approval. *For to this you have been called, because Christ also suffered for you, leaving you an example, that you should follow in his steps.* (1 Peter 2:20–21)

Notice the all-important little phrase "for you". Christ suffered "for you". This is the substitutionary atonement. He took our place and did for us what we could not do for ourselves. "He himself bore our sins in his body on the tree" (1 Peter 2:24). This is a work nobody else but the Son of God could do for us (Romans 8:3). It cannot be initiated or duplicated. It happened once for all. "He appeared *once for all* at the end of the age to put away sin by the sacrifice of himself" (Hebrews 9:26). This is the foundation of all our hope and joy and freedom and love. Our sins are forgiven and we have eternal life (Ephesians 1:7; John 3:16). God is for us and nothing can separate us from him (Romans 8:31, 35–39).

Therefore when Peter says that Jesus left you "an example, that you should follow in his steps", he did not mean that you are called to make atonement for sin. He meant that you are called to love like Jesus, and be willing to suffer for doing right like he did. The pattern we follow is not the atonement but the love and the pain. The relationship between the two is crucial. The substitution is the foundation of the imitation, not vice versa. We do not earn our forgiveness by suffering like Jesus. We are freed to love like Jesus because our sins are forgiven. Because he suffered *for* us, we can suffer *like* him.

In fact Peter says, "To this [way of suffering] you have been *called*." It is our vocation. Don't make the mistake of saying: "Oh, that was addressed to slaves with cruel masters, and does not apply to us." This is a mistake because 1 Peter 3:8–9 is addressed to all believers but makes the same point: "Finally, *all of you* . . . do not return evil for evil or reviling for reviling; but on the contrary bless, *for to this you have been called*, that you may obtain a blessing." This is not only the calling of slaves. It is the calling of all Christians. The way Christ lived and suffered and died places a calling on us to show with our lives the supremacy of this love by living in the same way.

So Peter goes on to describe how Jesus handled unjust suffering. We are called to do it the way he did it: "He committed no sin; no guile was found on his lips. When he was reviled, he did not revile in return; when he suffered, he did not threaten; but he trusted to him who judges justly" (1 Peter 2:22–23).

Arm yourselves with this "thought"

Then to make the call even more clear Peter says later on, "Since therefore Christ suffered in the flesh, arm yourselves with the same thought" (1 Peter 4:1). The suffering of Christ is a call for a certain mindset toward suffering, namely, that it is normal, and that the path of love and missions will often require it. Thus Peter says, "Beloved, do not be surprised at the fiery ordeal which comes upon you to prove you, as though something strange were happening to you" (1 Peter 4:12). Suffering with Christ is not strange; it is your calling, your vocation. It is the "same experience of suffering required of your brotherhood through the world" (1 Peter 5:9). This is the "thought" that we need to put on like armor, lest we be vulnerable to suffering as something strange.

Preparing for suffering – now!

Richard Wurmbrand endured fourteen years of imprisonment and torture in his homeland of Romania between 1948 and 1964. He had led a secret underground ministry when the Communists seized Romania and tried to control the church for their purposes. Wurmbrand, like the apostle Peter, stresses the tremendous need to get spiritually ready to suffer.

What shall we do about these tortures? Will we be able to bear them? If I do not bear them I put in prison another fifty or sixty men whom I know, because that is what the Communists wish from me, to betray those around me. And here comes the great need for the role of preparation for suffering which must start now. *It is too difficult* to prepare yourself for it when the Communists have put you in prison . . .

I remember my last confirmation class before I left Romania. I took a group of ten to fifteen boys and girls on a Sunday morning, not to a church, but to the zoo. Before the cage of lions I told them, "Your forefathers in faith were thrown before such wild beasts for their faith. Know that you also will have to suffer. You will not be thrown before lions, but you will have to do with men who would be much worse than lions. Decide here and now if you wish to pledge allegiance to Christ." They had tears in their eyes when they said, "Yes".

We have to make the preparation now, before we are imprisoned. In prison you lose everything. You are undressed and given a prisoner's suit. No more nice furniture, nice carpets, or nice curtains. You do not have a wife any more and you do not have your children. You do not have your library and you never see a flower. Nothing of what makes life pleasant remains. Nobody resists who has not renounced the pleasures of life beforehand.[4]

Paul tried to prepare his converts for suffering. Like Peter he armed them with this "thought" – that suffering is our calling. He said to the newer believers in Thessalonica, "We set Timothy . . . to exhort you that no one be moved by these afflictions. You yourselves know that *this is to be our lot*" (1 Thessalonians 3:2–3). Literally verse 3

79

means, "we are appointed for this". That is, it's our calling.

Similarly, as Paul returned from his first missionary journey he stopped at the young churches and encouraged them with this "thought". "He strengthened the souls of the disciples, exhorting them to continue in the faith, and saying that *through many tribulations we must enter the kingdom*" (Acts 14:22). It was important for the new believers to be "armed with this thought": that the road to the kingdom is the Calvary road; there are many tribulations. There is a divine necessity: "We *must* enter" this way. It is our calling. "All who desire to live a godly life in Christ *will* be persecuted" (2 Timothy 3:12).

"Let us go forth with him outside the camp"

The writer to the Hebrews connects the atoning work of Christ and the pattern of his suffering the same way Peter does, only with vividly different words.

> So Jesus also suffered outside the gate in order to sanctify the people through his own blood. Therefore let us go forth with him outside the camp and bear the abuse he endured. For here we have no lasting city, but we seek the city which is to come. (Hebrews 13:12–14)

Jesus suffered first in a way that we can't: "to sanctify the people by his blood". The death of the Son of God is absolutely unique in its effect. But then notice the word "therefore". Because Jesus died for us in this way, *therefore* let us go forth with him outside the camp and bear the abuse he endured. It does not say: since he suffered for us, *therefore* we can have an easy life free from suffering and abuse and danger. Just the opposite. Jesus' suffering is the *basis* of our going with him and bearing the same abuse he bore.

Outside the camp means outside the borders of safety and comfort. It is above all a missionary text. Outside the camp are the "other sheep" that are not of this fold. Outside the camp are the unreached nations. Outside the camp are the places and the people who will be costly to reach and will require no small sacrifice. But to this we are called: "Let us go and bear the abuse he endured." It is our vocation.

Bearing the abuse he endured in Sudan

The abuse may range from the slightest ostracism to agony of torture and death. Both are probably happening every day in our world. We only hear a tiny fraction of the "abuse he endured". For example, *Mission Frontiers* carried this report in 1988.

> In 1983, the Sudan was declared an Islamic republic. At that time, Islamic Sharia law was imposed on all the country's citizens. Since then, dozens of Christian pastors have been killed and countless Christian churches burned . . .
>
> This past March [1987] 27 and 28, according to a 33 page report filed by Khartoum University professors, Drs. Ushari Ahmad Mahmud and Suleyman Ali Baldo (both Muslims), more than 100 Dinka men, women, and children were slaughtered and burned to death in the western Sudan town of Diein.
>
> The massacre erupted when 25 Christian Dinka worshipers were driven from their evening prayer service by a mob of Rizeigat Muslims wielding sticks, spears, axes, and Soviet-made Kalashnikov guns. That evening, five to seven Dinkas were murdered, and dozens of homes were burned.
>
> Early the next morning, as many Dinkas were being loaded into rail boxcars for safe evacuation from the troubled town, hundreds of armed Rizeigats converged on the train station and began attacking the defenseless Dinkas. Burning mattresses were heaped on the top of huddled Dinkas. Others were shot, mutilated, and clubbed to death. By nightfall, more than 1000 Dinkas were dead.[5]

As horrible as this is, Peter said that when the fiery ordeal comes we should not be surprised as though something strange were happening to us. We live in such relative ease that such thinking seems incomprehensible to us. But I believe God is calling us to arm ourselves with this very thought: Christ suffered outside the gate brutally and without justice, leaving us an example that we should follow in his steps.

May we spend the night on death row?

Charles Wesley gives us an example of how one might obey Hebrews 13:13 and go "outside the camp" and bear the abuse he endured. On July 18, 1738, two months after his conversion, Charles Wesley did an amazing thing. He had spent the week witnessing to inmates at the Newgate prison with a friend named "Bray" whom he described as "a poor ignorant mechanic". One of the men they spoke to was "a black [slave] that had robbed his master". He was sick with a fever and was condemned to die.

On Tuesday Charles and Bray asked if they could be locked in overnight with the prisoners who were to be executed the next day [this is outside the camp!]. That night they spoke the gospel. They told the men that "One came down from heaven to save lost sinners." They described the sufferings of the Son of God, his sorrows, agony and death.

The next day the men were loaded onto a cart and taken to Tyburn. Charles went with them. Ropes were fastened around their necks so that the cart could be driven off and leave them swinging in the air to choke to death.

The fruit of Wesley's and Bray's night-long labor was astonishing. Here is what Wesley wrote:

> They were all cheerful; full of comfort, peace and triumph; assuredly persuaded Christ had died for them, and waited to receive them into paradise ... The black ... saluted me with his looks. As often as his eyes met mine, he smiled with the most composed, delightful countenance I ever saw.
>
> We left them going to meet their Lord, ready for the Bridegroom. When the cart drew off, not one stirred, or struggled for life, but meekly gave up their spirits. Exactly at twelve they were turned off. I spoke a few suitable words to the crowd; and returned, full of peace and confidence in our friends' happiness. That hour under the gallows was the most blessed hour of my life.[6]

Two things amaze and inspire me in this story. One is the astonishing power of Wesley's message about the truth and love of Christ. All the condemned prisoners were converted. And they were so deeply converted that they could look death in the face (without any long period of "follow up" or "discipling") and give up their lives, with confidence that Christ would receive them. Their suffering was not for righteousness' sake. But the same dynamics were at work to

82

sustain them. They looked on their suffering as something they must pass through on the way to heaven, and the hope of glory was so real they died in peace. O, for such power in witness!

The other thing that amazes me is the sheer fact that Wesley went to the prison and asked to be locked up all night with condemned criminals who had nothing more to lose if they killed another person. Wesley had no supervisor telling him that this was his job. He was not a professional prison minister. It would have been comfortable and pleasant to spend the evening at home conversing with friends. Then why did he go?

God put it in his heart to go. And Wesley yielded. There are hundreds of strange and radical things God is calling his people to do in the cause of world missions. Not everyone will hear the same call. Yours will be unique. It may be something you never dreamed of doing. It may be something you have *only* dreamed of doing. But I urge you to listen to the leading of the Spirit to see where "outside the camp" he may be taking you "to bear the abuse he endured".

"I will show him how much he must suffer"

Afflictions are our vocation, whether we are missionaries or not. But this is especially the calling of those appointed to reach the unreached peoples of the world. Paul is the prototype of such missionaries. When the Lord sent Ananias to Paul in Damascus he sent him with the armor of this "thought" mentioned in 1 Peter 4:1. Only it was intensified for Paul. The Lord said, "Go, for he is a chosen instrument of mine to carry my name before the Gentiles and kings and the sons of Israel; for *I will show him how much he must suffer for the sake of my name*" (Acts 9:15–16). Then God kept on pressing this "thought" on Paul: "The Holy Spirit testifies to me in every city that *imprisonment and afflictions await me*" (Acts 20:23).

It was part of Paul's calling. It became so much a part of his identity and ministry that he took it as a badge of his apostolic authenticity. It was like part of his visa papers to prove his right to do what God had called him to do.

As servants of God we commend ourselves in every way: through great endurance, in afflictions, hardships, calamities, beatings, imprisonments, tumults, labors, watching, hunger ... in honor and dishonor, in ill repute and good repute. We are treated as imposters, and yet are true; as unknown, and yet well known; as dying, and behold we live; as punished, and yet not killed; as sorrowful, yet always rejoicing; as poor, yet making many rich; as having nothing, and yet possessing everything. (2 Corinthians 6:4–10)

The extraordinary suffering of the apostle Paul staggers the mind. The litany of 2 Corinthians 11:23–28 is overwhelming, especially if you think of the pain of each part and the multiplied pain upon pain as the parts mount up. It is a rare glimpse into the cumulative pain and sorrow of Paul's missionary life:

... with far greater labors, far more imprisonments, with countless beatings, and often near death. Five times I have received at the hands of the Jews the forty lashes less one. Three times I have been beaten with rods; once I was stoned. Three times I have been shipwrecked; a night and a day I have been adrift at sea; on frequent journeys, in danger from rivers, danger from robbers, danger from my own people, danger from Gentiles, danger in the city, danger in the wilderness, danger at sea, danger from false brethren; in toil and hardship, through many a sleepless night, in hunger and thirst, often without food, in cold and exposure. And, apart from other things, there is the daily pressure upon me of my anxiety for all the churches.

Lest we pass over this too quickly, without having the breath knocked out of us, consider what it meant to receive "forty lashes less one". It meant that he was stripped and tied to some kind of stake so that he would not run or fall. Then a person trained in flogging would take a whip, maybe with or without shards in the leather, and lash Paul's back thirty-nine times. Halfway through, or earlier perhaps, the skin would probably begin to break and tear. By the end there would be parts of Paul's back that were like jelly. The lacerations were not clean, as with a razor blade. The skin was torn and shredded, so that the healing was slow and perhaps complicated by infection. They knew nothing of sterilization in those days, and had no anti-septics. It would take months perhaps before his garments could hang on his back without pain.

Now, with that view, consider that this happened again a second time on the same back, opening all the scars. It healed more slowly the second time. Then consider that some months later it happened a third time. Imagine what his back must have looked like. Then it happened again. And finally it happened a fifth time. And this is just one of Paul's sufferings.

Does God allow or appoint the suffering of his messengers?

Why does God allow this? No, that is not quite the right question. We have to ask, Why does God *appoint* this? These things are part of God's plan for his people just as the suffering and death of Jesus was part of God's plan for salvation (Acts 4:27–28; Isaiah 53:10). It is true that Satan can be the more immediate agent of suffering, but even he may do nothing without God's permission.[7] Paul describes suffering as a gift of God: "It has been *given* to you that for the sake of Christ you should not only believe in him, but also *suffer for his sake*" (Philippians 1:29).

Twice Peter spoke of suffering as being God's will: "It is better to suffer for doing right, *if that should be God's will*, than for doing wrong ... Let those who suffer according to God's will do right and entrust their souls to a faithful Creator" (1 Peter 3:17; 4:19).

James placed all of life, including the seemingly acci-dental hindrances to our plans, under the sovereign will of God: "Come now, you who say, 'Today or tomorrow we will go into such and such a town and spend a year there and trade and get gain' ... Instead you ought to say, '*If the Lord wills* we shall live and we shall do this or that'" (James 4:13, 15). Flat tires, car accidents, road construction – whatever can keep you from doing your plan – are the will of God. "*If God wills* you will live and do this or that."

The writer to the Hebrews puts all our suffering under the banner of God's loving discipline. It is not an accident that he permits; it is a plan for our holiness.

In your struggle against sin you have not yet resisted to the point of shedding your blood. And have you forgotten the exhortation which addresses you as sons? – "My son, do not regard lightly the discipline of the Lord, nor lose courage when you are chastened by him. For the Lord disciplines him whom he loves, and chastises every son whom he receives." (Hebrews 12:4–6)

The suffering that missionaries meet is not something unforeseen by the Lord. He saw it clearly, embraced it for himself, and sent his disciples into the same danger. "Behold I send you out as sheep in the midst of wolves" (Matthew 10:16). "I will send them prophets and apostles, some of whom they will kill and persecute" (Luke 11:49). As Paul says in 1 Thessalonians 3:3, we are "appointed" or "set" for these things.

Six reasons God appoints suffering for his servants

So our question is: Why? Why did God appoint for Paul to suffer so much as the prototype of the frontier missionary? God is sovereign. As every child knows, he could toss Satan into the pit today if he wanted to and all his terrorizing of the church would be over. But God wills that the mission of the church advance through storm and suffering. What are the reasons? I will mention six.

Deeper faith and deeper holiness

First, as we have just seen in Hebrews 12, God disciplines his children through suffering. His aim is deeper faith and deeper holiness. "He disciplines us for our good that we may share his holiness" (Hebrews 12:10). Jesus experienced the same thing. "Although he was a Son, he learned obedience through what he suffered" (Hebrews 5:8). This does not mean that Jesus grew from disobedience to obedience. The same writer says he never sinned (Hebrews 4:15). It means that the process through which he demonstrated deeper and deeper obedience was the process of suffering. For us there is not only the need to have our obedience tested and proven deep, but also purified of all remnants of self-reliance and entanglement with the world.

Paul described this experience in his own life like this:

> We do not want you to be ignorant, brethren, of the affliction we experienced in Asia, for we were so utterly, unbearably crushed that we despaired of life itself. We felt that we had received the sentence of death, but *that was to make us rely not on ourselves, but on God who raises the dead.* (2 Corinthians 1:8–9)

Paul does not concede his suffering to the hand of Satan but says that God ordained it for the increase of his faith. God knocked the props of life out from under Paul's heart so that he would have no choice but to fall on God and get his hope from the promise of the resurrection. This is the first purpose of missionary suffering: to wean us from the world and set our hope fully in God alone (cf. Romans 5:3–4). Since the freedom to love flows from this kind of radical hope (Colossians 1:4–5), suffering is a primary means of building compassion into the lives of God's servants.

Thousands of missionaries through the centuries have found that the sufferings of life have been the school of Christ where lessons of faith were taught that could not be learned anywhere else. For example, Francis Xavier (1506–1552), who founded the Jesuit missionary movement and himself served in India and Japan, was always in pursuit of a deeper life with God. He died at 46 awaiting passage to the great forbidden China. Notice from one of his last letters how he longs for his ministry to benefit not only the Chinese but his own faith as well.

> The danger of all dangers would be to lose trust and confidence in the mercy of God for whose love and service we came to manifest the law of Jesus Christ, His Son, our Redeemer and Lord, as He well knows ... To distrust Him would be a far more terrible thing than any physical evil which all the enemies of God put together could inflict on us, for without God's permission neither the devils nor their human ministers could hinder us in the slightest degree ... We are therefore determined to make our way into China at all costs, and *I hope in God that the upshot of our journey will be the increase of our holy faith*, however much the devil and his ministers may persecute us. If God is for us who can overthrow us?[8]

87

Suffering makes your cup increase

Secondly, by enduring suffering with patience the reward of our experience of God's glory in heaven increases. This is part of Paul's meaning in 2 Corinthians 4:17–18.

> This slight momentary affliction is preparing for us an eternal weight of glory beyond all comparison, because we look not to the things that are seen but to the things that are unseen, for the things that are seen are transient, but the things that are unseen are eternal.

Paul's affliction is "preparing" or "effecting" or "bringing about" a weight of glory beyond all comparison. We must take seriously Paul's words here. He is not merely saying that he has a great hope in heaven that enables him to endure suffering. That is true. But here he says that the suffering has an effect on the weight of glory. There seems to be a connection between the suffering endured and the degree of glory enjoyed. Of course the glory outstrips the suffering infinitely, as Paul says in Romans 8:18: "I consider the sufferings of this present time *not worth comparing with the glory* that is to be revealed to us." Nevertheless the weight of that glory, or the experience of that glory, seems to be more or less, depending in part on the affliction we have endured with patient faith.

Jesus pointed in the same direction when he said, "Blessed are you when men revile you and persecute you and say all kinds of evil against you falsely on my account. Rejoice and be glad, for *your reward is great in heaven*" (Matthew 5:11–12). This would carry the greatest encouragement to rejoice if Jesus meant that the more we endure suffering in faith, the greater will be our reward. If a Christian who suffers much for Jesus and one who does not suffer much experience God's final glory in exactly the same way and degree, it would seem strange to tell the suffering Christian to rejoice and be glad (in that very day, cf. Luke 6:23) because of the reward he would receive even if he did not suffer. The reward promised seems to be in response to the suffering and a specific recompense for it. If this is not explicit and certain here, it does seem to be implied in other passages of the New Testament. I will let

Jonathan Edwards bring them out as we listen to one of the most profound reflections on this problem I have ever read. Here Edwards deals, in a breathtaking way, with the issue of how there can be degrees of happiness in a world of perfect joy.

There are different degrees of happiness and glory in heaven ... The glory of the saints above will be in some proportion to their eminency in holiness and good works here [and patience through suffering is one of the foremost good works, cf. Romans 2:7]. Christ will reward all according to their works. He that gained ten pounds was made ruler over ten cities, and he that gained five pounds over five cities (Luke 19:17–19). "He that soweth sparingly, shall reap sparingly; and he that soweth bountifully shall reap also bountifully" (2 Corinthians 9:6). And the apostle Paul tells us that, as one star differs from another star in glory, so also it shall be in the resurrection of the dead (1 Corinthians 15:41). Christ tells us that he who gives a cup of cold water unto a disciple in the name of a disciple, shall in no wise lose his reward. But this could not be true, if a person should have no greater reward for doing many good works than if he did but few.

It will be no damp to the happiness of those who have lower degrees of happiness and glory, that there are others advanced in glory above them: for all shall be perfectly happy, every one shall be perfectly satisfied. Every vessel that is cast into this ocean of happiness is full, though there are some vessels far larger than others; and there shall be no such thing as envy in heaven, but perfect love shall reign through the whole society. Those who are not so high in glory as others, will not envy those that are higher, but they will have so great, and strong, and pure love to them, that they will rejoice in their superior happiness; their love to them will be such that they will rejoice that they are happier than themselves; so that instead of having a damp to their own happiness, it will add to it ...

And so, on the other hand, those that are highest in glory, as they will be the most lovely, so they will proportionally excel in divine benevolence and love to others, and will have more love to God and to the saints than those that are lower in holiness and happiness. And besides, those that will excel in glory will also excel in humility. Here in this world, those that are above others are the objects of envy, because . . . others conceive of them as being lifted up with it; but in heaven it will not be so, but those saints in heaven who excel in happiness will also [excel] in holiness, and consequently in humility . . . The exaltation of some in heaven above the rest will be so far from diminishing the perfect happiness and joy of the rest who are inferior, that they will be the happier for it; such will be the union in their society that they will be partakers of each other's happiness. Then will be fulfilled in its perfections that which is declared in 1 Corinthians 12:22, "If one of the members be honored all the members rejoice with it."[9]

Thus one of the aims of God in the suffering of the saints, is to enlarge their capacity to enjoy his glory both here and in the age to come. When their cup is picked up, as it were from the "refuse of the world" (1 Corinthians 4:13), and tossed into the ocean of heaven's happiness, it will hold more happiness for having been long weaned off the world and made to live on God alone.

The price of making others bold

Thirdly, God uses the suffering of his missionaries to awaken others out of their slumbers of indifference and make them bold. When Paul was imprisoned in Rome he wrote of this to the church at Philippi. "Most of the brothers have been made confident in the Lord because of my imprisonment and are much more bold to speak the word of God without fear" (Philippians 1:14). If he must, God will use the suffering of his devoted emissaries to make a sleeping church wake up and take risks for God.

The sufferings and dedication of young David Brainerd have had this effect on thousands. Henry Martyn recorded Brainerd's impact on his life again and again in his *Journal*. September 11, 1805: "What a quickening example has he often been to me, especially on this account, that he was of a weak and sickly constitution!" May 8, 1806: "Blessed be the memory of that holy man! I feel happy that I shall have his book with me in India, and thus enjoy, in a manner, the benefit of his company and example." May 12, 1806: "My soul was revived today through God's never-ceasing comparison, so that I found the refreshing presence of God in secret duties; especially was I most abundantly encouraged by reading D. Brainerd's account of the difficulties attending a mission to the heathen. Oh, blessed be the memory of that beloved saint! No uninspired writer ever did me so much good. I felt most sweetly joyful to labor amongst the poor natives here; and my willingness was, I think, more divested of those romantic notions, which have sometimes inflated me with false spirits."[10]

Five inspiring wives

In our own time it is hard to overstate the impact that the martyrdom of Jim Elliot, Nate Saint, Ed McCully, Pete Fleming, and Roger Youderian has had on generations of students. The word that appeared again and again in the testimonies of those who heard the Auca story was "dedication". But more than is often realized, it was the strength of the wives of these men that made many of us feel a surge of desire to be like that.

Barbara Youderian, the wife of Roger, wrote in her diary that night in January, 1956,

> Tonight the Captain told us of his finding four bodies in the river. One had tee-shirt and blue-jeans. Roj was the only one who wore them ... God gave me this verse two days ago, Psalm 48:14, "For this God is our God for ever and ever, He will be our Guide even unto death." As I came face to face with the news of Roj's death, my heart was filled with praise. He was worthy of his homegoing. Help me, Lord, to be both mummy and daddy.[11]

It is not hard to feel the Biblical point Paul was making. The suffering of the servants of God, borne with faith and even praise, is a shattering experience to apathetic saints whose lives are empty in the midst of countless comforts.

Applications doubled at his death

More recently the execution of Wycliffe missionary Chet Bitterman by the Colombian guerrilla group M-19 on March 6, 1981, unleashed an amazing zeal for the cause of Christ. Chet had been in captivity for seven weeks while his wife Brenda and little daughters Anna and Esther waited in Bogotá. The demand of M-19 was that Wycliffe get out of Colombia.

> They shot him just before dawn – a single bullet to the chest. Police found his body in the bus where he died, in a parking lot in the south of town. He was clean and shaven, his face relaxed. A guerrilla banner wrapped his remains. There were no signs of torture.

In the year following Chet's death "applications for overseas service with Wycliffe Bible Translators doubled. This trend was continued."[12] It is not the kind of missionary mobilization that any of us would choose. But it is God's way. "Unless a grain of wheat falls into the earth and dies, it remains alone; but if it dies it bears much fruit" (John 12:24).

"I complete what is lacking in Christ's afflictions"

Fourthly, the suffering of Christ's messengers ministers to those they are trying to reach and may open them to the gospel. This was one of the ways he brought the gospel to bear on the people in Thessalonica. "You know what kind of men we proved to be among you *for your sake*. And *you became imitators of us* and of the Lord, for *you received the word in much affliction* inspired by the Holy Spirit" (1 Thessalonians 1:5–6). They had imitated Paul by enduring much affliction with joy. And that is the kind of man Paul had proved to be among them. So it was his suffering that moved them and drew them to his authentic love and truth.

This is the kind of ministry Paul had in mind when he said, "As we share abundantly in Christ's sufferings, so through Christ we share abundantly in comfort too. If we are afflicted it is for your comfort and salvation" (2 Corinthians 1:5–6). His sufferings were the means God was using to bring salvation to the Corinthian church. They could see the suffering love of Christ in Paul. He was actually sharing in Christ's sufferings and making them real for the church.

This is part of what Paul meant in that amazing

statement in Colossians 1:24, "I rejoice in my sufferings for your sake, and in my flesh *I complete what is lacking in Christ's afflictions, for the sake of his body,* that is, the church." Christ's afflictions are not lacking in their atoning sufficiency. They are lacking in that they are not known and felt by people who were not at the cross. Paul dedicates himself not only to carry the message of those sufferings to the nations, but also to suffer with Christ and for Christ in such a way that what people see are "Christ's sufferings". In this way he follows the pattern of Christ by laying down his life for the life of the church. "I endure everything for the sake of the elect that they may obtain salvation in Christ Jesus with its eternal glory" (2 Timothy 2:10).

"When we saw your blistered feet"

While I was working on this book I had an opportunity to hear J. Oswald Sanders speak. His message touched deeply on suffering. He was 89 years old and had written a book a year since he turned 70! I mention that only to exult in the utter dedication of a life poured out for the gospel without thought of coasting in self-indulgence from sixty-five to the grave.

He told the story of an indigenous missionary who walked barefoot from village to village preaching the gospel in India. After a long day of many miles and much discouragement he came to a certain village and tried to speak the gospel but was spurned. So he went to the edge of the village dejected and lay down under a tree and slept from exhaustion.

When he awoke the whole town was gathered to hear him. The head man of the village explained that they came to look him over while he was sleeping. When they saw his blistered feet they concluded that he must be a holy man, and that they had been evil to reject him. They were sorry and wanted to hear the message that he was willing to suffer so much to bring them.

At the third beating the women wept

One of the unlikeliest men to attend the Itinerant Evangelists' Conference in Amsterdam sponsored by the Billy

Graham Association was a Masai warrior named Joseph. But his story won him a hearing with Dr. Graham himself. The story is told by Michael Card.

One day Joseph, who was walking along one of these hot, dirty African roads, met someone who shared the gospel of Jesus Christ with him. Then and there he accepted Jesus as his Lord and Savior. The power of the Spirit began transforming his life; he was filled with such excitement and joy that the first thing he wanted to do was return to his own village and share that same Good News with the members of his local tribe.

Joseph began going from door-to-door, telling everyone he met about the Cross of Jesus and the salvation it offered, expecting to see their faces light up the way his had. To his amazement the villagers not only didn't care, they became violent. The men of the village seized him and held him to the ground while the women beat him with strands of barbed wire. He was dragged from the village and left to die alone in the bush.

Joseph somehow managed to crawl to a waterhole, and there, after days of passing in and out of consciousness, found the strength to get up. He wondered about the hostile reception he had received from people he had known all his life. He decided he must have left something out or told the story of Jesus incorrectly. After rehearsing the message he had first heard, he decided to go back and share his faith once more.

Joseph limped into the circle of huts and began to proclaim Jesus. "He died for you, so that you might find forgiveness and come to know the living God" he pleaded. Again he was grabbed by the men of the village and held while the women beat him, reopening wounds that had just begun to heal. Once more they dragged him unconscious from the village and left him to die.

To have survived the first beating was truly remarkable. To live through the second was a miracle. Again, days later, Joseph awoke in the wilderness, bruised, scarred — and determined to go back.

He returned to the small village and this time, they attacked him before he had a chance to open his mouth. As they flogged him for the third and probably the last time, he again spoke to them of Jesus Christ, the Lord. Before he passed out, the last thing he saw was that the women who were beating him began to weep.

This time he awoke in his own bed. The ones who had so severely beaten him were now trying to save his life and nurse him back to health. The entire village had come to Christ.[13]

Surely this is something of what Paul meant when he said, "I complete what is lacking in Christ's afflictions, for the sake of his body."

Suffering enforces the missionary command to go

Fifthly, the suffering of the church is used by God to reposition the missionary troops in places they might not have otherwise gone. This is clearly the effect that Luke wants us to see in the story of the martyrdom of Stephen and the persecution that came after it. God spurs the church into missionary service by the suffering she endures. Therefore we must not judge too quickly the apparent setbacks and tactical defeats of the church. If you see things with the eyes of God, the Master Strategist, what you see in every setback is the positioning of troops for a greater advance and a greater display of his wisdom and power and love.

Acts 8:1 charts the divine strategy for the persecution: "On that day [the day of Stephen's murder] a great persecution arose against that church in Jerusalem; and they were all scattered throughout the region of *Judea and Samaria*, except the apostles." Up till now no one had moved out to Judea and Samaria in spite of what Jesus had said in Acts 1:8. "You shall receive power when the Holy Spirit has come upon you; and you shall be my witness in Jerusalem *and in all Judea and Samaria* . . ." It is no accident that these are the very two regions to which the persecution sends the church. What obedience will not achieve, persecution will.

To confirm this divine missionary purpose of the persecution, Luke refers back to it in Acts 11:19. "Now those who were scattered because of the persecution that arose over Stephen traveled as far as Phoenicia and Cyprus and Antioch, speaking the word to none except Jews." But in Antioch some spoke to Greeks also. In other words, the

95

persecution not only sent the church to Judea and Samaria (Acts 8:1), but also beyond to the nations (Acts 11:19).

The inertia of ease, the apathy of abundance

The lesson here is not just that God is sovereign and turns setbacks into triumphs. The lesson is that comfort and ease and affluence and prosperity and safety and freedom often cause a tremendous inertia in the church. The very things that we think would produce personnel and energy and creative investment of time and money for the missionary cause, instead produce the exact opposite: weakness, apathy, lethargy, self-centeredness, preoccupation with security.

The *Minneapolis Star Tribune* carried an article on Friday, May 3, 1991 that showed how the richer we are the smaller the percentage of our income we give to the church and its mission. The poorest fifth of the church give 3.4% of their income to the church and the richest fifth give 1.6% – half as much as the poorer church members. It is a strange principle, that probably goes right to the heart of our sinfulness and Christ's sufficiency – that hard times, like persecution, often produce more personnel, more prayer, more power, more open purses than easy times.

It is hard for a rich man to enter the kingdom of heaven, Jesus said (Matthew 19:23). It is also hard for rich people to help others enter. Jesus said as much in the parable of the soils. "The cares of the world, and *the delight in riches*, and *the desire for other things* enter in and choke the word and it proves unfruitful" (Mark 4:19). Unfruitful for missions and most every other good work.

Persecution can have harmful effects on the church. But prosperity, it seems, is even more devastating to the mission God calls us to. My point here is not that we should seek persecution. That would be presumption – like jumping off the temple. The point is that we should be very wary of prosperity and excessive ease and comfort and affluence. And we should not be disheartened but filled with hope if we are persecuted for righteousness' sake. Because the point of Acts 8:1 is that God makes persecution serve the mission of the church.

We must not be glib about this. The price of missionary advance is immense. Stephen paid for it with his life. And Stephen was one of the brightest stars in the Jerusalem sky. His enemies "could not withstand the wisdom and the Spirit with which he spoke" (Acts 6:10). Surely he was more valuable alive than dead, we would all reason. He was needed! There was no one like Stephen! But God saw it another way.

How Joseph Stalin served the cause

The way God brought whole Uzbek villages to Christ in the twentieth century is a great illustration of God's strange use of upheaval and displacement. Bill and Amy Stearns tell the story in their hope-filled book, *Catch the Vision 2000*. The key player was Joseph Stalin.

> Thousands of Koreans fled what is now North Korea in the 30's as the Japanese invaded. Many of these settled around Vladivostok. When Stalin in the late 30's and early 40's began developing Vladivostok as a weapons manufacturing center, he deemed the Koreans a security risk. So he relocated them in five areas around the Soviet Union. One of those areas was Tashkent, hub of the staunchly Muslim people called the Uzbeks. Twenty million strong, the Uzbeks had for hundreds of years violently resisted any Western efforts to introduce Christianity.
>
> As the Koreans settled around Tashkent, the Uzbeks welcomed their industry and kindness. Within a few decades, the Koreans were included in nearly every facet of Uzbek cultural life.
>
> As usual in God's orchestration of global events, He had planted within the relocated Koreans strong pockets of believers. Little did Stalin suspect that these Koreans would not only begin enjoying a wildfire revival among their own people, they would also begin bringing their Muslim, Uzbek and Kazak friends to Christ.
>
> The first public sign of the Korean revival and its break-through effects on the Uzbeks and Kazaks came on June 2, 1990, when in the first open air Christian meeting in the history of Soviet Central Asia, a young Korean from America preached to a swelling crowd in the streets of Alma-Ata, capital of Kazakhstan.[14]

The result of these roundabout, decades-long maneuverings by God to position his people in inaccessible places is that Muslims, who would not receive missionaries, are confessing that Isa (Jesus) is the way, the truth and the life. This was a costly strategy for many believers. To be uprooted from their homeland in Korea, and then again from their new home near Vladivostok, must have been a severe test of the Koreans' faith that God is good and has a loving plan for their lives. The truth was that God did have a loving plan, and not only for their lives but also for many unreached Muslims among the Uzbek and Kazak peoples.

Going forward by getting arrested

God's strange ways of guiding the missionary enterprise are seen similarly in the way Jesus told the disciples to expect arrest and imprisonment as God's deployment tactic to put them with people they would never otherwise reach. "They will lay their hands on you and persecute you, delivering you up to the synagogues and prisons, and you will be brought before kings and governors for my name's sake. *This will be a time for you to bear testimony*" (Luke 21:12–13; cf. Mark 13:9).

The June/July, 1989 issue of *Mission Frontiers* carried an article signed with the pseudonym, Frank Marshall, a missionary in a politically sensitive Latin American country. He told the story of his recent imprisonment. He and his co-workers had been beaten numerous times and thrown in jail before. This time federal agents accused him of fraud and bribing because they assumed he could not have gotten his official documents without lying. They did not believe that he had been born in the country.

In prison the Lord spared him from sexual assault by a huge man wrapped in a towel with four gold chains around his neck and a ring on every finger. When put in the cell with this man Frank began sharing the gospel with him and praying in his heart, "Lord, deliver me from this evil." The man changed color, shouted at Frank to shut up and told him to leave him alone.

Frank began to tell others about Christ when the men had free time in the courtyard. One Muslim named Satawa confessed Christ within the first week and invited Frank to answer questions with a group of fifteen other Muslims. In two weeks Frank finally was able to get a lawyer. He also asked for a box of Bibles. The next Sunday 45 men gathered in the courtyard to hear Frank preach. He spoke about how hard it was for him to be away from his family, and spoke of how much God loved his Son and yet gave him up for sinners so that we could believe and live. Thirty of these men stayed afterwards to pray and ask the Lord to lead them and forgive them. Frank was soon released and deported to the U.S. But he now knows firsthand the meaning of Jesus' words, "This will be a time for testimony."

Miracles in Mozambique

During the 1960s the Lord raised up an indigenous leader named Martinho Campos in the church in Mozambique. The story of his ministry, *Life Out of Death in Mozambique*, is a remarkable testimony to God's strange ways of missionary blessing.

Martinho was leading a series of meetings in the administrative area of Gurue, 60 miles from his own area of Nauela. The police arrested him and put him in jail without a trial. The police chief, a European, assumed that the gatherings were related to the emerging guerrilla group Frelimo. But even when the Catholic priest told him that these men were just "a gathering of heretics" he took no concern for justice, though he wondered why the common people brought so much food to the prisoner, as though he were someone important.

One night he was driving his truck with half a dozen prisoners in it and saw "what appeared to be a man in gleaming white, standing in the road, facing him". He swerved so sharply that the truck rolled over and he was trapped underneath. The prisoners themselves lifted the truck so that the police chief could get out.

After brief treatment in the hospital he returned to talk to Martinho because he knew there was some connection between this vision and the prisoner. He entered Martinho's cell and asked for forgiveness. Martinho told him about his need for God's forgiveness and how to have it. The police chief said humbly, "Please pray for me." Immediately the chief called for hot water that the prisoner might wash, took him out of solitary confinement, and saw to it that a fair trial was held. Martinho was released.

But the most remarkable thing was what followed: "Not only did the Chief of Police make plain his respect for what Martinho stood for, but granted him official permission to travel throughout the whole area under his jurisdiction, in order to preach and hold evangelical services."[15] There would have been no way that such a permission would have been given through the ordinary channels. But God had a way through suffering. The imprisonment was for the advancement of the gospel.

God was better served in prison

On January 9, 1985, Pastor Hristo Kulichev, a Congregational pastor in Bulgaria, was arrested and put in prison. His crime was that he preached in his church, even though the state had appointed as pastor another man whom the congregation did not elect. Kulichev's trial was a mockery of justice, and he was sentenced to eight months' imprisonment. During his time in prison he made Christ known every way he could.

When he got out he wrote, "Both prisoners and jailers asked many questions, and it turned out that we had a more fruitful ministry there than we could have expected in church. God was better served by our presence in prison than if we had been free."[16] In many places in the world the words of Jesus are as radically relevant as if they had been spoken yesterday. "They will deliver you to prison . . . This will be a time for you to bear testimony" (Luke 21:12–13). The pain of our shattered plans is for the purpose of scattered grace.

The supremacy of Christ manifest in suffering

Sixthly, the suffering of missionaries is meant by God to magnify the power and sufficiency of Christ. Suffering is finally to show the supremacy of God. When God declined to remove the suffering of Paul's "thorn in the flesh", he said to Paul, "My grace is sufficient for you; *my power is made perfect in weakness*." To this, Paul responded, "I will all the more gladly boast of my weaknesses, that the power of Christ may rest upon me. For the sake of Christ then I am content with weaknesses, insults, hardships, persecutions and calamities; for when I am weak then am I strong" (2 Corinthians 12:9–10).

Paul was strong in persecutions because "the power of Christ" rested upon him and was made perfect in him. In other words, Christ's power was Paul's only power when his sufferings brought him to the end of his resources and cast him wholly on Jesus. This was God's purpose in Paul's thorn, and it is his purpose in all our suffering. God means for us to rely wholly on him. "That was to make us rely not on ourselves but on God who raises the dead" (2 Corinthians 1:9). The reason God wants this is because this kind of trust shows his supreme power and love to sustain us when we can't do anything to sustain ourselves.

We began this chapter with this claim: loss and suffering, joyfully accepted for the kingdom of God, show the supremacy of God's worth more clearly in the world than all worship and prayer. We have seen this truth implicit in looking at six reasons why God appoints suffering for the messengers of his grace. But now we need to make explicit that the supremacy of God is the reason for suffering, running through and above all the other reasons. God ordains suffering because through all the other reasons it displays to the world the supremacy of his worth above all treasures.

Jesus makes crystal clear how we can rejoice in persecution. "Blessed are you when men revile you and persecute you and say all kinds of evil against you falsely on my account. Rejoice and be glad, *for great is your reward in heaven*" (Matthew 5:11–12). The reason we can rejoice in persecution is that the worth of our reward in heaven is so much greater than the worth of all that we lose through suffering on earth. Therefore suffering with joy proves to the world that our treasure is in heaven and not on the earth, and that this treasure is greater than anything the world has to offer.

The supremacy of God's worth shines through the pain that his people will gladly bear for his name.

Gladly will I boast of weakness and calamity

I use the word "gladly" because that's the way the saints speak of it. For example, we just saw Paul saying, "I will all the more gladly boast of my weaknesses . . . insults, hardships, persecutions and calamities" (2 Corinthians 12:9–10). He says the same thing in Romans 5:3, "We rejoice in our tribulations." And the reason he gives is that it produces patience and a tested quality of life and an unfailing hope (Romans 5:3–4). In other words, his joy flowed from his hope just the way Jesus said it should. And Paul makes clear that the reward is the glory of God. "We rejoice in our hope of the glory of God" (Romans 5:2). And so it is the supremacy of God's worth that shines through in Paul's joy in affliction.

Then you have the other apostles reacting the same way in Acts 5:41 after being beaten for their preaching: "Then they left the presence of the council, rejoicing that they were counted worthy to suffer dishonor for the sake of the name" (Acts 5:41). This fearless joy in spite of real danger and great pain is the display of God's superiority over all that the world has to offer.

You joyfully accepted the plundering of your property

Again, the early Christians who visited their friends in prison rejoiced even though it cost them their possessions. "For you had compassion on the prisoners, and you joyfully accepted the plundering of your property, since you knew that you yourselves had a better possession and an abiding one" (Hebrews 10:34). Joy in suffering flows from hope in a great reward. Christians are not called to live morose lives of burdensome persecution. We are called to rejoice. "Rejoice in so far as you share Christ's sufferings" (1 Peter 4:13). "Count it all joy, brothers, when you meet various trials" (James 1:2).

The love of God is better than life

The basis for this indomitable joy is the supremacy of God's love above life itself. "The steadfast love of the Lord is better than life" (Psalm 63:3). The pleasures in this life are "fleeting" (Hebrews 11:25) and the afflictions are "light and momentary" (2 Corinthians 4:17). But the steadfast love of the Lord is for ever. All his pleasures are superior and there will be no more pain. "In your presence there is fullness of joy, in your right hand are pleasures for evermore" (Psalm 16:11).

Glad suffering shines brighter than gratitude

It is true that we should bear testimony to the supremacy of God's goodness by receiving his good gifts with thanksgiving (1 Timothy 4:3). But for many Christians this has become the only way they see their lifestyles glorifying God. God has been good to them to give them so much. Therefore the way to witness to the reality of God is to take and be thankful.

But even though it is true that we should thankfully enjoy what we have, there is a relentless call in the Bible not to accumulate more and more things, but to give more and more, and to be deprived of things if love demands it. There are no easy rules to tell whether the call on our lives is the call of the rich young ruler to give away all that we have, or the call of Zacchaeus to give away half of what we have. What is clear from the New Testament is that, while we live on earth, suffering with joy, not gratitude in wealth, is the way the worth of Jesus shines most brightly.

Who can doubt that the supremacy of Christ's worth shines brightest in a life like this?

> But whatever gain I had, I counted as loss *for the sake of Christ*. Indeed I count everything as loss because of *the surpassing worth of knowing Christ Jesus my Lord. For his sake* I have suffered the loss of all things, and count them as refuse, in order *that I may gain Christ*. (Philippians 3:7–8)

You cannot show the preciousness of a person by being happy with his gifts. Ingratitude will certainly prove that the giver is not loved. But gratitude for gifts does not prove that the *giver* is precious. What proves that the giver is precious is the glad-hearted readiness to leave all his gifts

103

to be with him. This is why suffering is so central in the mission of the church. The goal of our mission is that people from all the nations worship the true God. But worship means cherishing the preciousness of God above all else, including life itself. It will be very hard to bring the nations to love God from a lifestyle that communicates a love of things. Therefore God ordains in the lives of his messengers that suffering sever our bondage to the world. When joy and love survive this severing, we are fit to say to the nations with authenticity and power: Hope in God.

How is hope in God made visible?

Peter talks about the visibility of this hope: "Hallow the Lord Christ in your hearts, ready always to give a reason to everyone who asks you for a word concerning the *hope* that is in you" (1 Peter 3:15). Why would people ask about hope? What kind of life are we to live that would make people wonder about our hope? If our security and happiness in the future were manifestly secured the way the world secures its future, no one would ask us about it. There would be no unusual hope to see. What Peter is saying is that the world should see a different hope in the lives of Christians – not a hope in the security of money or the security of power or the security of houses or lands or portfolios, but the security of "the grace that is coming to you at the revelation of Jesus Christ" (1 Peter 1:13).

Therefore God ordains suffering to help us release our hold on worldly hopes and put our "hope in God" (1 Peter 1:21). The fiery trials are appointed to consume the earthly dependencies and leave only the refined gold of "genuine faith" (1 Peter 1:7). "Let those who suffer according to God's will do right and entrust their souls to a faithful Creator" (1 Peter 4:19). It's the supremacy of God's great faithfulness above all other securities that frees us to "rejoice as [we] share in Christ's sufferings" (1 Peter 4:13). Therefore joy in suffering for Christ's sake makes the supremacy of God shine more clearly than all our gratitude for wealth.

Wartime austerity for the cause of missions

Jesus presses us toward a wartime lifestyle that does not

value simplicity for simplicity's sake, but values wartime austerity for what it can produce for the cause of world evangelization. He said, "Sell your possessions and give alms; provide yourselves with purses that do not grow old, with a treasure in the heavens that does not fail" (Luke 12:33). "Make friends for yourselves by means of unrighteous mammon, so that when it fails they may receive you into eternal habitations" (Luke 16:9). "Do not seek what you are to eat or what you are to drink, nor be of anxious mind. For all the nations of the world seek these things, and your Father knows that you need them. Instead seek his kingdom, and these things shall be yours as well" (Luke 12:29–31).

The point is: $70,000 salary does not have to be accompanied by a $70,000 lifestyle. God is calling us to be conduits of his grace, not cul-de-sacs. Our great danger today is thinking that the conduit should be lined with gold. It shouldn't. Copper will do. No matter how grateful we are, gold will not make the world think that our God is good; it will make people think that our God is gold. That is no honor to the supremacy of his worth.

The deadly desire for wealth

The desire for riches is deadly. Gehazi, Elisha's servant, was struck with Naaman's leprosy because he could not pass up a reward (2 Kings 5:26–27). Ananias dropped dead because desire for money prompted him to lie (Acts 5:5–6). The rich young ruler could not enter the kingdom of God (Mark 10:22–23). The rich man who feasted sumptuously and neglected Lazarus was tormented in Hades (Luke 16:23). Paul said that the desire to be rich plunges men into ruin and destruction (1 Timothy 6:9).

God's point in telling us about these tragedies is not to make us hate money, but to make us love him. The severity of punishment for loving money is a sign of the supremacy of God. We scorn the infinite worth of God when we covet. That is why Paul calls covetousness idolatry and says that the wrath of God is coming against it (Colossians 3:5–6).

"I had no shirt"

It is almost impossible for Christians in the West to come to terms with Jesus' commendation of the widow who "out of her poverty put in all the living that she had" (Luke 21:4). To see this spirit fleshed out we may have to leave our countries and go elsewhere. Stanford Kelly illustrates it from Haiti.

> The church was having a Thanksgiving festival and each Christian was invited to bring a love offering. One envelope from a Haitian man named Edmund held $13 cash. That amount was three months' income for a working man there. Kelly was as surprised as those counting a Sunday offering in the United States might be to get a $6,000 cash gift. He looked around for Edmund, but couldn't see him.
>
> Later Kelly met him in the village and questioned him. He pressed him for an explanation and found that Edmund had sold his horse in order to give the $13 gift to God. But why hadn't he come to the festival? He hesitated and didn't want to answer.
>
> Finally Edmund said, "I had no shirt to wear."[17]

Retirement and the unreached peoples

Two phenomena in America are emerging together: one is the challenge to give our all to do our part in finishing the task of world missions, and the other is a huge baby boom bulge in the population reaching peak earning years and coming toward "retirement". How will the Christians in this group respond to the typical American dream? Is it a Biblical dream?

Ralph Winter asks, "Where in the Bible do they see [retirement]? Did Moses retire? Did Paul retire? Peter? John? Do military officers retire in the middle of a war?"[18] I mentioned earlier that Oswald Sanders ministered around the world until he was 89 and wrote a book a year after he was 70.

Why Simeon's strength quadrupled at sixty

Charles Simeon, the pastor of Trinity Church, Cambridge, 200 years ago, learned a very painful lesson about God's attitude toward his "retirement". In 1807, after 25 years of ministry at Trinity Church, his health broke. He became very weak and had to take an extended leave from his labor. Handley Moule recounts the fascinating story of what God was doing in Simeon's life.

> The broken condition lasted with variations for thirteen years, till he was just sixty, and then it passed away quite suddenly and without any evident physical cause. He was on his last visit to Scotland . . . in 1819, and found himself to his great surprise, just as he crossed the border, "almost as perceptibly renewed in strength as the woman was after she had touched the hem of our Lord's garment". He saw in this revival no miracle, in the common sense of the word, yet as a distinct providence.
>
> He says that he had been promising himself, before he began to break down, a very active life up to sixty, and then a Sabbath evening [retirement!]; and that now he seemed to hear his Master saying: "I laid you aside, because you entertained with satisfaction the thought of resting from your labour; but now you have arrived at the very period when you had promised yourself that satisfaction, and have determined instead to spend your strength for me to the latest hour of your life, I have doubled, trebled, quadrupled your strength, that you may execute your desire on a more extended plan."[19]

How many Christians set their sights on a "Sabbath evening" of life – resting, playing, travelling, etc. – the world's substitute for heaven, since they do not believe that there will be one beyond the grave. The mindset is that we must reward ourselves in this life for the long years of labor. Eternal rest and joy after death are an irrelevant consideration. What a strange reward for a Christian to set his sights on! Twenty years of leisure(!) while living in the midst of the last days of infinite consequence for millions of unreached people. What a tragic way to finish the last lap before entering the presence of the king who finished his so differently!

Why not be like Raymond Lull?

Raymond Lull was born of an illustrious family at Palma on the island of Majorca of the Balearic group off Spain in

1235. His life as a youth was profligate. But all that changed as a result of five visions which compelled him to a life of devotion to Christ. He first entered monastic life but later became a missionary to Muslim countries in northern Africa. He learned Arabic which at the age of 79 he was teaching in Europe.

His pupils and friends naturally desired that he should end his days in the peaceful pursuit of learning and the comfort of companionship.

Such however was not Lull's wish. His ambition was to die as a missionary and not as a teacher of philosophy. Ever his favorite "Ars Major" had to give way to that *ars maxima* expressed in Lull's own motto, "He that lives by the life can not die" . . .

In Lull's contemplations we read . . . "Men are wont to die, O Lord, from old age, the failure of natural warmth and excess of cold; but thus, if it be Thy will, Thy servant would not wish to die; he would prefer to die in the glow of love, even as Thou wast willing to die for him."

The dangers and difficulties that made Lull shrink back from his journey at Genoa in 1291 only urged him forward to North Africa once more in 1314. His love had not grown cold, but burned the brighter "with the failure of natural warmth and the weakness of old age." He longed not only for the martyr's crown, but also once more to see his little band of believers [in Africa]. Animated by these sentiments he crossed over to Bugia on August 14, and for nearly a whole year labored secretly among a little circle of converts, whom on his previous visits he had won over to the Christian faith . . .

At length, weary of seclusion, and longing for martyrdom, he came forth into the open market and presented himself to the people as the same man whom they had once expelled from their town. It was Elijah showing himself to a mob of Ahabs! Lull stood before them and threatened them with divine wrath if they still persisted in their errors. He pleaded with love, but spoke plainly the whole truth. The consequences can be easily anticipated. Filled with fanatic fury at his boldness, and unable to reply to his arguments, the populace seized him, and dragged him out of the town; there by the command or at least the connivance, of the king, he was stoned on the 30th of June 1315.[20]

Lull was 80 years old when he gave his life for the Muslims of North Africa. As a hart longs for the flowing streams – and longs the more as the brook approaches and the smell sweetens and the thirst deepens – so longs the soul of the saint to see Christ and to glorify him in his dying (cf. John 21:19). It is beyond comprehension that soldiers of the cross would be satisfied in retiring from the battle just before the trumpet blast of victory – or just before admission to the coronation ceremony.

"Senior discounts" are for missionary travel

I am not saying that we can make professions and businesses keep us employed beyond 65 or 70. I am saying that a whole new chapter of life opens for most people at age 65. And if we have armed ourselves with the "thought" of the suffering Savior and saturated our mind with the ways of the supremacy of God, we will invest our time and our energy in this final chapter very differently than if we take our cues from the American dream. Millions of "retired" people should be engaged at all levels of intensity in hundreds of assignments around the world. Talk about travel! Park the car and use the senior discounts and "super savers" to fly wherever the agencies have need. Let the unreached peoples of the earth reap the benefits of a lifetime of earning. "You will be repaid at the resurrection of the just" (Luke 14:14).

"You'll be eaten by Cannibals"

An aging Christian once objected to John G. Paton's plan to go as a missionary to the South Sea Islands with the words, "You'll be eaten by Cannibals!" Paton responded:

> Mr. Dickson, you are advanced in years now, and your own prospect is soon to be laid in the grave, there to be eaten by worms; I confess to you, that if I can but live and die serving and honoring the Lord Jesus, it will make no difference to me whether I am eaten by Cannibals or worms; and in the Great Day my resurrection body will arise as fair as yours in the likeness of our risen Redeemer.[21]

When the world sees millions of "retired" Christians pouring out the last drops of their lives with joy for the sake of the unreached peoples and with a view toward heaven, then the supremacy of God will shine. He does not shine as brightly in the posh, leisure-soaked luxury homes on the outer rings of our cities.

Let there be no talk of ultimate self-denial

From the youngest to the oldest, Christ is calling his church to a radical, wartime engagement in world missions. He is making it plain that it will not happen without pain. But let there be no Christian self-pity, no talk of ultimate self-denial. It is simply amazing how consistent are the testimonies of missionaries who have suffered for the gospel. Virtually all of them bear witness to the abundant joy and overriding compensations. Those who have suffered most speak in the most lavish terms of the supreme blessing and joy of giving their lives away for others.

Lottie Moon said, "Surely there is no greater joy than saving souls." Sherwood Eddy said of Amy Carmichael, "Her life was the most fragrant, the most joyfully sacrificial, that I ever knew." Samuel Zwemer, after 50 years of labor (including the loss of two young children), said, "The sheer joy of it all comes back. Gladly would I do it all over again." And both Hudson Taylor and David Livingston, after lives of extraordinary hardship and loss, said, "I never made a sacrifice."[22]

From this discovery I have learned that the way of love is both the way of self-denial and the way of ultimate joy. We deny ourselves the fleeting pleasures of sin and luxury and self-absorption in order to seek the kingdom above all things. In doing so we bring the greatest good to others, we magnify the worth of Christ as a treasure chest of joy, and we find our greatest satisfaction.

God is most glorified in us when we are most satisfied in him. And the supremacy of that glory shines most brightly when the satisfaction that we have in him endures in spite of suffering and pain in the mission of love.

Notes

1. All the quotes in this account are taken from Henry Martyn, *Journal and Letters of Henry Martyn* (New York: Protestant

110

Episcopal Society for the Promotion of Evangelical Knowledge, 1851).

2. Dietrich Bonhoeffer, *The Cost of Discipleship* (New York: Macmillan, 1963), p. 99.

3. David Barrett, "Status of Global Mission, 1993", in *International Bulletin of Missionary Research*, 17/1, January, 1993, p. 23.

4. Richard Wurmbrand, "Preparing the Underground Church", in: *Epiphany Journal*, 5/4, Summer, 1985, pp. 46–48.

5. *Mission Frontiers*, 10/1, January, 1988, p. 29.

6. Charles Wesley, *Journal* (London: Thomas Jackson; reprinted by Grand Rapids: Baker Book House, 1908), Vol. 1, pp. 120–123.

7. Demons cannot even speak without the permission of Jesus: "He would not permit the demons to speak" (Mark 1:34). How much less may they do anything more harmful without permission, as Job 1:12, 21; 2:6–7, 10 makes plain. Nevertheless Satan does persecute the church. "Behold the devil is about to throw some of you in prison that you may be tested" (Revelation 2:10). For a more extensive treatment of this problem of how God's sovereignty relates to the evil things men do, see John Piper, *The Pleasures of God* (Portland: Multnomah Press, 1991), pp. 61–76.

8. From a letter to Father Perez in Francis M. DuBose, ed., *Classics of Christian Missions* (Nashville: Broadman Press, 1979), pp. 221f.

9. Jonathan Edwards, *The Works of Jonathan Edwards*, Vol. 2 (Edinburgh: Banner of Truth Trust, 1974), p. 902. The parable of the workers in the vineyard who all made the same wage (Matthew 20:1–16) need not be in conflict with what Edwards (and the texts he cites!) teaches here. What that text may imply is that all of us are thrown into the same ocean of happiness. Another point of that parable is that God is free to give anyone any degree of blessing more than he deserves, and if there is anyone who is self-pitying in or proud about his endurance, God is indeed free to exalt a person even above him so as to humble him and make him realize all of heaven is all of grace. I think Jonathan Edwards effectively answers Craig Blomberg's question: "Is it not fundamentally self-contradictory to speak of degrees of perfection?" ("Degrees of Reward in the Kingdom of Heaven", in *Journal of the Evangelical Theological Society*, 35/2, June, 1992, pp. 162–163). I do, however, want to side with Blomberg over against those who speak of "earning" rewards and who distort the conditional promises of heaven into promises of levels of reward in heaven.

10. *Journal and Letters of Henry Martyn*, pp. 240, 326–328.

11. Quoted in Elisabeth Elliot, *Through Gates of Splendor* (New

York: Harper and Row Publishers, 1957), pp. 235–236.

12. Steve Estes, *Called to Die* (Grand Rapids: Zondervan Publishing House, 1986), p. 252.

13. Michael Card, "Wounded in the House of Friends", *Virtue*, March/April, 1991, pp. 28–29, 69.

14. Bill and Amy Stearns, *Catch the Vision 2000* (Minneapolis: Bethany House Publishers, 1991), pp. 12–13.

15. Phyllis Thompson, *Life Out of Death in Mozambique* (London: Hodder and Stoughton, 1989), p. 111.

16. Herbert Schlossberg, *Called to Suffer, Called to Triumph* (Portland: Multnomah Press, 1990), p. 230.

17. Norm Lewis, *Priority One: What God Wants* (Orange, California: Promise Publishing, 1988), p. 120.

18. Ralph D. Winter, "The Retirement Booby Trap", *Missions Frontiers*, 7 July, 1985, p. 25.

19. Handley C. G. Moule, *Charles Simeon* (London: IVF, 1948, originally 1892), p. 125.

20. Samuel Zwemer, *Raymond Lull: First Missionary to the Moslems* (New York: Fleming H. Revell Company, 1902), pp. 132–145.

21. James Paton, ed., *John G. Paton: Missionary to the New Hebrides, An Autobiography* (London: Banner of Truth Trust, 1965, originally 1891), p. 56.

22. See John Piper, "The Battle Cry of Christian Hedonism", in: *Desiring God* (Portland: Multnomah Press, 1986), pp. 186–209.

Part two

Making God supreme in missions

The necessity and nature of the task

4

The supremacy of Christ as the conscious focus of all saving faith

Must people hear the gospel of Jesus Christ in order to be saved?

The supremacy of God in missions is affirmed Biblically by affirming the supremacy of his Son, Jesus Christ. It is a stunning New Testament truth that since the incarnation of the Son of God all saving faith must henceforth fix on him. This was not always true. And those times were called the "times of ignorance" (Acts 17:30). But now it is true, and Christ is made the conscious center of the mission of the church. The aim of missions is to "bring about the obedience of faith *for the sake of his name* among all the nations" (Romans 1:5). This is a new thing with the coming of Christ. God's will is to glorify his Son by making him the conscious focus of all saving faith.

Posing the question

The general question we are posing in this chapter is whether the supremacy of Christ means that he is the only way to salvation. But that general question really contains three questions. They are crucial for the missionary task of the Christian church. The three questions emerge as we hear different people answer and qualify the main question.

Will anyone experience eternal conscious torment under God's wrath?

Many today would affirm that Christ is man's only hope, but deny that there is eternal punishment for not believing in him. Some would say that everyone is going to be saved whether they hear about Christ in this life or not. For example, even though he has been dead since 1905 the preacher-novelist George MacDonald is being published and read as never before in America and is extending the influence of his brand of universalism. He makes hell into an extended means of self-atonement and sanctification. In hell the justice of God will eventually destroy all sin in his creatures. In this way God will bring everyone to glory.[1] Everyone will be saved. Hell is not eternal.

Others would say that while not everyone is saved, there is still no eternal, conscious punishment because the fire of judgment annihilates those who reject Christ. Thus they go out of existence and experience no conscious punishment. Hell is not a place of eternal punishment, but an event of annihilation. This is the direction that Clark Pinnock, John Stott, Edward Fudge[2] and others have chosen to go.

Therefore the question we must ask includes this one: Is eternal punishment at stake? That is, will anyone be eternally cut off from Christ and experience eternal conscious torment under the wrath of God?

Is the work of Christ necessary?

Others today would deny that Christ is man's *only* hope. They may believe that Christ is the provision that God has made for *Christians*, but for other religions there are other ways of getting right with God and gaining eternal bliss. The work of Christ is useful for Christians but not necessary for non-Christians.

For example, British theologian John Hick argues that different religions are "equals, though they each may have different emphases". Christianity is not superior, but one partner in the quest for salvation. We are not to seek one world religion but rather we look to the day when "the ecumenical spirit which has so largely transformed Christianity will increasingly affect relations between the world faiths".[3]

This means that the question we are asking must include: Is the work of Christ the *necessary* means provided by God for eternal salvation – not just for Christians, but for all people?

Some evangelicals say they just don't know.[4] Others, without denying the reality of eternal judgment or the necessity of Christ's saving work, would say, Yes, Christ is man's only hope, but he saves some of those who never hear of him through faith that does not have Christ for its conscious object. For example, Millard Erickson represents some evangelicals[5] who argue that, on the analogy of the saints in the Old Testament, some unevangelized persons today may "receive the benefit of Christ's death without conscious knowledge-belief in the name of Jesus".[6]

So we must make clear what we are really asking: Is it necessary for people *to hear of Christ* in order to be eternally saved? That is, can a person today be saved by the work of Christ even if he does not have an opportunity to hear about it?

Therefore when we ask, "Is Jesus Christ man's only hope for salvation?" we are really asking three questions:

1. Will anyone experience *eternal conscious torment* under God's wrath?

2. Is the work of Christ the *necessary* means provided by God for eternal salvation?

3. Is it necessary for people *to hear of Christ* in order to be eternally saved?

A nerve of urgency

Biblical answers to these three questions are crucial because in each case a negative answer would seem to cut a nerve of urgency in the missionary cause. Evangelicals like Erickson do not intend to cut that nerve, and their view is not in the same category with Hick or MacDonald. They insist that the salvation of anyone apart from the preaching of Christ is the exception rather than the rule and that preaching Christ to all is utterly important.

Nevertheless there is a felt difference in the urgency when one believes that preaching the gospel is absolutely the only hope that anyone has of escaping the penalty of sin and living for ever in happiness to the glory of God's grace. It does not ring true to me when William Crockett and James Sigountos argue that the existence of "implicit

Christians" (saved through general revelation without hearing of Christ) actually "should increase motivation" for missions. They say that these unevangelized converts are "waiting eagerly to hear more about [God]". If we would reach them "a strong church would spring to life, giving glory to God and evangelizing their pagan neighbors".[7] I cannot escape the impression that this is a futile attempt to make a weakness look like a strength. On the contrary, common sense presses another truth on us: the more likely it is that people can be saved without missions the less urgency there is for missions.

So with all three of these questions there is much as stake. Nevertheless, in the end it is not our desire to maintain the urgency of the missionary cause that settles the issue, but: What do the Scriptures teach?

My aim here is to provide the Biblical data that, in my judgment, compel a positive answer to each of these three questions. I hope to demonstrate that in the fullest sense Jesus Christ is man's only hope for salvation. To do this I will gather together into three groups the texts that relate most directly to the three questions we have posed. Some comment will be made along the way.

A hell of eternal conscious torment[8]

> And many of those who sleep in the dust of the earth shall awake, some to everlasting life, and some to shame and *everlasting contempt*. (Daniel 12:2)

It is true that the Hebrew *'ôlām* does not always mean "everlasting", but in this context it seems to because it points to a decisive division into joy or misery after death and resurrection. As the *life* is everlasting so the *shame and contempt* are everlasting.

> His winnowing fork is in his hand, and he will clear his threshing floor and gather his wheat into the granary, but the chaff he will burn with *unquenchable fire*. (Matthew 3:12 [Luke 3:17])

This is John the Baptist's prediction of the judgment that Jesus would bring in the end. He pictures a decisive separation. The term "unquenchable fire" implies a fire that will not be extinguished, and therefore a punishment that will not end. This is confirmed in Mark 9:43–48.

> And if your hand causes you to sin, cut it off; it is better for you to enter life maimed than with two hands to go to hell, to the *unquenchable fire*. And if your foot causes you to sin, cut it off; it is better for you to enter life lame than with two feet to be thrown into hell. And if your eye causes you to sin, pluck it out; it is better for you to enter the kingdom of God with one eye than with two eyes to be thrown into hell, *where their worm does not die, and the fire is not quenched.* (Mark 9:43–48)

Here the "unquenchable fire" is clearly hell, and the last line shows that the point is the unending misery of those who go there ("their worm does not die"). If annihilation (the teaching that some simply cease to exist after death)[9] were in view, why would the stress be laid on the fire not ever being quenched and the worm never dying? John Stott struggles to escape this by saying that the worm will not die nor the fire be quenched "until presumably their work of destruction is done".[10] That qualification is not in the text. But the focus on eternal duration is confirmed in Matthew 18:8.

> And if your hand or your foot causes you to sin, cut it off and throw it from you; it is better for you to enter life maimed or lame than with two hands or two feet to be thrown into the *eternal fire.* (Matthew 18:8)

Here the fire is not only unquenchable, but more explicitly, "eternal". That this fire is not merely a purifying fire of the age to come (as some take *aiōnion* to mean) will be shown in the subsequent sayings of Jesus, especially the one on the unforgivable sin.

> And do not fear those who kill the body but cannot kill the soul; rather fear him who can destroy both soul and body in hell. (Matthew 10:28 [Luke 12:4–5])

The "destruction" referred to here is decisive and final, but it does not have to mean obliterate or annihilate. The word *apollumi* frequently means "ruin" or "lose" or "perish" or "get rid of" (Matthew 8:25; 9:17; 10:6; 12:14). It does not imply annihilate. It is eternal ruin. (See on 2 Thessalonians 1:9 below.)

> Then he will say to those at his left hand, "Depart from me, you cursed, into the *eternal fire* prepared for the devil and his angels" . . . And they will go away into *eternal punishment*, but the righteous into eternal life. (Matthew 25:41, 46)

Here the eternal fire is explicitly "punishment". And its opposite is eternal life. It does not honor the full import of "eternal life" to say that it only refers to a quality of life without eternal connotations.[11] So it would fall short of truth to say that "eternal punishment" has no reference to eternal duration. As Leon Morris says, "It is not easy to see the fate of the wicked as anything less permanent than that of the believer."[12]

Not only that, but when you compare this text to Revelation 20:10 the case for conscious eternal torment is strengthened. Here in Matthew 25:41 the goats are sentenced to "eternal fire prepared *for the devil and his angels*". This is precisely what is described in Revelation 20:10, namely, the final destiny of the devil. The condition is clearly one of conscious torment (see below in this text).

> The Son of man goes as it is written of him, but woe to that man by whom the Son of man is betrayed! *It would have been better for that man if he had not been born.* (Matthew 26:24)

If Judas were destined for glory eventually (as in universalism), or even destined for extinction (as in annihilationism), it is difficult to imagine why it would have been better for him not to have been born.[13] In John 17:12 he is called the "son of perdition" – a term related to the word for "destroy" in Matthew 10:28.

> Whoever blasphemes against the Holy Spirit never has forgiveness, but is guilty of an *eternal sin*. (Mark 3:29)

> And whoever says a word against the Son of man will be forgiven; but whoever speaks against the Holy Spirit will not be forgiven, either in this age *or in the age to come.* (Matthew 12:32)

This rules out the idea that after a time of suffering in hell, sinners will then be forgiven and admitted to heaven. Matthew says that there will be no forgiveness in the age to come for the unforgivable sin, and so Mark calls it an *eternal* sin, which shows that the word "eternal" is indeed a temporal word of duration and not just a word referring to a limited period in the age to come.

> And besides all this, between us and you a great chasm has been fixed, in order that those who would pass from here to you may not be able, and *none may cross from there to us*. (Luke 16:26)

These are the words of Abraham in heaven speaking to the rich man in Hades. The point is that the suffering there cannot be escaped. There is no way out.

> For God will render to every man according to his works: to those who by patience in well-doing seek for glory and honor and immortality, he will give *eternal* life; but for those who are factious and do not obey the truth, but obey wickedness, there will be wrath and fury. (Romans 2:6–8)

This text is significant because wrath and fury are the alternative to "eternal life". This seems to imply that the wrath and fury are experienced instead of life "eternally" – for ever.

> They will suffer the punishment of *eternal destruction* and exclusion from the presence of the Lord and from the glory of his might, when he comes on that day to be glorified in his saints, and to be marveled at in all who have believed. (2 Thessalonians 1:9)

The word for "destruction" (*olethros*) means "ruin" (1 Timothy 6:9; 1 Corinthians 5:5). The picture is not of obliteration but of a ruin of human life out of God's presence for ever.

> Let us leave the elementary doctrines of Christ and go on to maturity, not laying again a foundation of repentance from dead works and of faith toward God, with instruction about ablutions, the laying on of hands, the resurrection of the dead, and *eternal judgment*. (Hebrews 6:1–2)

These are blemishes on your love feasts ... wild waves of the sea, casting up the foam of their own shame; wandering stars for whom the nether gloom of darkness has been reserved *for ever*. (Jude 12–13)

And the smoke of their torment goes up *for ever and ever*; and *they have no rest*, day or night, these worshipers of the beast and its image, and whoever receives the mark of its name. (Revelation 14:11)

There is no stronger Greek expression for eternity than this one: "unto ages of ages" (*eis aiomnas aiomnomn*).

Once more they cried, "Hallelujah! the smoke from her goes up *for ever and ever*." (Revelation 19:3)

And the devil who had deceived them was thrown into the lake of fire and brimstone where the beast and the false prophet were, and they will be tormented *day and night for ever and ever*. (Revelation 20:10)

Again the strongest of expressions are used for ever-lasting duration: "unto the ages of the ages" (*eis tous aiōnas tōn aiōnōn*). John Stott again struggles in vain to escape the clear intent of the eternal torments of the lake of fire. He says that Revelation 20:10 refers to the beast and false prophet who "are not individual people but symbols of the world in its varied hostility to God. In the nature of the case they cannot experience pain."[14]

But Stott fails to mention Revelation 20:15 where it says that "if *anyone*'s name [not just the beast and false prophet] was not found written in the book of life, he was thrown into the lake of fire". Similarly Revelation 21:8 says that it is *individual sinners* whose "lot shall be the lake that burns with fire and sulfur, which is the second death". And the torment that lasts "for ever and ever" in Revelation 14:10 is precisely the torment of people "with fire and sulfur" – that is, the tormnent of "the lake that burns with fire and sulfur" (21:8). In other words the "lake of fire" is in view not only, as Stott suggests, when the beast and false prophet and death and Hades (20:13) are cast out, but also when individual unbelievers are finally condemned

(14:10–11; 20:15; 21:8), and that shows decisively that individual unbelieving persons will experience eternal conscious torment.[15]

Conclusion

Hell is a dreadful reality. To speak of it lightly proves we do not grasp its horror. I know of no one who has over-stated the terrors of hell. We can scarcely surpass the horrid images Jesus used. We are meant to shudder.

Why? Because the infinite horrors of hell are intended by God to be a vivid demonstration of the infinite value of his glory which sinners have belittled. The Biblical assumption of the justice of hell is the clearest testimony to the infiniteness of the sin of failing to glorify God. All of us have failed. All the nations have failed. Therefore the weight of infinite guilt rests on every human head because of our failure to delight in God more than we delight in our own self-sufficiency.

The vision of God in Scripture is of a majestic and Sovereign God who does all things to magnify the great-ness of his glory for the everlasting enjoyment of his people. And the view of man in Scripture is that man suppresses this truth and finds more joy in his own glory than he does in God's.

When Clark Pinnock[16] and John Stott[17] repeat the centuries-old objection that an *eternal* punishment is dis-proportionate to a *finite* life of sinning, they disregard the essential thing that Jonathan Edwards saw so clearly. The essential thing is that degrees of blameworthiness come not from how long you offend dignity, but from how high the dignity is that you offend.

> The crime of one being despising and casting contempt on another, is proportionably more or less heinous, as he was under greater or less obligations to obey him. And there-fore if there be any being that we are under infinite obli-gation to love, and honor, and obey, the contrary towards him must be infinitely faulty.
>
> Our obligation to love, honor and obey any being is in proportion to his loveliness, honorableness, and authority ... but God is a being infinitely lovely, because he hath

123

infinite excellency and beauty . . .

So sin against God, being a violation of infinite obliga-
tions, must be a crime infinitely heinous, and so deserving
infinite punishment . . . The eternity of the punishment of
ungodly men renders it infinite . . . and therefore renders
it no more than proportionable to the heinousness of what
they are guilty of.[18]

One key difference between Edwards and our contemporary spokesmen who abandon the historic Biblical view
of hell is that Edwards was radically committed to
deriving his views of God's justice and love *from God*. But
more and more it seems contemporary evangelicals are
submitting to what "makes sense" to their own moral sentiments.[19] This will not strengthen the church or its mission. What is needed is a radical commitment to the
supremacy of God in determining what is real and what is
not.

The necessity of Christ's atonement for salvation

The second question we must ask as part of our enquiry is
whether Christ's work of atonement is necessary for the
salvation of whoever is saved. Are there people who can be
saved another way than by the efficacy of Christ's work?
Are other religions and the provisions they offer sufficient
for bringing people to eternal happiness with God?

The following Biblical texts lead us to believe that
Christ's atonement is necessary for the salvation of everyone who is saved. There is no salvation apart from the
salvation that Christ achieved in his death and resurrection.

If, because of one man's trespass, death reigned through
that one man, much more will those who receive the abundance of grace and the free gift of righteousness reign in
life through the one man Jesus Christ. Then as one man's
trespass led to condemnation for all men, so one man's act
of righteousness leads to acquittal and life for all men. For
as by one man's disobedience many were made sinners, so
by one man's obedience many will be made righteous.
(Romans 5:17–19)

The crucial point here is *the universality of the work of*

Christ. It is not done in a corner with reference merely to Jews. The work of Christ, the second Adam, corresponds to the work of the first Adam. As the sin of Adam leads to condemnation for all the humanity that are united to him as their head, so the obedience of Christ leads to righteousness for all humanity that are united to Christ as their head – "those who receive the abundance of grace" (v. 17). The work of Christ in the obedience of the cross is pictured as the divine answer to the plight of the whole human race.

> For as by a man came death, by a man has come also the resurrection of the dead. For as in Adam all die, so also in Christ shall all be made alive. But each in his own order: Christ the first fruits, then at his coming those who belong to Christ. (1 Corinthians 15:21–23)

In this text Christ's resurrection is made the answer to the universal human misery of death. Adam is the head of the old humanity marked by death. Christ is the head of the new humanity marked by resurrection. The members of this new humanity are "those who belong to Christ" (v. 23).[20] Christ is not a tribal deity relating merely to the woes of one group. He is given as God's answer to the universal problem of death. Those who attain to the resurrection of the dead attain it in Christ.

> There is one God, and there is one mediator between God and men, the man Christ Jesus, who gave himself a ransom for all. (1 Timothy 2:5)

The work of Christ corresponds to his role as sole Mediator in the universe between God and man.

> Worthy art thou to take the scroll and to open its seals, for thou wast slain and by thy blood didst ransom men for God from every tribe and tongue and people and nation, and hast made them a kingdom and priests to our God, and they shall reign on earth. (Revelation 5:9–10)

The whole book of Revelation pictures Christ as the King of kings and Lord of lords (17:14; 19:16) – the universal ruler over all peoples and powers. This verse shows that he purchased a people for himself from all the tribes and languages of the world. His atonement is the means in every culture by which men and women become part of his kingdom. (See John 11:51–52.)

> And there is salvation in no one else, for there is no other name under heaven given among men by which we must be saved. (Acts 4:12)

The work of Christ is not mentioned here explicitly, but the universality of his name as the only way to salvation would imply that whatever he did to win salvation for his people (namely, shed his blood, Acts 20:28) has universal significance. There are no other ways that a person in another religion can be saved. If anyone would be saved, he must be saved by the name of Christ.

> Since all have sinned and fall short of the glory of God, they are justified by his grace as a gift, through the redemption which is in Christ Jesus, whom God put forward as a propitiation by his blood, to be received by faith. (Romans 3:23–24)

Romans 3:9–20 establishes that all humans – Jew and Gentile – are under the power of sin and are speechless before the judgment of God. Therefore the death of Christ is set forth as an answer to this universal problem of sin. It is not one among many ways God deals with sin. It is the basis of the way God justifies any sinner.

Conclusion

In answer to our second question, the New Testament makes clear that the atoning work of Christ is not merely for Jews or merely for any one nation or tribe or language. It is the one and only way for anyone to get right with God. The problem of sin is universal, cutting people off from God. The solution to that problem is the atoning death of the Son of God offered once for all. This is the very foundation of missions. Since the work of Christ is the only basis for salvation,[21] it must be announced to all the nations, as Luke 24:46–47 says:

> Thus it is written, that the Christ should suffer and on the third day rise from the dead, and that repentance and

forgiveness of sins should be preached in his name to all nations, beginning from Jerusalem.

The necessity for people to hear of Christ in order to be saved

The question that concerns us here is whether some (perhaps only a few) people are quickened by the Holy Spirit and saved by grace through faith in a merciful Creator even though they will never hear of Jesus in this life. In other words, are there devout people in other religions who humbly rely on the grace of the God whom they know through nature (Romans 1:19–21), and thus receive eternal salvation?[22]

The "times of ignorance" and the "mystery of Christ"

Something of immense historical significance happened with the coming of the Son of God into the world. So great was the significance of this event that the focus of saving faith was henceforth made to center on Jesus Christ alone. So fully does Christ sum up all the revelation of God and all the hopes of God's people that it would henceforth be a dishonor to him should saving faith repose on anyone but him.[23]

Before his coming a grand "mystery" was kept secret for ages. With the uncovering of this mystery the "times of ignorance" ended and the call to repentance now sounds forth with a new specificity: Jesus Christ has been appointed Judge of all peoples by virtue of his resurrection from the dead. All appeals for mercy and acquittal must now come through him, and him alone. We turn now to the texts which lay this truth open for us.

The "mystery of Christ"

When you read this you can perceive my insight into the *mystery of Christ,* which was not made know to the sons of men in other generations as it has now been revealed to his holy apostles and prophets by the Spirit; that is, how the Gentiles are fellow heirs, members of the same body, and partakers of the promise in Christ Jesus *through the gospel.*

Of this gospel I was made a minister according to the gift of God's

grace which was given me by the working of his power. To me,
though I am the very least of all the saints, this grace was given,
to preach to the Gentiles the unsearchable riches of Christ, and to
make all men see what is the plan of the mystery hidden for ages in
God who created all things; that through the church the manifold
wisdom of God might now be made known to the principalities and
powers in the heavenly places. (Ephesians 3:4–10)

There was a truth that was not fully and clearly revealed before the coming of Christ. This truth, now revealed, is called the "mystery of Christ". It is the truth that *people from all the nations of the world would be full and complete partners with the chosen people of God* (Ephesians 3:6). It is called the "mystery of Christ" because it is coming true "through the gospel" (v. 6) which is about Christ.

Therefore the gospel is not the revelation that the nations already belong to God. The gospel is the instrument for bringing the nations into this equal status of salvation. The mystery of Christ (drawing the nations into inheritance of Abraham) is happening through the preaching of the gospel. Paul sees his own apostolic vocation as the means God is graciously using to declare the riches of the Messiah to the nations (v. 8).

So a massive change has occurred in redemptive history. Before the coming of Christ a truth was not fully revealed – namely, that the nations may enter with equal standing into the household of God (Ephesians 2:19). The time was not "full" for this revelation because Christ had not been revealed from heaven. The glory and honor of uniting all the peoples was being reserved for him in his saving work. It is fitting then that the nations be gathered in only through the preaching of the message of Christ, whose cross is the peace that creates the worldwide church (vv. 11–21).

In other words, there is a profound theological reason why salvation did not spread to the nations before the incarnation of the Son of God. The reason is that it would not have been clear that the nations were gathering for the glory of Christ. God means for his Son to be the center of worship as the nations receive the word of reconciliation. For this reason also we will see further on that the preaching of Christ is the means appointed by God for the ingathering of the nations.

> (25a) Now to him who is able to strengthen you (25b) according to my gospel and the preaching of Jesus Christ, (25c) according to the revelation of the mystery which was kept secret for long ages, (26a) but is now disclosed (26b) and through the prophetic writings is made known (26c) according to the command of the eternal God (26d) for the obedience of faith (26e) to all the nations – (27) to the only wise God be glory for evermore through Jesus Christ. Amen. (Romans 16:25–27)

This is a very complex sentence. But if we patiently examine its parts and notice how they relate to each other, the crucial meaning for missions emerges.

The verses are a doxology: "Now to him who is able to strengthen you . . ." But Paul gets so caught up in God that he does not come down again to the words of the doxology until verse 27: "to the only wise God be glory for evermore through Jesus Christ. Amen."

Sandwiched inside the two parts of the doxology is a massive statement about the meaning of Paul's gospel in relation to God's eternal purposes. The thought moves as follows. The strength that Paul prays will come to the Romans (v. 25a) accords with his gospel and the preaching of Christ (v. 25b). This means that God's power is revealed in the gospel Paul preaches and that's the power he prays for them to be strengthened by.

Then he says that this gospel preaching is in accord with the revelation of a mystery kept secret for ages and now revealed (vv. 25c, 26a). In other words what Paul preaches is not out of sync with God's purposes. It "accords" with them. It expresses and conforms to them. His preaching is a part of God's plan that is now being revealed in history.

How is it being revealed? It is being disclosed through the prophetic writings (v. 26c). This means that the mystery was not *totally* hidden in past ages. There were pointers in the prophetic writings. So much so that now these very Old Testament writings are used to make the mystery known. (See, for example, how Paul does this in Romans 15:9–13.)

In Paul's preaching of the gospel he uses the prophetic writings to help him make known the mystery.

What then is the mystery? Verse 26c–26e says that making known this mystery accords with "the command of the eternal God for the obedience of faith to all the nations". The most natural way to interpret this is to say that the mystery is the purpose of God to command all nations to obey him through faith.

But what makes this a mystery is that the command to the nations for the obedience of faith is specifically a command to have faith in Jesus the Messiah of Israel, and thus become part of the people of God and heirs of Abraham (Ephesians 2:19–3:6). In Romans 1:5 Paul describes his calling to the nations with these words: "We have received grace and apostleship to bring about the obedience of faith for the sake of [Christ's] name among all the nations." Here he makes plain that the term "obedience of faith" in Romans 16:26d is a call for the sake of Christ's name. It is thus a call to acknowledge and trust and obey Christ. This is the mystery hidden for ages – that all the nations would be commanded to trust in Israel's Messiah and be saved through him.

The word "now" in verse 26a is crucial. It refers to the fullness of time in redemptive history when God put Christ forward onto the center stage of history. From "now" on things are different. The time has come for the mystery to be revealed. The time has come to command all the nations to obey God through faith in Jesus the Messiah.

God is "now" doing a new thing. With the coming of Christ, God will no longer "allow the nations to walk in their own ways" (Acts 14:16, see below). The time has come for all nations to be called to repent and for the mystery to be fully revealed that through faith in Christ the nations are "fellow heirs, members of the same body, and partakers of the promises *through the gospel*" (Ephesians 3:6). Not without the gospel! But *through* the gospel. This will become increasingly obvious and crucial as we move on.

"The times of ignorance"

The times of ignorance God overlooked, but now he commands all men everywhere to repent, because he has fixed a day on which he will judge the world in righteousness by a man whom he has appointed, and of this he has given assurance to all men by raising him from the dead. (Acts 17:30–31)

This text comes from Paul's sermon to the Greeks on the Areopagus in Athens. He had noticed an "altar to an unknown god". So he said, "What therefore you worship as unknown, this I proclaim to you" (v. 23).

In other words, he goes so far as to say that they worship the true God unawares! This "ignorant" worship is what makes the past generations "times of ignorance" (v. 30). And we will see that the worship of the true God "ignorantly" is *not* a saving act.

The "times of ignorance" in Paul's sermon correspond to the ages in which the "mystery of Christ" has been kept secret (Romans 16:25; Colossians 1:26; Ephesians 3:5). These are the times in which, according to Acts 14:16, God has "allowed the nations to walk in their own ways". Or as Acts 17:30 says, the times that God "overlooked".

God's *overlooking* the "times of ignorance" does not mean that he ignores sins so as not to punish them. This would contradict Romans 1:18 ("the wrath of God is revealed from heaven against all ungodliness and wickedness of men") and Romans 2:12 ("those who have sinned without the law will also perish without the law").

Rather, God's overlooking the "times of ignorance" refers to his giving men over to their own ways. His overlooking is his sovereign decision to postpone an all-out pursuit of their repentance through the mission of his people. "The reason why men have wandered from the truth for so long is that God did not stretch forth His hand from heaven to lead them back to the way . . . Ignorance was in the world, as long as it pleased God to take no notice of it."[24]

This does not mean that the commands and instructions were not there in the Old Testament for Israel to bear witness to the nations of the grace of God and invite their participation (e.g., Psalm 67; Genesis 12:2–3). It means rather that for generations God did not intervene to overcome this disobedience, but for his own wise purposes

131

"allowed the nations to walk in their own ways" – and allowed his own nation to walk in the disobedience of missionary indifference.

God's ways are not our ways. Even today we live in a similar time of "hardening" – only now the tables are turned, and it is Israel that is passed over for a season.

> Lest you [Gentiles] be wise in your own conceits, I want you to understand this mystery, brethren: a hardening has come upon part of Israel, until the full number of the Gentiles come in and so all Israel will be saved. (Romans 11:25–26)

There was a time when the Gentiles were passed over while God dealt with Israel and now there is a time while Israel is largely passed over as God gathers the full number of his elect from the nations. In neither case are the people of God to neglect their saving mission toward Jew or Gentile "that they might save some" (Romans 11:14; 1 Corinthians 9:22). But God has his sovereign purposes in determining who actually hears and believes the gospel. And we may be sure that those purposes are wise and holy and will bring the greatest glory to his name.

We are given a glimpse in 1 Corinthians 1:21 of this divine wisdom:

> Since, *in the wisdom of God, the world did not know God through wisdom*, it pleased God through the folly of what we preach to save those who believe.

This says that it was God's wisdom that determined that men would not know him through their wisdom. In other words this is an instance and illustration of how God overlooked (i.e. glanced over) the times of ignorance and allowed men to go their own ways.

Why? To make crystal clear that men on their own, by their own wisdom (religion!) will never truly know God. An extraordinary work of God would be required to bring people to a true and saving knowledge of God, namely the preaching of Christ crucified: "It pleased God through the folly of what we preach to save those who believe." This is what Paul meant in Ephesians 3:6 when he said that the mystery of Christ is that the nations are becoming partakers of the promise "*through the gospel*". Thus 1 Corinthians 1:21 and Ephesians 3:6 are parallel ideas, and utterly crucial for seeing that in this "now" of redemptive history, knowing the gospel is the only way to become an heir of the promise.

All boasting is excluded by God's showing that man's own wisdom in all the nations – his own self-wrought religions – does not bring him to God. Rather, God saves now by means of preaching that is "a stumbling block to Jews and folly to Gentiles, but to those who are called, both Jews and Greeks, Christ the power of God and the wisdom of God" (1 Corinthians 1:23–24). In this way all boasting is excluded. For, left to himself, man does not come to God.

In his inspiring book, *A Vision for Missions*, Tom Wells tells the story of how William Carey illustrates this conviction in his own preaching. Carey was an English Baptist missionary, who left for India in 1793. He never came home, but persevered for 40 years in the gospel ministry.

> Once he was talking with a Brahman in 1797. The Brahman was defending idol worship, and Carey cited Acts 14:16 and 17:30.
>
> God formerly "suffered all nations to walk in their own ways," said Carey, "but now commandeth all men everywhere to repent."
>
> "Indeed," said the native, "I think God ought to repent for not sending the Gospel sooner to us."
>
> Carey was not without an answer. He said,
>
> "Suppose a kingdom had been long overrun by the enemies of its true king, and he though possessed of sufficient power to conquer them, should yet suffer them to prevail, and establish themselves as much as they could desire, would not the valour and wisdom of that king be far more conspicuous in exterminating them, than it would have been if he had opposed them at first, and prevented their entering the country? Thus by the diffusion of Gospel light, the wisdom, power, and grace of God will be more conspicuous in overcoming such deep-rooted idolatries, and in destroying all that darkness and vice which have so universally prevailed in this country, than they would have been if all had not been suffered to walk in their own ways for so many ages past."[25]

Carey's answer to why God allowed nations to walk in their own ways is that in doing so the final victory of God will be all the more glorious. There is a divine wisdom in the timing of God's deliverances from darkness. We should humble ourselves to see it rather than presume to know better how God should deal with a rebellious world.

In Acts 17:30 how does Paul assess the ignorant worship of the unknown god (v. 23)? He says that the time has come for repentance in view of the impending judgment of the world by Jesus Christ ("He has fixed a day on which he will judge the world in righteousness by a man whom he has appointed", v. 31). In other words, Paul does not reveal to the worshipers in Athens that they are already prepared to meet their Judge because they render a kind of worship to the true God through their altar to the unknown god (v. 23). They are not ready. They must repent.

As Jesus said in Luke 24:47, from the time of the resurrection onward "repentance and forgiveness of sins should be preached *in his name* to all nations". What is to be preached is that through confessing the name of Jesus sins can be forgiven. This was not known before, because Jesus was not here before. But now the times of ignorance are over. Jesus has brought the purposes of God to fulfillment. In him all the promises are yes. At his throne every knee will bow. Therefore, henceforth he is the focus of saving faith. He is now openly installed and declared as Judge, and he alone can receive the appeals for acquittal.

What then are we saying so far? We are saying that the coming of Jesus Christ into the world is an event of such stupendous proportions that a change has occurred in the necessary focus of saving faith. Before his coming, saving faith reposed in the forgiving and helping mercy of God displayed in events like the Exodus and in the sacrificial offerings and in the prophetic promises like Isaiah 53. Jesus was not known. The mystery that the nations would be fully included through the preaching of *his name* was kept secret for ages. Those were times of ignorance. God let the nations go their own way.

But "now" – a key word in the turning of God's historic

work of redemption – something new has happened. The Son of God has appeared. He has revealed the Father. He has atoned for sin. He has risen from the dead. His authority as universal Judge is vindicated. And the message of his saving work is to be spread to all peoples. This turn in redemptive history is for the glory of Jesus Christ. Its aim is to put him at the center of all God's saving work. And therefore it accords with this purpose that henceforth Christ be the sole and necessary focus of saving faith. Apart from a knowledge of him, none who has the ability to know will be saved.[26]

This tremendously important turn in redemptive history from the "times of ignorance" and the hiddenness of the "mystery of Christ" is not taken seriously enough by those who say people can be saved *today* who do not know Christ because people were saved *in the Old Testament* who did not know Christ. For example, Millard Erickson argues this way but does not reckon seriously enough with the tremendous significance that the New Testament sees in the historical turning point of the incarnation that ends the "times of ignorance" and manifests the "mystery of Christ".

> If Jews possessed salvation in the Old Testament era simply by virtue of having the form of the Christian gospel without its content, can this principle be extended? Could it be that those who ever since the time of Christ have had no opportunity to hear the gospel, as it has come through the special revelation, participate in this salvation on the same basis?[27]

This would be a valid argument, perhaps, if the New Testament did not teach that the coming of Christ is a decisive turn in redemptive history that henceforth makes him the focus of all saving faith.

But is this conclusion supported by other New Testament teaching? What about the case of Cornelius? Was he not a Gentile, living after the resurrection of Christ and saved through his genuine piety without focusing his faith on Christ?

The case of Cornelius, Acts 10:1 – 11:18

The story of Cornelius the Gentile centurion could lead

135

some to believe that a man can be saved today apart from knowing the gospel and just by fearing God and doing the good that he can.

Cornelius is described as a "devout man who feared God with all his household, gave alms liberally to the people and prayed constantly to God" (10:2). On one occasion an angel says to him, "Cornelius, your prayer has been heard and your alms have been remembered before God. Send therefore to Joppa and ask for Simon who is called Peter" (10:31–32).

Meanwhile the apostle Peter has had a vision from the Lord designed to teach him that the ceremonial uncleanness of the Gentiles is not a hindrance to their acceptance by God. A voice said to Peter, "What God has cleansed, you must not call common" (10:15).

When Peter meets Cornelius he says, "Truly I perceive that God shows no partiality, but in every nation any one who fears him and does what is right is acceptable to him" (10:34–35). This is the sentence that might lead some to think that Cornelius was already saved from his sin even before he heard and believed the gospel. But in fact Luke's point in telling the story seems to be just the opposite.

It will be helpful to ask two questions that are really pressing in this story. One is this: Was Cornelius already saved before Peter preached Christ to him? The reason this is so pressing is that verses 34–35 have led many to say that he was. They are the beginning of Peter's sermon: "Truly I perceive that God shows no partiality, but in every nation any one who fears him and does what is right is acceptable to him."

You can see how readers would easily conclude that Cornelius was already accepted by God since verse 2 said that he indeed feared God and prayed and gave alms. Did Peter then just inform Cornelius about the acceptance and salvation that he already had? And can we draw the conclusion for missions that there are unreached people who already have a saving relationship with God before they hear the gospel of Christ?

So my first question is: Does verse 35 mean that Cornelius and people like him are already justified and reconciled to God and saved from wrath? My second question will assume the answer to this first one and bring us to the very pointed application of this story to world missions.

Does verse 35 mean that Cornelius and those like him are already in God's family, justified, reconciled, saved? Is that Peter's point in saying this and Luke's point in writing it?

Was Cornelius already saved?

Let me give you four reasons from the text for answering *no*.

1. Acts 11:14 says that the message Peter brought was the way Cornelius was saved. Look at 11:13–14 where Peter tells the story of the angel's appearing to Cornelius: "He told us how he had seen the angel standing in his house and saying, 'Send to Joppa and bring Simon called Peter; he will declare to you *a message by which you will be saved*, you and all your household.'"

Notice two things. First, notice that the message itself is essential. The gospel is the power of God unto salvation. Then notice that the tense of the verb is future: ". . . a message by which you *will* be saved . . ." In other words the message was not simply the informing of Cornelius that he already was saved. If he sends for Peter and hears the message and believes on the Christ of that message then he *will* be saved. And if he does not he won't be.

This surely is why the whole story is built around God's miraculously getting Cornelius and Peter together. There was a message that Cornelius needed to hear to be saved (10:22, 33).

So Acts 10:35 probably does not mean that Cornelius is already saved when it says that people in unreached ethnic groups who fear God and do right are acceptable to God. Cornelius had to hear the gospel message to be saved.

2. Peter makes this point at the end of his sermon in 10:43. He brings the message to a close with these words: "To him (i.e., to Christ) all the prophets bear witness that *every one who believes in him receives forgiveness of sins through his name*."

Forgiveness of sins is salvation. No one is saved whose

sins against God are not forgiven by God. And Peter says that forgiveness comes through believing in Christ, and it comes through the name of Christ.

He does not say, "I am here to announce to you that those of you who fear God and do right are already forgiven." He says, "I am here so that you may hear the gospel and receive forgiveness in the name of Christ by believing in him." So again it is very unlikely that verse 35 means that Cornelius and his household were already forgiven for their sins before they heard the message of Christ.

3. Elsewhere in the book of Acts even those who are the most God-fearing and ethical are told that they must repent and believe in order to be saved, namely, the Jews. The Jews at Pentecost were called "devout men" (2:5) like Cornelius was called a devout man (in 10:2). But Peter ended his message in Acts 2 by calling even devout Jews to repent and be baptized in the name of Jesus for the forgiveness of their sins (2:38). The same is true in Acts 3:19 and 13:38–39.

So Luke is not trying to tell us in this book that devout, God-fearing people who practice what's right as best they know how are already saved and without any need of the gospel. The gospel got its start among the most devout people in the world, namely the Jews. They had more advantages in knowing God than any of the other peoples of the earth. Yet they were told again and again: devoutness and works of righteousness and religious sincerity do not solve the problems of sin. The only hope is to believe on Jesus.

4. The fourth reason for saying that verse 35 does not mean Cornelius and others like him are already saved is found in Acts 11:18. When the people hear Peter tell the story about Cornelius their initial misgivings are silenced, Luke says, "And they glorified God, saying, Then to the Gentiles also God has granted *repentance unto life*."

"Repentance unto life" means that their repentance led to eternal life. They did not already have eternal life. They received it when they heard the message about Christ and turned to believe and follow him.

138

So I conclude that Acts 10:35 does not mean that Cornelius was already saved because he was in some sense a God-fearer and did many right and noble things. That's the answer to my first question.

How was Cornelius "acceptable" to God?

The second is simply: What then does it mean when Peter says, "In every nation any one who fears God and does what is right is acceptable to him" (10:35)? And what does this have to do with our commitment to world evangelization?

In trying to answer this question my first thought was that what Peter means in verse 35 is what God meant in the vision about the unclean animals, namely, the lesson of verse 15: "What God has cleansed, you must not call common." But something stopped me and made me think again.

Consider verse 28. Peter is explaining to the Gentiles why he was willing to come and says, "You yourselves know how unlawful it is for a Jew to associate with or to visit any one of another nation; but God has shown me that I should not call *any man* common or unclean."

What this means is that Christians should never look down on a person from any race or ethnic group and say: they are unfit to hear the gospel from me. Or: they are too unclean for me to go into their house to share the gospel. Or: they are not worth evangelizing. Or: they have too many offensive habits to even get near them.

But the phrase that makes verse 28 so powerful is the phrase "any man" or "any one": "God has shown me that I should not call *any human being* common or unclean." In other words, Peter learned from his vision on the housetop in Joppa that God rules no one out of his favor on the basis of race or ethnic origin or mere cultural distinctives or physical distinctives. "Common and unclean" meant rejected, despised, taboo. It was like leprosy.

And Peter's point here in verse 28 is that there is not one human being on the face of the earth that we should think about that way. Not one. That's the amazing thing in this verse. Our hearts should go out to every single person whatever the color, whatever the ethnic origin, whatever the physical traits, whatever the cultural distinctives. We are not to write off anybody. "God has shown me that I should not call any one – not one – common or unclean."

Now that is *not* what Peter says in verse 35. This is what kept me from assuming that verse 35 simply meant: all people are acceptable as candidates for salvation, no matter their ethnic background. In verse 35 Peter says, "*In* every nation (note those words!) any one who fears him and does what is right is acceptable to God." Here he is not talking about every person like he was in verse 28. Here he is talking about some *in* every nation. "*In* every nation any one who fears him and does what is right is acceptable to God."

So the acceptability Peter has in mind here is something more, it seems, than merely not being common or unclean. That's everybody. Peter said, "Call *no one* common or unclean." Here he says that only *some* in every nation fear God and do right. And these are acceptable to God.

So now we know two things which verse 35 does not mean. First, it does not mean that these God-fearing doers of good are saved. We saw four reasons why it can't mean that. And secondly, it does not mean merely that they are acceptable candidates for evangelism (not common or unclean, not taboo), because verse 28 already said that's true of everybody, not just some. But verse 35 says that only some are God-fearing, doing what is right and thus acceptable.

So the meaning probably lies somewhere between these two: between being saved and being a touchable, lovable human candidate for evangelism.

My suggestion is that Cornelius represents a kind of unsaved person among an unreached people group who is seeking God in an extraordinary way. And Peter is saying that God *accepts* this search as genuine (hence "acceptable" in verse 35) and works wonders to bring that person the gospel of Jesus Christ the way he did through the visions of both Peter on the housetop and Cornelius in the hour of prayer.

A modern Cornelius

This "extraordinary searching" still happens today. Don Richardson, in his book *Eternity in Their Hearts*, tells of a conversion very similar to Cornelius'. The Gedeo people of south-central Ethiopia were a tribe of a half-million coffee-growing people who believed in a benevolent being called *Magano*, the omnipotent Creator of all that is. Few of the Gedeo people prayed to Magano, being concerned instead to appease an evil being they called *Sheit'an*. But one Gedeo man, Warrasa Wanga, from the town of Dilla on the edge of Gedeo tribal land, prayed to Magano to reveal himself to the Gedeo people.

Then Warrasa Wanga had a vision: two white-skinned strangers came and built flimsy shelters for themselves under the shade of a sycamore tree near Dilla. Later they built more permanent shiny-roofed structures which eventually dotted an entire hillside. Warrasa had never seen anything like these structures, since all of the Gedeo dwellings were grass-roofed. Then Warrasa heard a voice say, "These men will bring you a message from Magano, the God you seek. Wait for them." In the last scene of his vision, Warrasa saw himself remove the center pole from his own house, carry it out of the town, and set it in the ground next to one of the shiny-roofed dwellings of the men. In Gedeo symbolism, the center pole of a man's house stands for his very life.

Eight years later, in December 1948, two Canadian missionaries, Albert Brant and Glen Cain, came to Ethiopia to begin a work among the Gedeo people. They intended to ask permission from Ethiopian officials to place their new mission in the center of the Gedeo region, but they were advised by other Ethiopians that their request would be refused due to the current political climate. The advisors told them to ask permission only to go as far as Dilla, on the extreme edge of Gedeo tribal land. Permission was granted, and when they reached Dilla, the missionaries set up their tents under an old sycamore tree.

Thirty years later there were more than 200 churches among the Gedeo people, with each church averaging more than 200 members. Almost the entire Gedeo tribe has been influenced by the gospel.[28] Warrasa was one of the first converts, and the first to be imprisoned for his faith.[29]

The fear of God that is acceptable to God

The main evidence that Luke is talking about this kind of "acceptable" unsaved person who seeks the true God and his messengers is found in verse 31 where Cornelius says that the angel said to him, "Cornelius, *your prayer has been heard* and your alms have been remembered before God. Send *therefore* to Joppa and ask for Simon who is called Peter." Notice: Your prayers have been heard . . . *therefore* send for Peter. This implies that the prayers were for God to send him what he needed in order to be saved.

So the fear of God that is acceptable to God in verse 35 is a true sense that there is a holy God, that we have to meet him some day as desperate sinners, that we cannot save ourselves and need to know God's way of salvation, and that we pray for it day and night and seek to act on the light we have. This is what Cornelius was doing. And God accepted his prayer and his groping for truth in his life (Acts 17:27), and worked wonders to bring the saving message of the gospel to him. Cornelius would not have been saved if no one had taken him the gospel. And no one who can apprehend revelation (see note 26) will be saved today without the gospel.

Therefore Cornelius does not represent persons who are saved without hearing and believing the gospel; rather he illustrates God's intention to take out a people for his name from "every nation" (Acts 10:35) through the sending of gospel messengers across cultural lines which had once been taboo.

We should learn with the Jewish church in Jerusalem, that "to the Gentiles also God has granted repentance unto life" (11:18). But we must be sure that we learn this the way they learned it: they inferred this from the fact that the Gentiles have *believed the gospel that Peter preached* and have received the Holy Spirit. They do not infer the acceptance of the Gentiles from their fear of God and their good deeds.

It appears therefore that Luke's intention in telling the Cornelius story is to show that Gentiles can become part of the chosen people of God through faith in Christ in spite of their ceremonial "uncleanness". The point is *not* that Gentiles are already part of God's chosen people because they fear God and do many good deeds. The key sentence is Acts 11:14 – "He will declare to you a *message by which you will be saved.*"

"No other name under heaven", Acts 4:12

The reason this message saves is that the message proclaims the *name* that saves – the name of Jesus. Peter said that God visited the Gentiles "to take out of them a people *for his name*" (Acts 15:14). It stands to reason then that the proclamation by which God takes a people for his name would be a message that hinges on the name of his Son Jesus.

This is, in fact, what we saw in Peter's preaching at the house of Cornelius. The sermon comes to its climax with these words about Jesus: "Every one who believes in him receives forgiveness of sins *through his name*" (Acts 10:43).

The implicit necessity of hearing and embracing the name of Jesus which we see in the story of Cornelius, is made explicit in Acts 4:12 in the climax of another sermon by Peter, this time before the Jewish rulers in Jerusalem:

> And there is salvation in no one else, for there is no other name under heaven given among men by which we must be saved.

The situation behind this famous sentence is that the risen Jesus healed a man through Peter and John. The man had been lame from birth, but he got up and ran through the Temple praising God. A crowd gathered and Peter preached. His message makes it obvious that what is at stake here is not merely a local religious phenomenon. It has to do with everybody in the world.

Then according to Acts 4:1 the priests and the captain of the temple and the Sadducees came and arrested Peter and John and put them in custody overnight. The next morning the rulers and elders and scribes gathered and interrogated Peter and John. In the course of the interrogation Peter drew out the implication of the universal lordship of

Jesus: "There is salvation in no one else, for there is no other name under heaven given among men by which we must be saved."

We need to feel the force of this universal claim by taking several phrases very seriously. The reason there is salvation in no one else is that there is no other name *under heaven* (not just no other name in Israel, but no other name under heaven, including the heaven over Greece and Rome and Spain, etc.) given *among men* (not just among Jews, but among all humans everywhere) by which we must be saved. These two phrases, "under heaven" and "among men", press the claim of universality to its fullest extent.

But there is even more here that we need to see. Commentators usually interpret Acts 4:12 to mean that without believing in Jesus a person cannot be saved. In other words, Acts 4:12 is seen as a crucial text in answering the question whether those who have never heard the gospel of Jesus can be saved. But Clark Pinnock represents others who say that "Acts 4:12 does not say anything about [this question] . . . It does not comment on the fate of the heathen. Although it is a question of great importance to us, it is not one on which Acts 4:12 renders a judgment, either positive or negative."[30] Rather, what Acts 4:12 says is that "salvation in its fullness is available to humankind only because God in the person of his Son Jesus provided it".[31] In other words, the verse says that salvation comes only through the *work* of Jesus but not only through faith in Jesus. His work can benefit those who relate to God properly without him, for example, on the basis of general revelation in nature.

The problem with Pinnock's interpretation is that it does not reckon with the true significance of Peter's focus on the "*name*" of Jesus. "There is no other *name* under heaven *by which* we must be saved." Peter is saying something more than that there is no other *source* of saving power that you can be saved by under some *other* name. The point of saying, "There is no other *name*", is that we are saved by calling on the name of the Lord Jesus. Calling on his name is our entrance into fellowship with God. If one is saved by Jesus incognito, one does not speak of being saved *by his name*.

We noticed above that Peter said in Acts 10:43, "*Every one who believes in him* receives forgiveness of sins *through his name*." The name of Jesus is the focus of faith and repentance. In order to believe on Jesus for the forgiveness of sins, you must believe on his name. Which means that you have heard of him and know who he is as a particular man who did a particular saving work and rose from the dead.

The point of Acts 4:12 for missions is made explicit by the way Paul picks up on this very issue of "the name of the Lord" Jesus in Romans 10:13–15. We turn to this passage now and see that missions is essential precisely because "Every one who calls on *the name of the Lord* will be saved. But how are men to call upon him in whom they have not believed and how are they to believe in him of whom they have never heard? And how are they to hear without a preacher?"

"How are they to believe in him whom they have not heard? And how are they to hear without a preacher?"

For our purposes the crucial thing to see in the sequence of thought from Romans 9:30 to 10:9 is that faith in Jesus Christ comes to stand in the place of the faith in God that was required in the Old Testament and is referred to in 9:32 as the way to righteousness. We trace this sequence of thought briefly so that the point of 10:6–9 will become plain, namely, that Christ is the goal of the Old Testament message and that all faith must now be focused on him for salvation.

In Romans 9:30 – 10:21 Paul shows that the chosen people Israel have failed to attain righteousness even though they were taught the message of faith in the Old Testament all along. In other words the fall of Israel (Romans 11:12–15) is not owing to a failure of God to reveal to them what they needed to know. Rather Romans 9:32 tells us why Irael did not attain to the righteousness taught in the law. The reason was that they pursued it "not from faith but *as though* it were from works".

This "as though" shows that the true intention of the law was never to be a system of works by which men try to earn their righteousness. Rather its intention was to be a "law of faith" – it taught that Israel should trust the mercy of God

145

and that all obedience should be the "obedience of faith" (Romans 1:5; 16:26) and all works should be the "works of faith" (1 Thessalonians 1:3; 2 Thessalonians 1:11).[32]

But Israel stumbled over this teaching and distorted it into a legalistic system called "works of law" (Romans 3:28; cf. 9:32). Another way to say this is to say that Israel was "ignorant" of the righteousness of God offered to faith, but instead sought to establish their own righteousness (10:3).

In 10:4 Paul brings this age-old distortion of the law into relation to Christ. He says that Christ is the goal of the law. He means that Christ is the climactic expression of what the law was teaching all along, namely the message of faith. Christ is the stone of stumbling referred to in 9:33. Therefore it is not surprising that Israel rejected Christ because they had already rejected the true meaning of the law (faith!) which came to fulfillment in him.[33]

In Romans 10:6–8 Paul refers to Deuteronomy 30:11–14 and treats Christ as the essence of the commandment. The point of Deuteronomy 30:11–14 is that the commandment of the law is not too hard to be kept. "For this commandment which I command you this day is not too hard for you, neither is it far off" (Deuteronomy 30:11). It does not require heroic moral efforts. The implication is that it only requires faith.

Now Paul says that Christ is the fulfillment of this truth: that the requirement of God is not hard – it is not too far off or too deep. Rather it is as close as your lips and your heart, which he takes to mean as close as the confession of your lips and the belief of your heart. Hence the statement in Romans 10:9: "If you confess with your lips that Jesus is Lord and believe in your heart that God raised him from the dead, you will be saved."

Thus we can see that in this sequence of thought from 9:30 to 10:9 faith in Jesus Christ has come to stand in the place of the faith in God. This is the point of 10:6–9. Christ is the goal of the Old Testament message and all faith must now be focused on him for salvation.

So when Romans 10:11 quotes Isaiah 28:16, "No one who believes in him will be put to shame", the reference is clearly to Jesus, the predicted cornerstone. And when

Romans 10:13 quotes Joel 2:32, "Everyone who calls upon the name of the Lord will be saved", Jesus is the "Lord" referred to, even though in Joel 2:32 "Yahweh" is in view. The reason we know this is that Romans 10:9 said, "If you confess with your lips that Jesus is Lord . . . you shall be saved."

So Paul is making clear that in this new era of redemptive history, Jesus is the goal and climax of Old Testament teaching, and therefore Jesus now stands as Mediator between man and Yahweh as the object of saving faith.

The flow of thought from Romans 10:14 to 21 is not easy to grasp. The sequence of questions in verses 14–15 is very familiar, and is often cited in relation to missionary work:

> Therefore how are men to call upon him in whom they have not believed? And how are they to believe in him whom they have never heard?[34] And how are they to hear without a preacher? And how can men preach unless they are sent? As it is written, "How beautiful are the feet of those who preach good news!"

But how do these verses fit into the flow of Paul's thought? Why do they begin with the word "therefore" (*oun*)? How does asking a series of questions communicate an inference? Why does the next verse (v. 16) begin with "*But* (or *nevertheless*) they have not all obeyed the gospel"?

The answer seems to be this: the "therefore" at the beginning of verse 14 and the "nevertheless" at the beginning of verse 16 point to the fact that the series of questions in verses 14–15 is really making a statement to the effect that God has already worked to bring about these conditions for calling on the Lord Jesus for salvation. We could paraphrase as follows:

> (10–13) Salvation is richly available to both Jews and Gentiles – to everyone who calls upon the name of the Lord Jesus. (14–15) *Therefore*, God has taken steps to provide the prerequisites for calling on the Lord. He is sending those who preach so that Christ can be heard and people can believe and call on the Lord Jesus. (16) Nevertheless, this has not led to obedience, as Isaiah predicted: "Lord, who has believed our report?"

So far then the main point of verses 14–16 would be that

even though God has taken steps to provide the prerequisites for calling on the Lord, *nevertheless* most have not obeyed.

But who is in view here when Paul says they have not believed? The answer to this question divides two different ways of construing Paul's line of reasoning in the whole passage. John Murray and Charles Hodge represent these two lines.

Murray says, "At verse 16 the apostle returns to that subject which permeates this section of the epistle, the unbelief of Israel."[35] Similarly Murray says the focus on Israel's unbelief continues to the end of the paragraph. So, for example, verse 18 also refers to Israel, "But I ask, have they not heard? Indeed they have, for 'Their voice has gone out to all the earth and their words to the ends of the world.'" He says the quote from Psalm 19:4 (which originally referred to works of nature declaring God's glory) is used by Paul to describe the worldwide spread of the gospel of Jesus. And the point is that if the gospel is going out to all the world, "it cannot then be objected that Israel did not hear".[36] So the focus stays on Israel. The point of Paul's thought throughout Romans 10 is that Israel knows the gospel and is nevertheless rejecting it and is thus accountable.

Charles Hodge, on the other hand, sees the focus differently in verses 11–21. "Paul's object in the whole context is to vindicate the propriety of extending the gospel call to all nations." He sees both verses 16 and 18 as references not to Israel but to the nations. "The 16th verse refers to the Gentiles, 'They have not all obeyed the gospel', and therefore this verse [18], 'Have they not heard?' cannot, without any intimation of change, be naturally referred to a different subject ... In the following verse [19], where the Jews are really intended, they are distinctly mentioned, 'Did not Israel know?'"[37]

In spite of this difference between Murray and Hodge the important thing for our purpose remains fairly clear, and both agree. Whether Paul is focusing in a narrower way on the accountability of Israel or more broadly on the availability of the gospel to the nations (and therefore also to Israel), both agree that calling on the name of the Lord Jesus is necessary for salvation (v. 13).

So necessary is it that Paul feels compelled to show that all the necessary prerequisites for calling on the Lord are being put in place by God (vv. 14–15). Even more relevant for our immediate question is the implication that "calling on the Lord" in a saving way is not something that a person can do from a position of ignorance. One cannot do it from another religion. This is made plain in the questions of verses 14–15.

Each succeeding question rules out an argument from those who say that there can be salvation without hearing the gospel of Jesus. First, "How are men to call upon him whom they have not believed?" shows that effective calling presupposes faith in the one called. This rules out the argument that one might call on God savingly without faith in Christ.

Second, "And how are they to believe in him whom they have never heard?" shows that faith presupposes hearing Christ in the message of the gospel. This rules out the argument that a person might have saving faith without really knowing or meeting Christ in the gospel.

Third, "And how are they to hear without a preacher?" shows that hearing Christ in the gospel presupposes a proclaimer of the gospel. This rules out the argument that one might somehow meet Christ or hear Christ without a messenger to tell the gospel.

Millard Erickson does not seem to take the force of this sequence seriously enough when he suggests that the quote from Psalm 19:4 in Romans 10:18 teaches that general revelation in nature is all that some need to receive salvation, apart from missionary proclamation.[38] At first this suggestion may seem compelling. Paul says that people must hear in order to call on the Lord. Then he asks in verse 18, "Have they not heard?" And he answers with the words of Psalm 19:4: "Indeed they have, for 'Their voice has gone out to all the earth and their words to the end of the world.'"

In the original context of Psalm 19 "their voice" and "their words" refer to what is communicated through "night" and "day" and "heavens" and "firmament". So one might conclude that the "hearing" that is necessary for saving faith (v. 17) is effectively provided through natural revelation. This is what Erickson concludes.[39]

The problem with this is that it creates an insurmountable tension with the point of verse 14. There Paul says, "How shall they hear without a preacher?" If Erickson were right that a hearing which is effective to save comes through nature, then Paul's question is misleading: "How shall they hear without a preacher?" He clearly means that one cannot hear what one needs to hear for salvation unless a preacher is sent. He would contradict this if he meant in verse 18 that preachers are not essential for salvation, because an effective message of salvation comes through nature.

Therefore, as most commentators agree, it is unlikely that Paul intends for verse 18 to teach that natural revelation fulfills the saving role of the "word of Christ" which gives rise to faith (v. 17). Murray and Hodge agree that Paul uses the words of the Psalm to draw a parallel between the universality of general revelation and the universal spread of the gospel.[40] The point is that God has set in motion a missionary movement (the sending of v. 15) that will reach to all the peoples of the earth on the analogy of the universal spread of God's glory through natural revelation.[41]

Summing up our thoughts on Romans 10, the theological assumption behind Paul's missionary conviction is that Christ is the fulfillment of all that the Old Testament was pointing toward. Before Christ, faith was focused on the mercy of God to forgive sins and to care for his people. As revelation progressed, faith could move more easily from the animal sacrifices on to the promised sin-bearer of Isaiah 53. But when Chirst came, all faith narrowed in its focus to him alone as the One who purchased and guaranteed all the hopes of the people of God. From the time of Christ onward, God wills to honor Christ by making him the sole focus of saving faith. Therefore, people must call upon him and believe in him and hear him and be sent messengers with the "word of Christ".

Paul's conception of his own missionary vocation

The indispensability of hearing the gospel of salvation is seen in the Biblical texts that show how Paul conceived of his own missionary vocation.

At his conversion Paul received a commission from the Lord that clarifies the condition of those without Christ. He refers to this in Acts 26:15–18.

> And I said, "Who are you, Lord?" And the Lord said, "I am Jesus, whom you are persecuting. But rise and stand upon your feet; for I have appeared to you for this purpose, to appoint you to serve and bear witness to the things in which you have seen me and to those in which I will appear to you, delivering you from the people and from the Gentiles – to whom *I send you to open their eyes, that they may turn from darkness to light and from the power of Satan to God, that they may receive forgiveness of sins* and a place among those who are sanctified by faith in me."

Here we see what was at stake in Paul's ministry. Without making any distinctions, the Lord says that those who do not yet have the gospel are in darkness and in the power of Satan and without the forgiveness of sins. Christ commissioned Paul with a word of power that actually opens the eyes of the spiritually blind, not so that they can see they *are* forgiven, but so that they can *be* forgiven. His message delivers from the power of Satan. The picture of nations without the gospel is that they are blind and in the darkness and in bondage to Satan and without forgiveness of sins and unacceptable to God because they are unsanctified.

This accords with what Paul says elsewhere about the condition of man without the power of the gospel: all are under sin with their mouths stopped before God (Romans 3:9–19); they are in the flesh and unable to submit to God or please God (Romans 8:7–8); they are natural and not spiritual and therefore unable to receive the things of the Spirit (1 Corinthians 2:14–16); they are dead in trespasses, and children of wrath (Ephesians 2:3–5); and they are darkened and alienated from God and hard in heart (Ephesians 4:17–18).

Now with the coming of Christ, there is a message that has power to save (Romans 1:16; 1 Thessalonians 2:16; 1 Corinthians 15:2) and bear fruit (Colossians 1:6) and triumph (2 Thessalonians 3:1), and it is the mission of Paul and all his heirs to preach that message to the nations. "Since in the wisdom of God the world did not know God through wisdom [or false religion], it pleased God through the folly of what we preach to save those who believe" (1 Corinthians 1:21).

Salvation is at stake when Paul speaks to Jews in the synagogue as well. Paul does not assume that God-fearing Gentiles or Jews are saved by virtue of their knowing the Old Testament Scriptures. What does he say in the synagogue at Antioch of Pisidia?

> Let it be known to you therefore, brethren, that through this man forgiveness of sins is proclaimed to you, and by him everyone that believes is freed from everything from which you could not be freed by the law of Moses. (Acts 13:38–39)

Paul does not tell them that even the best of them are already forgiven by virtue of their Old Testament religion. He offers them forgiveness through Christ. And he makes "freeing" ("justification") from sin conditional upon believing on Christ. When the synagogue later opposes this message, Paul says in Acts 13:46–48,

> It was necessary that the word of God should be spoken first to you. Since you thrust it from you, and judge yourselves unworthy of eternal life, behold, we turn to the Gentiles. For so the Lord has commanded us, saying, "I have set you to be a light for the Gentiles, that you may bring salvation to the uttermost parts of the earth." And when the Gentiles heard this they were glad and glorified the word of God; and as many as were ordained to eternal life believed.

Paul's vocation is to bring salvation to the end of the earth. The assumption is that salvation is not already at the end of the earth. Paul is to take it. Paul's message is the means of salvation. There is no salvation without it: as many as were ordained to eternal life believed Paul's message, and were saved. God has ordained that salvation come to the nations through sent messengers whose obedient preaching of the gospel brings salvation to the nations.

Through Paul's preaching God is now doing the sovereign work that he had "overlooked" for so long during the "times of ignorance". He is bringing Gentiles to faith according to his preordained plan. He is opening their hearts to the gospel (Acts 16:14) and granting them repentance (Acts 11:18) and cleansing their hearts by faith (Acts 15:9).

Before this time of gospel privilege these things were not possible, for God was allowing the nations to go their own way (Acts 14:16). But now a great movement is under way to gather a people for his name from all the nations, and God himself is active in the ministry of his messengers to sanctify a people for himself.

This becomes wonderfully clear in Romans 15 where Paul describes his own vocation in its relation to the work of Christ in and through him.

> But on some points I have written to you very boldly by way of reminder because of the grace given me by God to be a minister of Christ Jesus to the Gentiles in the priestly service of the gospel of God, so that the offering of the Gentiles may be acceptable, sanctified by the Holy Spirit. In Christ Jesus, then, I have reason to exult in my work for God. For I will not venture to speak of anything except what Christ has wrought through me to win obedience from the Gentiles, by word and deed. (Romans 15:15–18)

Notice the initiative of God in these verses. First, God gave Paul the grace of apostleship and called him to the ministry of the gospel (vv. 15–16). Second, the Gentiles who believed Paul's message are acceptable to God because they are sanctified by the Holy Spirit (v. 16). Third, it is not Paul himself who has won obedience from the Gentiles; it is what Christ has "wrought through him" (v. 18).

So the Gentile mission is the new work of God. It is the fulfillment of divine prophecy that once God allowed the nations to go their own way, but *now* . . .

God has visited the Gentiles to take out of them a people for his name. And with this the words of the prophets agree, as it is written,

> After this I will return,
> and I will rebuild the dwelling of David, which has fallen;
> I will rebuild its ruins,
> and I will set it up,
> *that the rest of men may seek the Lord,*
> and all the Gentiles who are called by my name,
> says the Lord, who has made these things known from of
> old.

(Acts 15:14–18)

A new day has come with Jesus Christ. The people of God are being rebuilt in such a way that they will no longer fail in their task of reaching the nations. In this new day God will not suffer his people to neglect their mission; he will no longer allow the nations to go their own way. He is establishing a church "that the rest of men may seek the Lord".

And he will now gather in all those among the nations who are called by his name! It is *his* new work! All those who are predestined *will* be called (Romans 8:30). All those who are foreordained to eternal life *will* believe (Acts 13:48). All those who are ransomed *will* be gathered from every people under heaven (Revelation 5:9). God himself is the chief agent in this new movement and he *will* take out a people for his name among the nations (Acts 15:14).

The writings of John

John's conception of the new missionary task parallels Paul's. Just as Paul said no one could believe in a Christ they have not heard (Romans 10:14), so Jesus says in John 10:27, "My sheep hear my voice, and I know them, and they follow me" (cf. 10:4, 14). In other words, Jesus gathers his redeemed flock by calling them with his own voice. The true sheep hear his voice and follow and he gives them eternal life (10:28).

Whom does Jesus have in mind when he speaks of those who will hear his voice and follow him? He means more than the Jews that actually heard him on earth. He says, "I have *other sheep that are not of this fold*; them I must bring also; and they will heed my voice. So there shall be one flock and one shepherd" (10:16). By "other sheep that are not of this fold" he means Gentiles who are not part of the Jewish fold.

But how will these Gentiles hear his voice? The answer is the same as with Paul: they hear the voice of Jesus, not in nature or in an alien religion, but in the voice of Christ's messengers. We see this in the way Jesus prays for his future disciples in John 17:20: "I do not pray for these only, but also for those *who believe in me through their word*, that they may all be one." We infer from this then that the "sheep that are not of this fold" will hear the voice of the Shepherd through the voice of his messengers.

So eternal life comes only to those who hear the voice of the Shepherd and follow him. "My sheep hear my voice, and I know them, and they follow me; and I give them eternal life" (10:27–28). This hearing is through the messengers of the Shepherd. This is what Jesus meant in John 14:6 when he said, "I am the way, the truth and the life; no one comes to the Father but by me." "By me" does not mean that people in other religions can get to God because Jesus died for them, though they don't know about it. The "by me" must be defined in the context of John's gospel as believing in Jesus through the word of his disciples (John 6:35; 7:38; 11:25; 12:46; 17:20).

Eternal life is owing to the death of Jesus for his sheep (10:15) – a death that atoned not for a few Jewish sheep only but for sheep from every nation. We see this in John 11:51–53 where John interprets the words of Caiaphas, "Being the high priest that year he prophesied that Jesus should die for the nation, and *not for the nation only, but to gather into one the children of God who are scattered abroad.*"

The "children of God scattered abroad" (11:52) are the "other sheep that are not of this fold" (10:16). And when we look at John's picture of the consummation of the missionary cause in Revelation we see that these "sheep" and "children" are truly from all the nations.

> And they sang a new song, saying,
> Worthy art thou to take the scroll and to open its seals,

> for thou wast slain and by thy blood didst ransom men
>   for God
> *from every tribe and tongue and people and nation*
> *and hast made them a kingdom and priests to our God,*
> *and they shall reign on earth.*

(Revelation 5:9–10)

Here we see the true extent of the word "scattered" in John 11:52. He died to gather the "children of God" who are scattered among "every tribe and tongue and people and nation".

The implication is that the messengers of the Shepherd *must* (Mark 13:10) and *will* (Matthew 24:14) reach every people under neaven with the message of the gospel and the voice of the Shepherd. The redeemed in heaven from all the peoples are not redeemed without knowing it. Rather, as Revelation 7:14 makes clear, those "from every nation, and all tribes and peoples and tongues" (Revelation 7:9) are those who "have washed their robes and made them white in the blood of the Lamb" (Revelation 7:12; 22:14). They are those who "keep the commandments of God and bear testimony to Jesus" (Revelation 12:17). The gospel of the blood crucified for sinners and risen in victory must be preached to all the nations so they can believe and be saved.

Conclusion

The question we have been trying to answer in this section is whether some people are quickened by the Holy Spirit and saved by grace through faith in a merciful Creator even though they never hear of Jesus in this life. Are there devout people in religions other than Christianity who humbly rely on the grace of a God whom they know only through nature or non-Christian religious experience?

The answer of the New Testament is a clear and earnest No. Rather, the message throughout is that with the coming of Christ a major change has occurred in redemptive history. Saving faith was once focused on the mercy of God known in his redemptive acts among the people of Israel, and in the system of animal sacrifices and in the prophecies of coming redemption. Outside Israel we hear of Melchizedek (Genesis 14) who seems to know the true God apart from connection with special revelation in the line of Abraham.

But now the focus of faith has narrowed down to one Man, Jesus Christ, the fulfillment and guarantee of all redemption and all sacrifices and all prophecies. It is to his honor now that henceforth all saving faith shall be directed to him.

Therefore, this great turn in redemptive history is accompanied by a new mission thrust ordained by God. God no longer allows the nations to walk their own way (Acts 14:16), but sends his messengers everywhere calling all to repent and believe the gospel (Acts 17:30).

God in Christ is himself the power behind this mission. He has ordained his people to life (Acts 13:48) and ransomed them by laying down his life for them (John 10:15; Revelation 5:9). Now he is commissioning Spirit-filled messengers to preach to them (Romans 10:15; 1:5) and he is speaking through these messengers with power (Luke 12:12; 21:15; 1 Thessalonians 2:13) and calling the lost effectually to faith (1 Corinthians 1:24; Romans 8:30) and keeping them by his almighty power (Jude 24).

Those who affirm that people who today have no access to the gospel may nevertheless be saved without knowing Christ try to argue that this idea "enhances our motivation to evangelize the lost". As we saw above ("A nerve of urgency", pp. 117–118) it is a futile effort. The arguments fall apart as you pick them up. For example, John Ellenberger of Alliance Theological Seminary cites four ways our motivation will be "enhanced".

1. Citing Acts 18:10 ("I have many people in this city"), he says that "the knowledge that the Holy Spirit has been working in the hearts of people prior to hearing the good news should encourage us".[42] I agree. But that's not the issue. Working in someone's heart to prepare them to respond to the gospel is very different from working in their hearts so that they are saved apart from the gospel. The first motivates missions, the second doesn't.

2. Unintelligibly, he argues that "because the great majority have not responded to general revelation, they

need to be confronted by the claims of Jesus".[43] This amounts to saying that if you believe some are saved apart from the claims of special revelation, you will be more motivated to share those claims because most aren't saved that way. A natural interpretation of these words would mean: where Ellenberger's claim (that some are saved without knowing Christ) does *not* apply, there it will increase motivation. This argument is incomprehensible to me.

3. Third, he argues that believing that some are saved apart from the preaching of the gospel "broadens our understanding of the whole gospel".[44] In other words, if we are going to still pursue missions with zeal it will need to be for reasons wider than merely providing escape from hell (which some already have before we get there). We will need to desire to bring the blessings of salvation in this life. I suppose this is true. But why should we assume that the church will be more motivated to bring *these* blessings to people than they are to bring the blessing of eternal life? The risk I am willing to take to save a person from execution is not increased by telling me, "He is no longer on death row, but surely you will want to feel all the same urgency to help him find a good life."

4. Finally, Ellenberger argues that believing some are saved apart from the preaching of the gospel "reaffirms love as the primary motivation". Again this is unintelligible to me, since it seems to assume that the urgency of missions driven by the desire to rescue people from eternal torment is not love. How does saying some are saved without the gospel make a greater appeal to love?

So I affirm again that the contemporary abandonment of the universal necessity of hearing the gospel for salvation does indeed cut a nerve in missionary motivation. I say "a nerve" rather than "the nerve" because I agree that the universal lostness of man is not the only focus for missionary motivation. Arching over it is the great goal of bringing glory to Christ.

Therefore the church is bound to engage with the Lord of glory in his cause. Charles Hodge is right that "the solemn question, implied in the language of the apostle,

HOW CAN THEY BELIEVE WITHOUT A PREACHER? should sound day and night in the ears of the churches."[45] It is our unspeakable privilege to be caught up with him in the greatest movement in history – the ingathering of the elect "from all tribes and tongues and peoples and nations" until the full number of the Gentiles come in, and all Israel is saved, and the Son of man descends with power and great glory as King of kings and Lord of lords and the earth is full of the knowledge of his glory as the waters cover the sea for ever and ever. Then the supremacy of Christ will be manifest to all and he will deliver the kingdom to God the Father, and God will be all in all.

Notes

1. See for example his sermon on "Justice" in *Creation in Christ* (ed. Rolland Hein [Wheaton: Harold Shaw Publishers, 1976], pp. 63–81) where he argues forcefully that "Punishment is for the sake of amendment and atonement. God is bound by His love to punish sin in order to deliver His creature: He is bound by his justice to destroy sin in His creation" (p. 72). I have given an extended critique of MacDonald's view of divine justice, self-atonement, and universalism in *The Pleasures of God* (Portland: Multnomah Press, 1991), pp. 170–174, 180 note 10, 182–183 note 13.

2. Clark Pinnock and Delwin Brown, *Theological Crossfire: An Evangelical/Liberal Dialogue* (Grand Rapids: Zondervan Publishing House, 1990), pp. 226–227. "I was led to question the traditional belief in everlasting conscious torment because of moral revulsion and broader theological considerations, not first of all on scriptural grounds. It just does not make any sense to say that a God of love will torture people forever for sins done in the context of a finite life ... It's time for evangelicals to come out and say that the biblical and morally appropriate doctrine of hell is annihilation, not everlasting torment."

   In David L. Edwards and John Stott, *Evangelical Essentials* (Downers Grove: IVP, 1988), pp. 314–320, John Stott says: "Emotionally, I find the concept [of eternal conscious torment] intolerable and do not understand how people can live with it without either cauterizing their feelings or cracking under the strain." He gives four arguments that he says suggest "Scripture points in the direction of annihilation, and that 'eternal conscious torment' is a tradition which has to yield to the supreme authority of Scripture ... I do not dogmatise about the position to which I have come. I hold it tentatively. But I do plead for frank dialogue among Evangelicals on the basis of Scripture. I also believe that the ultimate annihilation of the wicked should at least be accepted as a legitimate, biblically founded alternative to their eternal conscious torment."

Edward William Fudge, *The Fire That Consumes* (Houston: Providential Press, 1982).

3. John Hick, "Whatever Path Men Choose Is Mine", in *Christianity and Other Religions*, eds. John Hick and Brian Hebblethwaite (Philadelphia: Fortress Press, 1980), p. 188. Hick ends with a quote from the Bhagavad Gita, iv, 11, "Howsoever men may approach me, even so do I accept them; for, on all sides, whatever path they may choose is mine."

Similarly John Parry, the Other Faiths Secretary of the World Church and Mission Department of the United Reformed Church in London, wrote in 1985, "It is to the faith of Jesus Christ that we are called. The change of preposition from in to of is signficant. It is a faith that is shown in one's trust in God, in surrender to God's purposes, in giving oneself. Such a response of faith I have witnessed among my friends of other faiths. I cannot believe they are far from the kingdom of heaven, what is more, as Dr. Starkey writes '... people will not be judged for correct doctrinal beliefs but for their faith. Those who will enter the kingdom on the day of judgment are those who in faith respond to God's love by loving others.'" ("Exploring the Ways of God with Peoples of Faith", in *International Review of Missions*, Vol. lxxiv, No. 296, October, 1985, p. 512.)

4. For example, John Stott says, "I believe the most Christian stance is to remain agnostic on this question ... The fact is that God, alongside the most solemn warnings about our responsibility to respond to the gospel, has not revealed how he will deal with those who have never heard it." David L. Edwards and John Stott, *Evangelical Essentials* (Downers Grove: IVP, 1988), pp. 327. In the collection of essays edited by William V. Crockett and James G. Sigountos, *Through No Fault of Their Own* (Grand Rapids: Baker Book House, 1991), Timothy Phillips, Aida Besancon Spencer, and Tite Tienou "prefer to leave the matter in the hands of God" (p. 259, note 3).

5. William V. Crockett and James G. Sigountos, eds., *Through No Fault of Their Own* (Grand Rapids: Baker Book House, 1991), include some essays by evangelicals who take the view that those who have never heard are in fact led to salvation through general revelation. Their conclusion is "Those who hear and reject the gospel are lost. And those who do embrace the light of general revelation must be willing to

turn from their dead idols to serve the living God (1 Thessalonians 1:9). General revelation, then, creates in them a desire to reject their pagan religion; it does not help them see the saving significance of their own" (p. 260).

6. Erickson argues from the revelation available in nature according to Romans 1–2 and 10:18. The essential elements in the "gospel message" in nature are: "1) The belief in one good powerful God. 2) The belief that he (man) owes this God perfect obedience to his law. 3) The consciousness that he does not meet this standard, and therefore is guilty and condemned. 4) The realization that nothing he can offer God can compensate him (or atone) for this sin and guilt. 5) The belief that God is merciful, and will forgive and accept those who cast themselves on his mercy.

"May it not be that if a man believes and acts on this set of tenets he is redemptively related to God and receives the benefits of Christ's death, whether he consciously knows and understands the details of that provision or not? Presumably that was the case with the Old Testament believers . . .

"If this is possible, if Jews possessed salvation in the Old Testament era simply by virtue of having the form of the Christian gospel without its content, can this principle be extended? Could it be that those who ever since the time of Christ have had no opportunity to hear the gospel, as it has come through the special revelation, participate in this salvation on the same basis? On what other grounds could they fairly be held responsible for having or not having salvation (or faith)?" But here he is very tentative, for he goes on to say, "What Paul is saying in the remainder of Romans is that very few, if any, actually come to such a saving knowledge of God on the basis of natural revelation alone."

He is following here A. H. Strong, "Whoever among the heathen are saved must in like manner [i.e., like the patriarchs of the Old Testament] be saved by casting themselves as helpless sinners upon God's plan of mercy, dimly shadowed forth in nature and providence." *Systematic Theology* (Westwood, New Jersey: Fleming H. Revell, 1907), p. 842. This is a departure from the older Reformed theologian, Charles Hodge, who argued that only through the word of God heard or read does the effectual call to salvation come. *Systematic Theology*, Vol. 2 (Grand Rapids: Wm. B. Eerdmans Publishing Co., 1952), p. 646.

7. William V. Crockett and James G. Sigountos, eds., *Through No Fault of Their Own*, p. 260.

8. For a thorough assessment of the recent departures from historic belief in hell as eternal conscious torment of the ungodly I (along with J. I. Packer who wrote the Foreword for both works) recommend Ajith Fernando, *Crucial Questions*

about Hell (Eastbourne: Kingsway Publications, 1991), and Larry Dixon, *The Other Side of the Good News: Confronting the Contemporary Challenges to Jesus' Teaching on Hell* (Wheaton: Victory Books, 1992).

9. Clark Pinnock of McMaster Divinity College argues that "the 'fire' of God's judgment consumes the lost . . . God does not raise the wicked in order to torture them consciously forever, but rather to declare his judgment upon the wicked and to condemn them to extinction, which is the second death" ("Fire, Then Nothing", *Christianity Today*, March 20, 1987, p. 49).

10. David L. Edwards and John Stott, *Evangelical Essentials* (Downers Grove: IVP, 1988), p. 317.

11. Scot McKnight devotes extensive treatment to Matthew 25:46 in view of recent efforts (like John Stott's) to see the eternal consequence of unrighteousness as annihilation. His conclusion is solid: "The terms for eternal in Matthew 25:46 pertain to the final age, and a distinguishing feature of the final age, in contrast to this age, is that it is eternal, endless, and temporally unlimited. It follows then that the most probable meaning of Matthew 25:46 is that just as life with God is temporally unlimited for the righteous, so punishment for sin and rejection of Christ is also temporally unlimited . . . the final state of the wicked is conscious, eternal torment." "Eternal Consequences or Eternal Consciousness," in William V. Crockett and James G. Sigountos, eds., *Through No Fault of Their Own* (Grand Rapids: Baker Book House, 1991), p. 157.

12. Leon Morris, "The Dreadful Harvest," *Christianity Today*, Vol. 35, No. 6, May 27, 1991, p. 36.

13. In David Edwards and John Stott, *Evangelical Essentials*, p. 314, John Stott tries to honor this text by saying, "We surely have to say that this banishment from God will be real, terrible (so that 'it would have been better for him if he had not been born', Mark 14:21) and eternal." But he gives us no idea of why a man who eats, drinks and is merry for 70 years and then ceases to have any consciousness would have been better off not to have existed.

14. *Evangelical Essentials*, p. 318.

15. John Stott has been gracious enough to correspond with me personally about this issue of the eternal fate of the lost. To be fair to one I count a brother and a theological and pastoral mentor for the last 29 years of my life, I want to give his perspective on what I have written from a personal letter dated March 1, 1993. He writes:

"I cannot honestly say that I think you have done justice to what I have written in *Evangelical Essentials* . . . For example, I do strongly affirm all the 'eternal' and 'unquenchable' verses which you quote, and do believe in 'eternal punishment'. It is not the eternity, but the nature, of the punishment which is under discussion. You do not make this clear.

"I also believe in torment in the interim state (as the Dives and Lazarus story shows), and that there will be terrible 'weeping and gnashing of teeth' when the lost learn their fate. I think I believe as strongly as you do that 'it is a fearful thing to fall into the hands of the living God'.

"What troubles me is the way you tend to quote proof texts as knock-down arguments, when they are capable of alternative interpretation. I just find you over-dogmatic, as I wrote in my earlier letter, leaving no room for the humble agnosticism which allows that God has not revealed everything as plainly as you make out."

I mentioned to Dr. Stott in an earlier letter that my less than positive attitude toward "agnosticism" and "tentativity" is probably influenced by the sea of relativism that I am trying to navigate, both inside and outside the church. I do not want to communicate an unwillingness to learn or to change as new light on the Scripture emerges. But my diagnosis of the sickness of our times inclines me less toward "humble agnosticism" and more toward (I hope) humble affirmation. Whether I have moved from warranted and well-grounded firmness of conviction into unwarranted and poorly argued dogmatism, I leave for others to judge.

16. "It just does not make sense to say that a God of love will torture people forever for sins done in the context of a finite life." (Clark Pinnock and Delwin Brown, *Theological Crossfire: An Evangelical/Liberal Dialogue* [Grand Rapids: Zondervan Publishing House, 1990], p. 226.)

17. "Would there not be serious disproportion between sins consciously committed in time and torment consciously experienced throughout eternity?" *Evangelical Essentials*, p. 318.

18. "The Justice of God in the Damnation of Sinners", *The Works of Jonathan Edwards*, Vol. 1 (Edinburgh: Banner of Truth Trust, 1974), p. 669.

19. See Pinnock's quote in note 2, and Stott's quote in note 3 above. Also see my critique on the way Pinnock follows the same procedure concerning the omniscience of God in my book *The Pleasures of God*, p. 70 note 6. Another thing overlooked is that in hell the sins of the unrepentant go on for ever and ever. They do not become righteous in hell. They are given over to the corruption of their nature so that they continue rebelling and deserving eternal punishment eternally. This latter insight was suggested to me by my colleague Tom Steller.

20. Note that it would be an incorrect, superficial reading of this text, as well as of Romans 5:17–19, to assume that it is teaching universalism in the sense that all human beings will

be saved. The "all" who are acquitted in Romans 5 are defined in Romans 5:17 as "those who receive the abundance of grace". And the "all" who are made alive in 1 Corinthians 15:22 are defined as "those who belong to Christ". Moreover the other texts cited in this chapter make it highly unlikely that Paul means to teach here that all humans are saved.

21. For further study of the significance of Christ's death consider the following texts: Mark 10:45; Matthew 26:28; John 1:29; 6:51; Romans 4:25 – 5:1; 5:6, 8–10; 1 Corinthians 15:3; 2 Corinthians 5:18–21; Galatians 1:4; 4:4; Ephesians 1:7; 2:1–5, 13, 16, 18; 5:2, 25; Colossians 1:20; 1 Thessalonians 5:9; 1 Timothy 4:10; Titus 2:14; Hebrews 1:3; 9:12, 22, 26; 10:14; 12:24; 13:12; 1 Peter 1:19; 2:24; 3:18; 1 John 2:2; Revelation 1:5.

22. See notes 7 and 8 above for representatives of this view. Clark Pinnock embraces the idea that people from other religions will be saved without knowing Christ. "We do not need to think of the church as the ark of salvation, leaving everyone else in hell; we can rather think of it as the chosen witness to the *fullness* of salvation that has come into the world through Jesus" (italics added). (Clark Pinnock, "Acts 4:12 – No Other Name Under Heaven", in William V. Crockett and James G. Sigountos, eds., *Through No Fault of Their Own*, p. 113.) He is following others with similar views: Charles Kraft, *Christianity in Culture* (Maryknoll, N.Y.: Orbis, 1979), pp. 253–257; J. N. D. Anderson, *Christianity and World Religions* (Downers Grove: IVP, 1984), chapter 5; and John E. Sanders, "Is Belief in Christ Necessary for Salvation?", *Evangelical Quarterly*, 60 (1988), pp. 241–259. For a short survey of representatives on both sides of the question see Malcolm J. McVeigh, "The Fate of Those Who've Never Heard? It Depends," *Evangelical Missions Quarterly*, Vol. 21, No. 4 (Oct., 1985), pp. 370–379.

23. There is a continuity between God's path to salvation in the Old Testament times and the path through faith in Jesus during the New Testament times. Even before Christ, people were not saved apart from special revelation given by God. (See Ajith Fernando, *The Christian's Attitude Toward World Religions* [Wheaton: Tyndale House Publishers, 1987], pp. 136–139.)

It is not as though general revelation through nature was effective in producing faith before Christ but ceased to be effective after Christ. According to Romans 1:18–23 general revelation through nature has always been *sufficient* to make people accountable to glorify and thank God, but not *efficient* to do so. The reason given is that people in their natural condition suppress the truth. See note 39. Thus special revelation has always been the path to salvation and this special revelation was centered in Israel, the promise of a

Redeemer, and the foreshadowings of this salvation in the sacrificial system of the Old Testament. Jesus is now the climax and fulfillment of that special revelation so that saving faith, which was always focused on special revelation, is now focused on him.

24. John Calvin, *The Acts of the Apostles, 14–28*, trans. John W. Fraser (Grand Rapids: Wm. B. Eerdmans Publishing Company, 1973), p. 123.

25. Tom Wells, *A Vision for Missions* (Edinburgh: Banner of Truth Trust, 1985), pp. 12–13.

26. I state it like this so as to leave open salvation for infants and imbeciles who do not have the physical ability to even apprehend that there is any revelation available at all. The principle of accountability in Romans 1:20 (God makes knowledge available *"in order that* they might be without excuse"*) is the basis for this conviction. The Bible does not deal with this special case in any detail and we are left to speculate that the fitness of the connection between faith in Christ and salvation will be preserved through the coming to faith of children whenever God brings them to maturity in heaven or in the age to come.

27. Millard Erickson, "Hope for Those Who Haven't Heard? Yes, But ...", *Evangelical Missions Quarterly*, Vol. 11, No. 2 (April, 1975), pp. 124–125.

28. Don Richardson, *Eternity in Their Hearts* (Ventura, California: Regal Books, 1981), pp. 56–58.

29. Harold W. Fuller, *Run While the Sun is Hot* (Cedar Grove: Sudan Interior Mission, 1967), pp. 183–184.

30. Clark Pinnock, "Acts 4:12 – No Other Name under Heaven", in William V. Crockett and James G. Sigountos, eds., *Through No Fault of Their Own*, p. 110. Pinnock acknowledges that the commentators (e.g., Bruce, Haenchen, Longenecker, Conzelmann) take Acts 4:12 to support the "exclusivist paradigm".

31. Clark Pinnock, "Acts 4:12 – No Other Name under Heaven," p. 109.

32. See Daniel Fuller, *Unity of the Bible: Unfolding God's Plan for Humanity* (Grand Rapids: Zondervan Publishing House, 1992), pp. 353–357, 465–467, for a more extensive treatment of Paul's argument in Romans 9:30–33.

33. See Daniel Fuller, *Gospel and Law: Contrast or Continuum?* (Grand Rapids: Wm. B. Eerdmans Publishing Company, 1980), pp. 65–120, for a detailed exegetical defense of this understanding of the law in the thinking of Paul.

34. The Greek verb for "hear" (*akouō*) followed by a person in the genitive case means *hear the person*, not merely hear about him. Most commentators are agreed on this (e.g. Meyer, Murray, Cranfield).

35. John Murray, *The Epistle to the Romans*, Vol. 2 (Grand Rapids:

Wm. B. Eerdmans Publishing Company, 1965), p. 60.

36. John Murray, *The Epistle to the Romans*, Vol. 2, p. 62.

37. Charles Hodge, *Commentary on the Epistle to the Romans* (New York: A. C. Armstrong and Son: 1893), p. 548.

38. See note 8 above.

39. He finds support for this conclusion also in Romans 1:18–21. But the problem with this is that though these verses teach the reality of general revelation that is sufficient to hold humanity accountable to glorify God (v. 21), nevertheless they also teach that men suppress this truth in unrighteousness (v. 18) and do *not* thank God or honor him the way they should (v. 21) and are therefore without excuse (v. 20). General revelation is sufficient to hold all men accountable to worship God but not efficient to bring about the faith that saves. That is why the gospel must be preached to all peoples. God wills to honor his Son by accompanying the preaching of his name with heart-awakening power.

40. John Murray, *The Epistle to the Romans*, Vol. 2, p. 61. "Since the gospel proclamation is not to all without distinction, it is proper to see the parallel between the universality of general revelation and the universalism of the gospel. The former is the pattern now followed in the sounding forth of the gospel to the uttermost parts of the earth. The application which Paul makes of Psalm 19:4 can thus be seen to be eloquent not only of this parallel but also of that which is implicit in the parallel, namely, the widespread diffusion of the gospel of grace."

Charles Hodge, *Commentary on the Epistle to the Romans*, p. 549. "This verse, therefore, is to be considered as a strong declaration that what Paul had proved ought to be done, had in fact been accomplished. The middle wall of partition had been broken down, the gospel of salvation, the religion of God, was free from its trammels, the offers of mercy were as wide and general as the proclamation of the heavens ... His object in using the words of the Psalmist was, no doubt, to convey more clearly and affectingly to the minds of his hearers the idea that the proclamation of the gospel was now as free from all nations or ecclesiastical restrictions, as the instructions shed down upon all people by the heavens under which they dwell. Paul, of course, is not to be understood as quoting the Psalmist as though the ancient prophet was speaking of the preaching of the gospel. He simply uses scriptural language to express his own ideas, as is done involuntarily almost by every preacher in every sermon."

41. The words, "Their voice has gone out", do not have to mean that the spread of the message is finished. In Paul's context the natural meaning is that the gospel has been propelled into the world to reach all peoples. Olshausen

suggests that "their voice has gone out" is to be understood as prophetically spoken; "that which is begun is viewed as if already completed, and therefore we need not seek for any further explanation how it is that St. Paul can represent Christ's messengers as spread all over the earth, whereas, when he wrote these words, they had not so much as carried the preaching of Christ through the whole of the Roman empire". Hermann Olshausen, *Studies in the Epistle to the Romans* (Minneapolis: Klock and Klock Christian Publishers, Inc., 1983, originally 1849), p. 354.

42. John Ellenberger, "Is Hell a Proper Motivation for Missions?" in: William V. Crockett and James G. Sigountos, eds., *Through No Fault of Their Own*, p. 225.
43. John Ellenberger, "Is Hell a Proper Motivation for Missions?" p. 226.
44. Ibid.
45. Charles Hodge, *Commentary on the Epistle to the Romans*, p. 553.

5

The supremacy of God among "all the nations"

Can love decide?

How do we decide what the task of missions is, or even if there should be such a thing as missions? One answer would be that love demands it and love defines it. If people all over the world are under condemnation for sin and cut off from eternal life (Ephesians 2:2–3, 12; 4:17; 5:6), and if calling on Jesus is their only hope for eternal, joyful fellowship with God (as chapter four shows), then love demands missions.

But can love define missions? Not without consulting the strange ways of God. Sometimes the ways of God are not the way we would have done things with our limited views. But God is love, even when his ways are puzzling. It may not look like love for your life if you sold all that you had and bought a barren field. But it might, in fact, be love from another perspective, namely, that there is a treasure buried in the field. So, of course, love will consult God's perspective on missions. Love will refuse to define missions with a limited human perspective. Love will test its logic by the larger picture of God's ways.

Two sinking ocean liners

The limits of love's wisdom become plain when we imagine missions as a rescue operation during a tragedy at sea.

Suppose there were two ocean liners on the sea, and both began to sink at the same time with large numbers of people on board who did not know how to swim. There are some lifeboats but not enough. And suppose you were in charge of a team of ten rescuers in two large boats.

You arrive on the scene of the first sinking ship and find yourself surrounded by hundreds of screaming people, some going down before your eyes, some fighting over scraps of debris, others ready to jump into the water from the sinking ship. Several hundred yards farther away the very same thing is happening to the people on the other ship.

Your heart breaks for the dying people. You long to save as many as you can. So you cry out to your two crews to give every ounce of energy they have. There are five rescuers in each boat and they are working with all their might. They are saving many. There is lots of room in the rescue boats.

Then someone cries out from the other ship, "Come over and help *us*!" What would love do? Would love go or stay?

I cannot think of any reason that love would leave its life-saving labor and go to the other ship. Love puts no higher value on distant souls than on nearer souls. In fact, love might well reason that in the time it would take to row across the several hundred yards to the other ship, an overall loss of total lives would result.

Love might also reason that the energy of the rescuers would be depleted by rowing between ships, which would possibly result in a smaller number of individuals being saved. Not only that, from past experience you may know that the people on that other boat were usually all drunk by this time in the evening and would be less cooperative with your saving efforts. This too might mean fewer lives saved.

So love, by itself, may very well refuse to leave its present rescue operation. It may stay at its present work in order to save as many individuals as possible.

This imaginary scene on the sea is not, of course, a perfect picture of the church in the world, if for no other reason than that the rescue potential of the church is *not* fully engaged even where it is. But the point of the illustration still stands: that love alone (from our limited human perspective) may not see the missionary task the way God does.

God may have another view

God may have in mind that the aim of the rescue operation should be to gather saved sinners from every people in the world (from *both* ocean liners), even if some of the successful rescuers must leave a fruitful *reached* people (the first ocean liner), in order to labor in a (possibly less fruitful) *unreached* people (the second ocean liner).

In other words, the task of missions may not be merely to win[1] as many individuals as possible from the most responsive people groups of the world, but rather to win individuals from *all* the people groups of the world. It may not be enough to define missions as leaving the safe shore of our own culture to do rescue operations on the strange seas of other languages and cultures. Something may need to be added to that definition which impels us to leave one rescue operation to take up another.

What we are going to see in this chapter is that God's call for missions in Scripture *cannot* be defined in terms of crossing cultures to maximize the total number of individuals saved. Rather God's will for missions is that every people group be reached with the testimony of Christ and that a people be called out for his name from all the nations.[2]

It may be that this definition of missions will in fact result in the greatest possible number of white-hot worshipers for God's Son. But that remains for God to decide. Our responsibility is to define missions his way and then obey.

That means a careful investigation of how the New Testament portrays the special missionary task of the church. More specifically it means that we must assess Biblically the widespread concept of "unreached peoples" as the focus of missionary activity.

The indictment of 1974: people blindness

Since 1974 the task of missions has increasingly focused on evangelizing[3] unreached *peoples* as opposed to evangelizing unreached *territories*. One reason for this is that at the Lausanne Congress on World Evangelization that year Ralph Winter indicted the Western missionary enterprise with what he called "people blindness". Since that time he and others have relentlessly pressed the "people group" focus onto the agenda of most mission-minded churches and agencies. The "shattering truth" that he revealed at Lausanne was this: in spite of the fact that every *country* of the world has been penetrated with the gospel, four out of

170

five non-Christians are still cut off from the gospel because the barriers are cultural and linguistic, not geographic.

> Why is this fact not more widely known? I'm afraid that all our exultation about the fact that every *country* of the world has been penetrated has allowed many to suppose that every *culture* has by now been penetrated. This misunderstanding is a malady so widespread that it deserves a special name. Let us call it "people blindness", that is, blindness to the existence of separate *peoples* within *countries* – a blindness, I might add, which seems more prevalent in the U.S. and among U.S. missionaries than anywhere else.[4]

Winter's message was a powerful call for the church of Christ to reorient its thinking so that missions would be seen as the task of evangelizing unreached *peoples*, not the task of merely evangelizing more territories. In a most remarkable way in the next fifteen years the missionary enterprise responded to this call. In 1989 Winter was able to write, "now that the concept of Unreached Peoples has taken hold very widely, it is immediately possible to make plans . . . with far greater confidence and precision".[5]

A milestone definition, 1982

Probably the most significant united effort to define what a "people group" is came in March, 1982, as a result of the work of the Lausanne Strategy Working Group. This meeting defined a "people group" as

> a significantly large grouping of individuals who perceive themselves to have a common affinity for one another because of their shared language, religion, ethnicity, residence, occupation, class or caste, situation, etc. or combinations of these . . . [It is] the largest group within which the Gospel can spread as a church planting movement without encountering barriers of understanding or acceptance.[6]

We should be aware that this definition was developed not merely on the basis of Biblical teaching about the specific nature of people groups, but also on the basis of what would help missionaries identify and reach various groups. This is a legitimate method for advancing evangelistic strategy. But we need to distinguish it from the method I will use in this chapter.[7]

We also need to make clear at the outset that I am not going to use the term "people group" in a precise sociological way as distinct from "people". I agree with those who say that the Biblical concept of "peoples" or "nations" cannot be stretched to include individuals grouped on the basis of things like occupation or residence or handicaps. These are sociological groupings that are very relevant for evangelistic strategy but do not figure into defining the *Biblical* meaning of "peoples" or "nations". Harley Schreck and David Barrett have proposed distinguishing the sociological category "people group" from the ethnological category "peoples".[8] I agree with the category distinction but have found the terminology to be a linguistic strait-jacket that I can't wear. The singular "people" in the English language does not clearly signify a distinctive grouping. Therefore when I use "people group" I am only calling attention to the group concept over against individuals. The context will make clear the nature of the grouping.

"Test all things" – including people group thinking

My aim is to test the people group focus by the Scriptures. Is the specifically missionary mandate of the Bible (1) a command to reach as many individuals as possible, or is it (2) a command to reach all the "fields", or is it (3) a command to reach all the "people groups" of the world, as the Bible defines people groups? Is the emphasis that has dominated discussion since 1974 a Biblical teaching, or is it simply a strategic development that gives mission effort a sharper focus?

So we turn now to the basic question of this chapter: Is it Biblical to define the missionary task of the church as reaching all the unreached[9] *peoples* of the world? Or is it sufficient to say that missions is simply the effort to reach as many individuals as possible in places different from our own?

The most famous commission, Matthew 28:18–20

> (18) And Jesus came and said to them, "All authority in heaven and on earth has been given to me. (19) Go therefore and make disciples of all nations, baptizing them in the name of the Father and of the Son and of the Holy Spirit, (20) teaching them to observe all that I have commanded you; and lo, I am with you always, to the close of the age."

This passage is often called the Great Commission. The first thing to make clear about it is that it is still binding on the modern church. It was not merely given to the apostles for their ministry, but was given to the church for its ministry as long as this age lasts.

The basis for saying this comes from the text itself. The undergirding promise of verse 20 says, "And behold, I am with *you* always, to the close of the age." The people referred to in the word "you" cannot be limited to the apostles, since they died within one generation. The promise extends to "the close of the age", that is, to the day of judgment at Christ's second coming (cf. Matthew 13:39–40, 49). So Jesus is speaking to the apostles as representatives of the church that would endure to the end of the age. He is assuring the church of his abiding presence and help as long as this age lasts.

This is significant because the promise of verse 20 is given to sustain and encourage the command to make disciples of all nations. Therefore if the sustaining promise is expressed in terms that endure to the end of the age, we may rightly assume that the command to make disciples also endures to the end of the age. It was not given merely to the apostles. They received the commission as representatives of the church that endures to the end of the age.

I conclude then that the Great Commission was given not just to the apostles but to the church that would endure to the end of the age. This is further buttressed by the authority he claims in verse 18. He lays claim to "all authority in heaven and on earth". This enables him to do what he had earlier promised in Matthew 16:18 when he said, "I will build my church." So the abiding validity of the Great Commission rests on the ongoing authority of Christ

173

over all things (Matthew 28:18), and on the purpose of Chirst to build his church (Matthew 16:18), and on the promise to be present and help in the mission of the church to the end of the age (Matthew 28:20).

Therefore, these words of the Lord are crucial for deciding what the missionary task of the church should be today. Specifically the words "make disciples of all nations" must be closely examined. They contain the very important phrase "all nations" which is often referred to in the Greek form *panta ta ethnē* (*panta* = all, *ta* = the, *ethnē* = nations). The reason this is such an important phrase is that *ethnē*, when translated as "nations", sounds like a political or geographic grouping. That is its most common English usage. But we will see that this is not what the Greek means. Nor does the English always mean this. For example, we say the Cherokee nation or the Sioux nation. This means something like: people with a unifying ethnic identity. In fact the word "ethnic" comes from the Greek word *ethnos* (singular of *ethnē*). Our inclination then might be to take *panta ta ethnē* as a reference to "all the ethnic groups". "Go and disciple all the ethnic groups."

But this is precisely what needs to be tested by a careful investigation of the wider Biblical context and especially the use of *ethnos* in the New Testament and its Old Testament background.

The singular use of *ethnos* in the New Testament

In the New Testament the singular *ethnos* never refers to an individual.[10] This is a striking fact. Every time the singular *ethnos* does occur it refers to a people group or "nation" – often the *Jewish* nation, even though in the plural it is usually translated "Gentiles" in distinction from the Jewish people.[11]

Here are some examples to illustrate the corporate meaning of the singular use of *ethnos*.

Nation (*ethnos*) will rise against nation (*ethnos*) and kingdom against kingdom, and there will be famines and earthquakes in various places. (Matthew 24:7)

Now there were dwelling in Jerusalem devout men from

every nation (*ethnous*) under heaven. (Acts 2:5)

There was a man named Simon who . . . amazed the nation (*ethnos*) of Samaria. (Acts 8:9)

You are a chosen race, a royal priesthood, a holy nation (*ethnos*), God's own people. (1 Peter 2:9)

By your blood you ransomed men for God from every tribe and tongue and people and nation (*ethnous*). (Revelation 5:9)

What this survey of the singular establishes is that the word *ethnos* very naturally and normally carried a corporate meaning in reference to people groups with a certain ethnic identity. In fact the reference in Acts 2:5 to "every nation" is very close in form to "all the nations" in Matthew 28:19. And in Acts 2:5 it must refer to people groups of some kind. So at this stage we find ourselves leaning toward a corporate "people group" understanding of "all the nations" in the Great Commission of Matthew 28:19.

The plural use of *ethnos* in the New Testament

Here we meet a change. Unlike the singular, the plural of *ethnos* does not always refer to "people groups". It sometimes simply refers to Gentile individuals.[12] Many instances are ambiguous. What is important to see is that in the plural the word can refer either to an ethnic group or simply to Gentile individuals who may not make up an ethnic group. For example, to illustrate the meaning of Gentile individuals consider the following texts.

Acts 13:48 – When Paul turns to the Gentiles in Antioch after being rejected by the Jews, Luke says, "And when *the Gentiles* heard this, they were glad and glorified the word of God." This is a reference not to nations but to the group of Gentile individuals at the synagogue who heard Paul.

1 Corinthians 12:2 – "You know that when you were *Gentiles*, you were led astray to dumb idols." In this verse "you" refers to the individual Gentile converts at Corinth. It

would not make sense to say, "When you were nations . . ."

Ephesians 3:6 – Paul says that the mystery of Christ is "how *the Gentiles* are fellow heirs, members of the same body . . ." It would not make sense to say that "nations" are fellow heirs and *members* (a definite reference to individuals) of the same body. Paul's conception is that the local body of Christ has many *individual* members who are *Gentiles*.

These are perhaps sufficient to show that the plural of *ethnos* does not *have to* mean nation or "people group". On the other hand the plural, like the singular, certainly can, and often does, refer to "people groups". For example:

Acts 13:19 – Referring to the taking of the promised land by Israel, Paul says, "And when he had destroyed seven nations (*ethnē*) in the land of Canaan, he gave them their land as an inheritance."

Romans 4:17–18 – "As it is written, I have made you the father of many nations." Here Paul is quoting Genesis 17:4–5 where "father of many nations" does not refer to individuals but to people groups. *Ethnōn* is a Greek translation of the Hebrew *gôyîm* which virtually always means nations or people groups. For example, in Deuteronomy 7:1 Moses says that God will "clear away many *nations* before you, Hittites, Girgashites, Amorites, Canaanites, Perizzites, Hivites and Jebusites". The word "nations" here is *gôyîm* in Hebrew and *ethnē* in Greek.

Revelation 11:9 – "For three and a half days men from the peoples, tribes, tongues and nations (*ethnōn*) gaze at their dead bodies." In this sequence it is clear that "nations" refers to some kind of ethnic grouping, not just to Gentile individuals.

What we have seen then is that in the plural *ethnē* can mean Gentile individuals who may not be part of a single people group, or it can mean (as it always does in the singular) a people group with ethnic identity. This means that we cannot yet be certain which meaning is intended in Matthew 28:19. We cannot yet answer the question whether the task of missions is merely reaching as many individuals as possible or reaching all the people groups of the world.

Nevertheless, the fact that in the New Testament the singular *ethnos* never refers to an individual but always refers to a people group should perhaps incline us toward the people group meaning unless the context leads us to think otherwise. This will be all the more true when we put before us the Old Testament context and the impact it had on the writings of John and Paul. But first we should examine the New Testament use of the crucial phrase *panta ta ethnē* ("all the nations").

The use of *panta ta ethnē* in the New Testament

Our immediate concern is with the meaning of *panta ta ethnē* in Matthew 28:19, "Go and make disciples of *all nations*." Since this is such a crucial phrase in the understanding of missions, and since it is tossed about as a Greek phrase today even in non-technical writings, I think it's important to make all the uses of it readily accessible for the reader without a knowledge of Greek to consider. Therefore in what follows I will provide all the texts where the combination of *pas* (all) and *ethnos* (nation/ Gentile) occurs in the New Testament, either in the singular ("every nation") or plural ("all nations/Gentiles"). The different forms of *pan, panta, pasin* and *pantōn* are simply changes in the grammatical case of the same word to agree with the various forms of the noun *ethnos* (*ethnē, ethnesin*).

Matthew 24:9 – "You will be hated by *pantōn tōn ethnōn* for my sake."

Matthew 24:14 (= Mark 13:10) – "This gospel of the kingdom will be preached throughout the whole world, as a testimony to *pasin tois ethnesin*; and then the end will come."

Matthew 25:32 – "Before him will be gathered *panta ta ethnē*, and he will separate them one from another as a shepherd separates the sheep from the goats." (This context seems to demand the meaning "Gentile individuals", not people groups, because it says that Jesus will "separate them from one another as a shepherd separates the sheep

177

from the goats". This is a reference to individuals who are being judged as the "cursed" and the "righteous" who enter hell or eternal life. Cf. verses 41, 46.)

Matthew 28:19 – "Make disciples of *panta ta ethnē*."

Mark 11:17 – "My house shall be called a house of prayer for *pasin tois ethnesin*." (This is a quote from Isaiah 56:7. The Hebrew phrase behind *pasin tois ethnesin* is *lᵉkol hā'ammîm*, which has to mean "all peoples" rather than "all people".)

Luke 12:29–30 – "Do not seek what you are to eat and what you are to drink, nor be of anxious mind. For *panta ta ethnē* of the world seek these things."

Luke 21:24 – "They will fall by the edge of the sword, and be led captive among *ta ethnē panta*." (This warning echoes the words of Ezekiel 32:9 where the corresponding Hebrew word is *gôyîm* which means nations or people groups. See also Deuteronomy 28:64.)

Luke 24:47 – "Repentance and forgiveness of sins should be preached in his name to *panta ta ethnē*, beginning from Jerusalem."

Acts 2:5 – "Now there were dwelling in Jerusalem Jews, devout men from *pantos ethnous* under heaven." (This must clearly refer to people groups rather than individuals. The reference is to various ethnic or national groups from which the diaspora Jews had come to Jerusalem.)

Acts 10:35 – "In *panti ethnei* any one who fears him and does what is right is acceptable to him." (Again this must be a reference to people groups or nations, not to individual Gentiles, because the individuals who fear God are "*in* every nation".)

Acts 14:16 – "In past generations he allowed *panta ta ethnē* to walk in their own ways."

Acts 15:16–17 – "I will rebuild the dwelling of David which has fallen ... that the rest of men may seek the Lord, and *panta ta ethnē* upon whom is called my name upon them." (I render the verse at the end with this awkwardly literal translation simply to highlight the fact that this is a quotation from Amos 9:12, which in Greek follows the Hebrew with similar literalness. Again the Hebrew word behind *ethnē* is *gôyîm* which means nations or people groups.)

Acts 17:26 – "And he made, from one, *pan ethnos* of men to live on all the face of the earth." (As with Acts 2:5 and 10:35 this is a reference to "every people group" rather than individuals because it says that every nation is made up "of men". It would not make sense to say that every individual Gentile was made up "of men". Nor does the suggestion of some that it means "the whole human race" fit the meaning of *ethnos* or the context.)[13]

Romans 1:5 – "We have received grace and apostleship to bring about the obedience of faith for the sake of his name among *pasin tois ethnesin*."

Galatians 3:8 – "And the Scripture, foreseeing that God would justify the Gentiles by faith, preached the gospel beforehand to Abraham, saying, 'In you shall *panta ta ethnē* be blessed.'" (This is a quote from Genesis 12:3 which clearly refers to people groups. The corresponding Hebrew phrase, *kōl mišpᵉḥōt*, means "all families". See below on Genesis 12:3 for more discussion of Paul's translation.)

2 Timothy 4:17 – "But the Lord stood by me and gave me strength to proclaim the word fully, that *panta ta ethnē* might hear it."

Revelation 12:5 – "She brought forth a male child, one who is to rule *panta ta ethnē* with a rod of iron." (Cf. Psalm 2:9. The Old Testament allusion makes it likely that the Old Testament reference to nations in Psalm 2:8 is intended here as well.)

Revelation 15:4 – "Who shall not fear and glorify thy name, O Lord. For thou alone art holy. *Panta ta ethnē* shall come and worship thee, for thy judgments have been revealed." (Cf. Psalm 86:9; LXX[14] 85:9. Again the Old Testament allusion suggests a corporate understanding of nations coming to worship the Lord.)

179

Out of these eighteen uses of *panta ta ethnē* (or its variant) only the one in Matthew 25:32 would seem to demand the meaning "Gentile individuals". (See the comments above on that verse.) Three others demand the people group meaning on the basis of the context (Acts 2:5; 10:35; 17:26). Six others require the people group meaning on the basis of the Old Testament connection (Mark 11:17; Luke 21:24; Acts 15:17; Galatians 3:8; Revelation 12:5; 15:4). The remaining eight uses (Matthew 24:9, 14; 28:19; Luke 12:30; 24:47; Acts 14:16; 2 Timothy 4:17; Romans 1:5) could go either way.

What can we conclude so far concerning the meaning of *panta ta ethnē* in Matthew 28:19 and its wider missionary significance?

The singular use of *ethnos* in the New Testament always refers to a people group. The plural use of *ethnos* sometimes must be a people group and sometimes must refer to Gentile individuals, but usually can go either way. The phrase *panta ta ethnē* must refer to Gentile individuals only once, but must refer to people groups nine times. The remaining eight uses may refer to people groups. The combination of these results suggests that the meaning of *panta ta ethnē* leans heavily in the direction of "all the nations (people groups)". It cannot be said with certainty that it always carries this meaning wherever it is used, but it is far more likely to than not in view of what we have seen so far.

This likelihood increases even more when we realize that the phrase *panta ta ethnē* occurs in the Greek Old Testament some 100 times and virtually never carries the meaning of Gentile individuals but always carries the meaning "all the nations" in the sense of people groups outside Israel.[15] That the New Testament vision for missions has this focus will appear even more probable when we turn now to the Old Testament background.

The Old Testament hope

The Old Testament is replete with promises and expectations that God would one day be worshipped by people from all the nations of the world. We will see that these promises form the explicit foundation of New Testament missionary vision.

All the families of the earth will be blessed

Foundational for the missionary vision of the New Testament was the promise which God made to Abram in Genesis 12:1–3.

> (1) Now the LORD said to Abram, "Go from your country and your kindred and your father's house to the land that I will show you. (2) And I will make of you a great nation and I will bless you and make your name great, so that you will be a blessing. (3) I will bless those who bless you, and him who curses you I will curse; and by you *all the families* of the earth shall be blessed."

This promise for universal blessing to the "families" of the earth is essentially repeated in Genesis 18:18; 22:18; 26:4; 28:14.

In 12:3 and 28:14 the Hebrew phrase for "all the families" (*kōl mišpᵉḥōt*) is rendered in the Greek Old Testament by *pasai hai phulai*. The word *phulai* means "tribes" in most contexts. But *mišpāḥâ* can be, and usually is, smaller than a tribe.[16] For example when Achan sinned, Israel is examined in decreasing order of size: first by tribe, then by *mišpāḥâ* (family) then by household (Joshua 7:14).

So the blessing of Abraham is intended by God to reach to fairly small groupings of people. We need not define these groups with precision in order to feel the impact of this promise. The three other repetitions of this Abrahamic promise in Genesis use the phrase "all the nations" (Hebrew: *kōl gôyê*) which the Septuagint translates with the familiar *panta ta ethnē* in each case (18:18; 22:18; 26:4). This again suggests strongly that the term *panta ta ethnē* in missionary contexts has the ring of people groups rather than Gentile individuals.

The New Testament explicitly cites this particular Abrahamic promise twice. In Acts 3:25 Peter says to the Jewish crowd: "You are the sons of the prophets and of the covenant which God gave to your fathers, saying to

Abraham, 'And in your posterity shall *all the families* of the earth be blessed.'"

The Greek phrase in Acts 3:25 for "all the families" is *pasai hai patrai*. This is an independent translation of Genesis 12:3, differing from both the Greek Old Testament (*pasai hai phulai*) and the way Paul translates it in Galatians 3:8 (*panta ta ethnē*).[17] But by choosing another word that refers to people groups (*patriai*) the writer confirms that the promise was understood in the early church in terms of people groups not in terms of Gentile individuals. *Patria* can be a subgroup of a tribe, or more generally a clan or tribe.

The other New Testament quotation of the Abrahamic promise is in Galatians 3:6–8.

> (6) Thus Abraham "believed God, and it was reckoned to him as righteousness". (7) So you see that it is men of faith who are the sons of Abraham. (8) And scripture, foreseeing that God would justify the Gentiles (*ta ethnē*) by faith, preached the gospel beforehand to Abraham, saying, "In you shall all the nations (*panta ta ethnē*) be blessed."

Interestingly all the English versions translate the word *ethnē* differently in its two uses in verse 8; in the first case, "Gentiles" and the next, "nations".

One could try to argue that Paul's use of the promise to support the justification of individual "Gentiles" means he did not see people groups in the Abrahamic promise, since it is individuals who are justified.

But that is not a necessary conclusion. More likely is the possibility that Paul recognized the Old Testament meaning of *panta to ethnē* in Genesis 18:18 (the closest Old Testament parallel) and drew out the inference that individual Gentiles are necessarily implied. So the English versions are right to preserve the different meaning in the two uses of *ethnē* in Galatians 3:8.

Paul's use of the promise alerts us not to get so swept up into people group thinking that we forget the truth that the "blessing of Abraham" is indeed experienced by *individuals*, or not at all.

What we may conclude from the wording of Genesis

12:3 and its use in the New Testament is that God's purpose for the world is that the blessing of Abraham, namely, the salvation achieved through Jesus Christ, the seed of Abraham, would reach to all the ethnic people groups of the world. This would happen as people in each group put their faith in Christ and thus become "sons of Abraham" (Galatians 3:7) and heirs of the promise (Galatians 3:29). This event of individual salvation as persons trust Christ will happen among "all the nations". The size and make-up of the "nations" or people groups referred to in this promise and its New Testament usage are not precise. But the words point to fairly small groupings, since the reference to "all the nations" in Genesis 18:18 (= Galatians 3:8) is an echo of "all the families" in Genesis 12:3.

The smallness of the people groups envisioned in the Old Testament hope is brought out again by the phrase "families of the nations" in Psalm 22:27 (LXX 21:28) and 96:7 (LXX 95:7).

> All the ends of the earth shall remember and turn to the Lord; and *all the families of the nations* shall worship before him. For dominion belongs to the LORD, and he rules over the nations. (Psalm 22:27–28)

The phrase "all the families of the nations" is *pasai hai patriai tōn ethnōn*. So the hope in view is not just that "all the nations" (*panta ta ethnē*) would respond to the truth and worship God, but that even smaller groupings, "all the families of the nations". "Family" does not carry our modern meaning of nuclear family but something more like clan.[18] This will be confirmed when we look at the hope expressed in Revelation 5:9 where worshipers have been redeemed not only from every "nation" (*ethnous*) but also from every "tribe" (*phulēs*).

The hope of the nations

One of the best ways to discern the scope of the Great Commission as Jesus gave it and the apostles pursued it is to immerse ourselves in the atmosphere of hope which they felt in reading their Bible, the Old Testament. One overwhelming aspect of this hope is its expectation that the truth of God would reach to all the people groups of the world and that these groups would come and worship the true God. This hope was expressed in people group terminology again and again (peoples, nations, tribes, families, etc.). Here is a sampling from the Psalms and Isaiah of the kind of hope that set the stage for Jesus' Great Commission. The texts fall into four categories of exhortation, promise, prayers and plans.

"Declare his glory among the nations!"

The first category of texts expressing the hope of the nations is a collection of *exhortations* that God's glory be declared and praised among the nations and by the nations.

Sing praises to the LORD, who dwells in Zion! Tell among the *peoples* his deeds! (Psalm 9:11)

Clap your hands, *all peoples*! Shout to God with loud songs of joy! (Psalm 47:1)

Bless our God, O *peoples*, let the sound of his praise be heard. (Psalm 66:8)

Declare his glory among the *nations*, his marvelous works among *all the peoples*! (Psalm 96:3)

Ascribe to the LORD, *O families of the peoples*, ascribe to the Lord glory and strength! Say among the *nations*, "the LORD reigns! Yea, the world is established, it shall never be moved; he will judge the *peoples* with equity." (Psalm 96:7, 10)

O give thanks to the LORD, call on his name, make known his deeds among the *peoples*! (Psalm 105:1)

Praise the LORD, *all nations*! Extol him, *all peoples*! (Psalm 117:1)

And you will say in that day: "Give thanks to the LORD, call upon his name; make known his deeds among the *nations*, proclaim that his name is exalted." (Isaiah 12:4)

Draw near, *O nations*, to hear, and hearken, *O peoples*! Let the earth listen, and all that fills it; the world, and all that comes from it. (Isaiah 34:1)

"Nations shall come to your light!"

The second category of texts expressing the hope of the nations is a collection of *promises* that the nations will one day worship the true God.

I shall give thee the *nations* for thine inheritance. (Psalm 2:8; cf. 111:6)

I will cause your name to be celebrated in all generations; therefore the *peoples* will praise you[19] for ever and ever. (Psalm 45:17)

The *princes of the peoples* gather as the people of the God of Abraham. For the shields of the earth belong to God; he is highly exalted! (Psalm 47:9)

All nations whom thou hast made shall come and worship before thee, O LORD; and shall glorify thy name. (Psalm 86:9)

The LORD records as the registers the *peoples*, "This one was born there." (Psalm 87:6)

The *nations* will fear the name of the LORD, and all the kings of the earth thy glory. (Psalm 102:15)

Peoples gather together, and kingdoms, to worship the LORD. (Psalm 102:22)

He has shown his people the power of his works, in giving them the heritage of the *nations*. (Psalm 111:6)

In that day the root of Jesse shall stand as an ensign to the *peoples*; him shall the *nations* seek, and his dwellings shall be glorious. (Isaiah 11:10)

On this mountain the LORD of hosts will make for *all peoples* a feast of fat things, a feast of wine on the lees, of fat things full of marrow, of wine on the lees well refined. And he will destroy on this mountain the covering that is cast over all *peoples*, the veil that is spread over all *nations*. (Isaiah 25:6–7)

[The LORD] says: "It is too light a thing that you should be my servant to raise up the tribes of Jacob and to restore the preserved of Israel; I will give you as a light to the *nations*, that my salvation may reach to the end of the earth." (Isaiah 49:6)

My deliverance draws near speedily, my salvation has gone forth, and my arms will rule the *peoples*; the coastlands wait for me, and for my arm they hope. (Isaiah 51:5)

The LORD has bared his holy arm before the eyes of all the *nations*; and all the ends of the earth shall see the salvation of our God. (Isaiah 52:10)

So shall [my Servant] startle *many nations*; kings shall shut their mouths because of him; for that which has not been told them they shall see, and that which they have not heard they shall understand. (Isaiah 52:15)

Behold, you shall call *nations* that you know not, and *nations* that knew you not shall run to you, because of the LORD your God, and of the Holy One of Israel, for he has glorified you. (Isaiah 55:5)

These I will bring to my holy mountain, and make them joyful in my house of prayer; their burnt offerings and their sacrifices will be accepted on my altar; for my house shall be called a house of prayer for *all peoples*. (Isaiah 56:7)

And *nations* shall come to your light, and kings to the brightness of your rising. (Isaiah 60:3)

For I know their works and their thoughts, and I am coming to gather *all nations and tongues*; and they shall come and shall see my glory. (Isaiah 66:18)

I am coming to gather *all nations* and tongues; and they shall come and see my glory, and I will set a sign among them. And from them I will send survivors to the *nations*, to Tarshish, Put, and Lud, who draw the bow, to Tubal and Javan, to the coastlands afar off, that have not heard my fame or seen my glory; and they shall declare my glory among the *nations*. (Isaiah 66:18–19)

"Let all the peoples praise thee, O God!"

The third category of texts that express the hope of the nations does so with confident *prayers* that God be praised among the nations.

> May God be gracious to us and bless us and make his face to shine upon us, that thy way may be known upon earth, thy saving power among all nations. Let the *peoples* praise thee, O God; let *all the peoples* praise thee! Let the *nations* be glad and sing for joy, for thou dost judge the *peoples* with equity and guide the *nations* upon earth. Let the *peoples* praise thee, O God; let *all the peoples* praise thee! (Psalm 67:1–5)

> May all the kings fall down before him, *all nations* serve him! (Psalm 72:11)

> May his name endure for ever, his fame continue as long as the sun! May men bless themselves by him, *all nations* call him blessed! (Psalm 72:17)

"I will sing praises to thee among the nations"

The fourth category of texts that express the hope of the nations announces the plans of the psalmist to do his part in making God's greatness known among the nations.

> For this I will extol thee, O LORD, among the *nations*, and sing praises to thy name. (Psalm 18:49)

> I will give thanks to thee, O LORD, among the *peoples*; I will sing praises to thee among the *nations*. (Psalm 57:9)

> I will give thanks to thee, O LORD, among the *peoples*, I will sing praises to thee among the *nations*. (Psalm 108:3)

Blessed to be a blessing

What these text demonstrate is that the blessing of forgiveness and salvation that God had granted to Israel was meant eventually to reach all the people groups of the world. Israel was blessed in order to be a blessing among the nations. This is expressed best in Psalm 67:1–2, "May God be gracious to us and bless us and make his face to shine upon us, [*Why?*] that thy way may be known upon earth, thy saving power among *all nations*." Blessing came to Israel as a means of reaching the nations. This is the hope of the Old Testament: the blessings of salvation are for the nations.

The missionary God vs. the reluctant prophet

One of the most vivid Old Testament confirmations and illustrations of God's saving purposes for the nations is found in the book of Jonah. The prophet was commissioned to preach to the pagan city of Nineveh. He tried to run away because he knew God would be gracious to the people and forgive them. The point of the book is not the fish. It's about missions and racism and ethnocentrism. The point is: be merciful like God, not miserly like Jonah. For Jonah, "be merciful" meant be a missionary.

Nineveh did in fact repent at the begrudging preaching of Jonah. When God saw the repentance of Nineveh "God repented of the evil which he had said he would do to them; and he did not do it" (Jonah 3:10). This is what Jonah was afraid of. "It displeased Jonah exceedingly, and he was angry. And he prayed to the LORD and said, 'I pray thee, LORD, is not this what I said when I was yet in my country? That is why I made haste to flee to Tarshish; for I knew that thou art a gracious God and merciful, slow to anger, and abounding in steadfast love, and repentest of evil. Therefore now, O LORD, take my life from me, I beseech thee, for it is better for me to die than to live'" (Jonah 4:1–3).

Jonah is not the model missionary. His life is an example of how not to be. As he sulks on the outskirts of town, God appoints a plant to grow up over Jonah to give him shade. When the plant withers Jonah pities the plant! So God comes to him with these words: "You pity the plant, for which you did not labor, nor did you make it grow, which came into being in a night, and perished in a night. And should not I pity Nineveh, that great city, in which there are more than a hundred and twenty thousand persons who do not know their right hand from their left, and also much cattle?" (Jonah 4:10–11).

The missionary implications of Jonah are not merely

that God is more ready to be merciful to the nations than his people are, but also that Jesus identifies himself as "one greater than Jonah" (Matthew 12:39–41). He is greater not only because his resurrection is greater than surviving a fish's belly, but also because he stands in harmony with the mercy of God and extends it now to *all the nations*. Thomas Carlisle's poem "You, Jonah" closes with these lines:

> And Jonah stalked
> to his shaded seat
> and waited for God
> to come around
> to his way of thinking.
> And God is still waiting for a host of Jonahs
> in their comfortable houses
> to come around
> to his way of loving.[20]

To see what power this Old Testament hope had on the missionary vision of the New Testament we turn now to the apostle Paul and his idea of the missionary task. The Old Testament hope is the explicit foundation of his life's work as a missionary.

Paul's idea of the missionary task

We treated Paul's use of Genesis 12:3 (Galatians 3:8) earlier in this chapter. He saw the promise that in Abraham all the nations would be blessed, and he reasoned that Christ was the true offspring of Abraham and thus the heir of the promises (Galatians 3:16). Further he reasoned that all who are united to Christ by faith also become sons of Abraham and heirs of their promise. "It is men of faith who are the sons of Abraham . . . If you are Christ's then you are Abraham's offspring, heirs according to the promise" (Galatians 3:7, 29). This is how Paul saw Abraham's blessing coming to the nations. It came through Christ who was the seed of Abraham. By faith people are united to Christ and inherit the blessing of Abraham. "Christ redeemed us from the curse of the law . . . that in Christ Jesus the blessing of Abraham might come upon the Gentiles" (Galatians 3:13–14). So the promise of Genesis 12:3

189

comes true as the missionaries of the Christian church extend the message of the gospel to all the families of the earth.

How would Abraham be the father of many nations?

But Paul saw another connection between the promise to Abraham and Paul's own calling to reach the nations. He read in Genesis 17:4–5 that God promised to make Abraham the father of a multitude of nations. "Behold, my covenant is with you and you shall be *the father of a multitude of nations*. No longer shall your name be Abram, but your name shall be Abraham, for I have made you *the father of a multitude of nations*."

We saw earlier that "nations" here refers to people groups not Gentile individuals. But how was this promise supposed to come true? How could a Jew become the father of a multitude of nations? It would not be enough to say that Abraham became the great grandfather of the twelve tribes of Israel plus the father of Ishmael and his descendants plus the grandfather of Esau and the Edomites. Fourteen does not make a multitude.

Paul's answer to this was that all who believe in Christ become the children of Abraham. In this way Abraham becomes the father of a multitude of nations, because believers will be found in every nation as missionaries reach all the unreached people groups. Paul argues like this: in Romans 4:11 he points out that Abraham received circumcision as the sign of righteousness which he had by faith before he was circumcised. "The purpose was to make him *the father of all who believe* without being circumcised and who thus have righteousness reckoned to them" (Romans 4:11). In other words, the decisive thing that happened to Abraham in his relation to God happened before he received the distinguishing mark of the Jewish people, circumcision. So true spiritual sonship to Abraham is to share his faith, not his Jewish distinctives.

So the way Abraham becomes the father of many nations is by those nations coming to share his faith and being united to the same source of blessing that flows through the covenant God made with him. So Paul says in Romans

4:16–17, "That is why it depends on faith, in order that the promise may rest on grace and be guaranteed to all his descendants – not only to the adherents of the law (that is, Jews) but also to those who share the faith of Abraham (that is, the non-Jewish nations), for he is *the father of us all*, as it is written, 'I have made you *the father of many nations*.'"

When Paul read that Abraham would be made "the father of many nations" he heard the Great Commission. These nations would only come into their sonship and enjoy the blessing of Abraham if missionaries reached them with the gospel of salvation by faith in Jesus Christ. It is not surprising then to find Paul supporting his own missionary calling with other Old Testament promises that predicted the reaching of the nations with God's light and salvation.

"I have set you to be a light to the nations"

For example, in Acts 13:47 Paul's explanation of his ministry to the Gentile nations is rooted in the promise of Isaiah 49:6 that God would make his servant a light to the nations. As Paul preached in the synagogue of Antioch of Pisidia on his first missionary journey, the Jews "were filled with jealousy and contradicted what was spoken by Paul and reviled him" (Acts 13:45). So Paul and Barnabas turn away from the synagogue and focus their ministry on the people from other people groups. To give an account of this decision Paul cites Isaiah 49:6, "Since you thrust [the word of God] from you, and judge yourselves unworthy of eternal life, behold, we turn to the Gentiles. For so the Lord has commanded us, saying, 'I have set you to be a light for the Gentiles (*ethnōn*, nations), that you may bring salvation to the uttermost parts of the earth'" (Acts 13:46–47).

It is difficult to know why the English versions don't preserve the Old Testament sense of Isaiah 49:6 and translate, "I have set you to be a light for the *nations*." The Hebrew word in Isaiah 49:6 is *gôyîm* which means people groups, not Gentile individuals. Then Paul would be doing just what he apparently did in Galatians 3:8. He would be drawing a necessary inference about individual "Gentiles" from an Old Testament reference to "nations". Thus we see that Paul's own missionary vision was guided by his mediating not only on the promises to Abraham, but also on the wider Old Testament hope that salvation would come to all the nations.

Paul's passion for unreached peoples

This is remarkably confirmed in Romans 15. Here it becomes crystal clear that Paul saw his specifically missionary calling as reaching more and more people groups not just more and more Gentile individuals.

In Romans 15:8–9 Paul states the twofold purpose for Christ's coming: "For I tell you that Christ became a servant to the circumcised [that is, became incarnate as a Jew] to show God's truthfulness, in order [1] *to confirm the promises given to the patriarchs*, in order [2] *that the Gentiles (ta ethnē) might glorify God for his mercy*." So the first purpose for Christ's coming was to prove that God is truthful and faithful in keeping, for example, the promises made to Abraham. And the second purpose for Christ's coming is that the nations might glorify God for his mercy.

These two purposes overlap since clearly one of the promises made to the patriarchs was that the blessing of Abraham would come to "all the families of the earth". This is in perfect harmony with what we saw in the Old Testament hope. *Israel* is blessed that the *nations* might be blessed (Psalm 67). In the same way Christ comes to *Israel* so that the *nations* might receive mercy and give God glory.

Saturated with the hope of the nations

Then to support this claim of God's purpose for the nations, Paul gathers four Old Testament quotations about the *ethnē*, all of which in their Old Testament context refer to *nations* not just to Gentile individuals.

As it is written, "Therefore I will praise thee among the nations (*ethnesin*) and sing to thy name." (Romans 15:9 = Psalm 18:49)

Rejoice, *nations* (*ethnē*), with his people. (Romans 15:10 = Deuteronomy 32:43)

Praise the Lord, *all the nations (panta ta ethnē)*, and let all the *peoples* praise him. (Romans 15:11 = Psalm 117:1)

The root of Jesse shall come, he who rises to rule the *nations (ethnōn)*; in him shall *nations (ethnē)* hope. (Romans 15:12 = Isaiah 11:10)

What is so remarkable about this series of texts which Paul strings together here is that Paul either had them memorized or took the trouble to find them in the Old Testament – without a concordance! Either way it shows that he was intent on seeing his missionary calling in the light of the Old Testament hope that all the nations would be reached with the gospel. The people group focus of these texts is unmistakable from the Old Testament context.

From Jerusalem to Illyricum: the work is finished!

What we see next therefore is how the people group focus governed Paul's missionary practice. Was his aim to win as many Gentile individuals as possible or to reach as many people groups or "nations" as possible? Romans 15:18–21 gives a startling answer.

For I will not venture to speak of anything except what Christ has wrought through me to win obedience from the nations (*ethnōn*), by word and deed, by the power of signs and wonders, by the power of the Holy Spirit, so that *from Jerusalem and as far round as Illyricum I have fulfilled the gospel of Christ*, thus making it my ambition to preach the gospel, *not where Christ has already been named*, lest I build on another man's foundation, but as it is written, "They shall see who have never been told of him, and they shall understand who have never heard of him."

Literally Paul says, "From Jerusalem and around to Illyricum I have *fulfilled (peplērōkenai)* the gospel." What can that possibly mean? We know that there were thousands of souls yet to be saved in that region because this is Paul's and Peter's assumption when they wrote letters to the churches in those regions. It is a huge area that stretches from southern Palestine to northern Italy. Yet

Paul says he has *fulfilled the gospel* in that whole region even though his work of evangelism is only ten or fifteen years old.

We know that Paul believed work was still needed there because he left Timothy in Ephesus (1 Timothy 1:3) and Titus in Crete (Titus 1:5) to do the work. Nevertheless, he says he has *fulfilled the gospel* in the whole region. In fact, he goes so far as to say in Romans 15:23, "But now, since *I no longer have any room for work in these regions* . . . I hope to see you as I go to Spain." This is astonishing! How can he say not only that he has fulfilled the gospel in that region, but also that he has no more room for work? He is finished and going to Spain (Romans 15:24). What does this mean?

It means that Paul's conception of the *missionary task* is not merely the winning of more and more people to Christ (which he could have done very efficiently in these familiar regions), but the reaching of more and more peoples or nations. His focus was not primarily on new geographic areas. Rather, he was gripped by the vision of unreached peoples. Romans 15:9–12 (just quoted) shows that his mind was saturated with Old Testament texts that relate to the hope of the nations.

Driven by prophetic vision of hope

What was really driving Paul when he said in Romans 15:20 that his aim is to preach not where Christ has been named "*in order that I might not build on another's foundation*"? One could uncharitably assume a kind of ego-drive that likes to be able to take all the credit for a church planting effort. But this is not the Paul we know from Scripture; nor is it what the context suggests.

The next verse (Romans 15:21) shows what drives Paul. It is the Old Testament conception of God's worldwide purpose that gives Paul his vision as a pioneer missionary. He is driven by a prophetic vision of hope. He quotes Isaiah 52:15, "They shall see who have never been told of him, and they shall understand who have never heard of him."

In the Old Testament these words are immediately preceded by: "So shall he startle *many nations* (*ethnē polla*): kings shall shut their mouths because of him" (Isaiah 52:15). No doubt Paul reflected on the fact that his commission from the Lord came to him in similar words. In a close parallel to Isaiah 52:15, the risen Lord Jesus had said to Paul that he is "to carry [Christ's] name before the *nations (ethnōn)* and *kings*" (Acts 9:15).

In other words, Paul is being driven by a personal commission from the Lord which has been richly buttressed and filled out with a prophetic vision of hope. He was gripped by the Old Testament purpose of God to bless all the nations of the earth (Galatians 3:8) and to be praised by all the peoples (Romans 15:11), and to send salvation to the end of the earth (Acts 13:47), and to make Abraham the father of many nations (Romans 4:17), and to be understood in every group where he is not known (Romans 15:21).[21]

So Paul's conception of his specific missionary task was that he must press on beyond the regions and peoples where Christ is now preached to places like Spain, and to peoples "who have never been told of him". God's missionary "grace" for Paul was to be a foundation-layer in more and more places and peoples. His aim was not to reach as many Gentile individuals as he could but to reach as many unreached peoples as he could. This was Paul's specifically missionary vision.

Obedience for the sake of his name among all the nations

Against this backdrop the missionary statements at the beginning and ending of the book of Romans take on a distinct people group coloring. Earlier we had said that *panta ta ethnē* in these two verses was ambiguous. But from what we have seen now, from its use in the Old Testament and from Paul's dependence on that Old Testament hope, it is very likely that Paul has in view "nations" or people groups and not just Gentile individuals.

> Through [Christ] we have received grace and apostleship to bring about the obedience of faith for the sake of his name among *all the nations (pasin tois ethnesin)*. (Romans 1:5)

> The mystery ... is now disclosed, and through the prophetic writings is made known to *all nations (panta ta ethnē)*,

according to the command of the eternal God, to bring
about the obedience of faith. (Romans 16:26)

Paul saw his special missionary "grace and apostleship"
as one of God's appointed means of fulfilling the "command" that the obedience of faith be pursued among all
the nations. To this he gave his life.

John's vision of the missionary task

The vision of the missionary task in the writings of the
apostle John confirms that Paul's grasp of the Old Testament hope of reaching all the peoples was not unique
among the apostles. What emerges from Revelation and
the Gospel of John is a vision that assumes the central
missionary task of reaching people groups, not just Gentile
individuals.

The decisive text is Revelation 5:9–10. John is given a
glimpse of the climax of redemption as redeemed people
worship at the throne of God. The composition of that
assembly is crucial.

> The four living creatures and the twenty-four elders ...
> sang a new song, saying, "You are worthy to take the scroll
> and to open its seals, for you were slain and by your blood
> ransomed men for God *from every tribe and tongue and people
> and nation*, and made them a kingdom and priests to our
> God, and they shall reign on earth."

The missionary vision behind this scene is that the task of
the church is *to gather the ransomed from all peoples, tongues,
tribes and nations*.[22] All peoples must be reached because
God has appointed people to believe the gospel whom he
has ransomed through the death of his Son. The design of
the atonement prescribes the design of mission strategy.
And the design of the atonement (Christ's ransom, v. 9) is
universal in the sense that it extends to all peoples and
definite in that it effectually ransoms some from each of
these peoples. Therefore the missionary task is to gather
the ransomed from all the peoples through preaching the
gospel.

Gathering the scattered children

This understanding of John's vision of missions is powerfully confirmed from his Gospel. In John 11:51–52 Caiaphas, the high priest, admonishes the irate Jewish council to get Jesus out of the way because "it is expedient for you that one man should die for the people, and that the whole nation should not perish". Then John comments on this word from Caiaphas. His words are crucial for understanding John's missionary vision. John says,

> [Caiaphas] did not say this of his own acord, but being high priest that year he prophesied that Jesus should die for the nation, and not for the nation only, but *to gather into one the children of God who are scattered abroad.*

This ties in remarkably with John's conception of missions in Revelation 5:9. There it says that Christ's death ransomed men "*from* every tribe and tongue and people and nation". Here in John 11:52 it says that Christ's death gathers the children of God who are scattered among all those nations. In other words, both texts picture the missionary task as gathering in those who are ransomed by Christ. John calls them "the children of God".

Therefore "scattered" (in John 11:52) is to be taken in its fullest sense: the "children of God" will be found as widely scattered as there are *peoples* of the earth. The missionary task is to reach them in every tribe, tongue, people, and nation. The way they are to be reached is by the preaching of missionaries. This is what Jesus implies when he says in John 17:20, "I do not pray for these only, but also for those who believe in me through their word." This parallels John 11:52 which says Jesus did not die for the nation only, but to gather into one the children of God who are scattered abroad. The saving power of his death will extend to people in all the nations of the world, but it will only do so through the word of those whom he sends.

I must bring the other sheep also!

The same conception also lies behind the missionary text in John 10:16. Jesus says, "I have other sheep that are not of this fold; I must bring them also, and they will heed my voice." "This fold" refers to the people of Israel. The "other sheep" refer to the "children of God" who are scattered abroad (John 11:52). These are the "ransomed from every tribe" in Revelation 5:9. Therefore the words "I *must* bring them also" are a very strong affirmation the Lord *will* see his missionary purpose completed. He will gather his "sheep" or "the children of God" or the "ransomed" from all the peoples of the earth. As he says in Matthew 16:18, he will build his church.

Thus the Gospel of John lends tremendous force to the missionary purpose and missionary certainty implied in Revelation 5:9. Jesus has *ransomed* persons in all the peoples of the world. He *died* to gather these "children of God" who are scattered among all the peoples. And therefore he *must* bring all these wandering sheep into his fold! And they will be brought in through the word preached by his messengers.

Again and again: nations, tribes, peoples and tongues

Four other passages from Revelation confirm that John understands the task of missions as reaching all the people groups of the world so that the redeemed can be gathered in.

> After this I looked, and behold, a great multitude which no man could number, from *every nation, from all tribes and peoples and tongues*, standing before the throne and before the lamb, clothed in white robes, with palm branches in their hands, and crying out with a loud voice, "Salvation belongs to our God who sits upon the throne, and to the Lamb!" (Revelation 7:9–10)

Unless you restrict this multitude to the converts of the great tribulation and say that God's missionary purpose at that time is different than it is now, the implication of God's worldwide purpose is clear: He aims to be worshiped by converts from all the nations, tribes, peoples and tongues.

> Then I saw another angel flying in midheaven, with an *eternal gospel to proclaim to those who dwell on earth, to every*

198

nation (pan ethnos) and tribe and tongue and people; and he said with a loud voice, "Fear God and give him glory, for the hour of his judgment has come; worship him who made heaven and earth, the sea and the fountains of water." (Revelation 14:6–7)

Again the intention is that the gospel be proclaimed not just to more and more individuals, but to "every nation, tribe, tongue and people".

Who shall not fear and glorify thy name, O Lord? For thou alone are holy. All nations (*panta ta ethnē*) shall come and worship thee, for thy judgments have been revealed. (Revelation 15:4)

In view of the Old Testament allusion here to Psalm 86:9,[23] and in view of the context of Revelation with its repeated use of *ethnos* in reference to "nations" (at least ten times) and not persons, *panta ta ethnē* in 15:4 no doubt refers to people groups and not merely to Gentile individuals. Therefore what John foresees as the goal of missions is a worshiping multitude of saints from all the peoples of the world.

And I heard a great voice from the throne saying, "Behold, the dwelling of God is with men. He will dwell with them, and they shall be his *peoples* (*laoi*), and God himself will be with them." (Revelation 21:3)

This is a surprising and remarkable glimpse of the new heaven and new earth. It pictures *peoples*, not just people, in the age to come. Though not certain, it seems that *laoi* (peoples) and not *laos* (people) is the genuine, original reading.[24] Therefore John (recording the angelic voice) seems to make explicit (in distinction from Leviticus 26:12, *laos*) that the final goal of God in redemption is not to obliterate the distinctions of the peoples but to gather them all into one *diverse* but unified assembly of "peoples".

We may conclude from this inquiry into John's writings that John's conception of the unique task of missions is to reach more and more people groups until there are converts from "every tribe and tongue and people and nation". It is a task that he is utterly certain will be accomplished, for

he sees it as already complete in the Lord's vision of the age
to come.

Did Paul and John get this focus on peoples from Jesus?

We ask now whether this focus on peoples was the intention of Jesus as he gave his apostles their final commission.
Paul's conception of his own missionary task, which he
received from the risen Lord, would certainly suggest that
this is what the Lord commanded, not only to him and all
the apostles as the special missionary task of the church.

The Great Commission: it was written!

But there is also evidence of this in the context of Luke's
record of the Lord's words in Luke 24:45–47.

> Then he opened their minds to understand the Scriptures,
> and said to them, "Thus it is written, that the Christ should
> suffer and on the third day rise from the dead, and that
> repentance and forgiveness of sins should be preached in
> his name to *all nations (panta ta ethnē)*, beginning from
> Jerusalem."

The context here is crucial for our purposes. First, Jesus
"opens their minds to understand the *Scriptures*". Then he
says "Thus *it is written*" (in the Old Testament), followed (in
the original Greek) by three coordinate infinite clauses
which make explicit what is written in the Old Testament:
first, that the Christ is *to suffer*, second, that he is *to rise* on
the third day; and third, that repentance and forgiveness
of sins are *to be preached* in his name to "all nations".

So Jesus is saying that his commission to take the message of repentance and forgiveness to *all nations* "is written" in the Old Testament "Scriptures". This is one of the
things he opened their minds to understand. But what is
the Old Testament conception of the worldwide purpose
of God (which we saw above)? It is just what Paul saw that it
was – a purpose to bless all the families of the earth and win
a worshiping people from "all nations".[25]

Therefore we have strong evidence that the *panta ta ethnē*
in Luke 24:47 was understood by Jesus not merely in terms
of Gentile individuals, but as an array of world peoples

who must hear the message of repentance for the forgiveness of sin.

Luke's other account of Jesus' commission in Acts 1:8 points in the same direction. Jesus says to his apostles just before his ascension,

> You shall receive power when the Holy Spirit has come upon you; and you shall be my witnesses in Jerusalem and in all Judea and Samaria and to the end of the earth.

This commission suggests that getting to all the unreached areas (if not explicitly people groups) is the special task of missions. There is a pressure to keep moving, not just to unconverted individuals nearby, but to places beyond, even to the end of the world. Not only that, the phrase "end of the earth" is sometimes in the Old Testament closely associated with all the peoples of the earth. For example, Psalm 22:27:

> All the ends of the earth shall remember and turn to the LORD; and all the families of the nations shall worship before him.

This parallel shows that "end of the earth" sometimes carried the association of distant peoples.[26] The apostles would probably not have heard the commission of Acts 1:8 as significantly different from the commission of Luke 24:47.

A house of prayer for all nations

Another pointer to the way Jesus thought about the worldwide missionary purposes of God comes from Mark 11:17. When Jesus cleanses the temple he quotes Isaiah 56:7:

> Is it not written, "My house shall be called a house of prayer for all the nations (*pasin tois ethnesin*)"?

The reason this is important for us is that it shows Jesus reaching back to the Old Testament (just like he does in Luke 24:45–47) to intepret the worldwide purposes of God. He quotes Isaiah 56:7 which in the Hebrew explicitly says, "My house shall be called a house of prayer for all peoples (*l^ekol hā'ammîm*)."

The people group meaning is unmistakable. Isaiah's point is not that every individual Gentile will have a right to dwell in the presence of God, but that there will be converts from "all peoples" who will enter the temple to worship. That Jesus was familiar with this Old Testament hope, and that he based his worldwide expectations on references to it (Mark 11:17; Luke 24:45–47), suggests that we should interpret his Great Commission along this line – the very same line we have found in the writings of Paul and John.

Back to the Great Commission in Matthew

We come back now to our earlier effort to understand what Jesus meant in Matthew 28:19 when he said, "Go and make disciples of *panta ta ethnē*." This command has its corresponding promise of success in Matthew 24:14, "And this gospel of the kingdom will be preached throughout the whole world, as a testimony to all nations (*pasin tois ethnesin*); and then the end will come." The scope of the command and the scope of the promise hang on the meaning of *panta ta ethnē*.

My conclusion from what we have seen in this chapter is that one would have to go entirely against the flow of the evidence to interpret the phrase *panta ta ethnē* as "all Gentile individuals" (or "all countries"). Rather the focus of the command is the discipling of all the people groups of the world. This conclusion comes from the following summary of our Biblical investigation:

1. In the New Testament the singular use of *ethnos* never means Gentile individuals, but always means people group or nation.
2. The plural *ethnē* can mean either Gentile individuals or people groups. Sometimes context demands that it mean one or the other. But in most instances it could carry either meaning.
3. The phrase *panta ta ethnē* occurs eighteen times in the New Testament. Only once must it mean Gentile individuals. Nine times it must mean people groups. The other eight times are ambiguous.
4. Virtually all of the some 100 uses of *panta ta ethnē* in

the Greek Old Testament refer to nations in distinction from the nation of Israel. See note 15.

5. The promise made to Abraham that in him "all the families of the earth" would be blessed and that he would be "the father of many nations" is taken up in the New Testament and gives the mission of the church a people group focus because of this Old Testament emphasis.

6. The Old Testament missionary hope is expressed repeatedly as exhortations, promises, prayers and plans for God's glory to be declared among the peoples and his salvation to be known by all the nations.

7. Paul understood his specifically missionary task in terms of this Old Testament hope and made the promises concerning peoples the foundation of his mission. He was devoted to reaching more and more people groups not simply more and more individuals. He interpreted Christ's commission to him in these terms.

8. The apostle John envisioned the task of missions as the ingathering of "the children of God" or the "other sheep" out of "every tribe, tongue, people, and nation".

9. The Old Testament context of Jesus' missionary commissions in Luke 24:46–47 shows that *panta ta ethnē* would most naturally have the meaning of "all the peoples or nations".

10. Mark 11:17 shows that Jesus probably thinks in terms of people groups when he envisions the worldwide purpose of God.

Therefore in all likelihood Jesus did not send his apostles out with a general mission merely to win as many individuals as they could, but rather to reach all the peoples of the world and thus to gather the "sons of God" which are scattered (John 11:52), and to call all the "ransomed from every tongue and tribe and people and nation" (Revelation 5:9), until redeemed persons from "all the peoples praise him" (Romans 15:11).

Thus when Jesus says in Matthew 24:14 that "the gospel must first be preached to *all nations (panta ta ethnē)*", there is no good reason for construing this to mean anything other than that the gospel must reach *all the peoples* of the world before the end comes. And when Jesus says, "Go and make disciples of all *the nations* (*panta ta ethnē*)", there is no good reason for construing this to mean anything other than that the missionary task of the church is to press on to all the unreached peoples until the Lord comes. Jesus commands it and he assures us that it will be done before he comes again. He can make that promise because he himself is building his church from all the peoples. All authority in heaven and on earth have been given to him for this very thing (Matthew 28:18).

What is a people group?

We have tried to establish that the special missionary task of the New Testament is the reaching of all the people groups of the world. But we have not defined precisely what a people group is. What we have found, in fact, is that a precise definition is probably not possible to give on the basis of what God has chosen to reveal in the Bible. God probably did not intend for us to use a precise definition of people groups so as to think we could ever stop doing pioneer missionary work just because we conclude that all the groups with our definition have been reached.

For example, the point of Matthew 24:14 ("This gospel of the kingdom will be preached throughout the whole world, as a testimony to all the nations and *then the end will come*") is not that we should reach all the "nations" as we understand them and then stop. The point rather is that as long as the Lord has not returned, there must be more people groups to reach, and we should keep on reaching them.

There are Biblical pointers to the nature of a people group. For example, in Revelation 5:9 John uses four terms to describe the people groups that will be represented at the throne of God: "By your blood you ransomed men for God from every *tribe* and *tongue* and *people* and *nation*." To these four the promise to Abraham adds another: "In you all the *families*[27] of the earth will be blessed."

What is a language?

From this we can say, for example, that at least every *language group* (tongue) should be sought out in the missionary task. But when does a dialect become so distinct that it is a different language? Questions like this show why there is such difficulty and disagreement over what a people group is. For years now Ralph Winter has put forward the number 24,000 as the total number of people groups in the world. David Barrett, on the other hand, in the *World Christian Encyclopedia* refers to 8,990 ethno-linguistic people groups.[28] Patrick Johnstone, however, says, "All distinct ethno-linguistic groups with a sufficient distinctiveness within each nation for which church planting may be necessary [total] 12,017."[29]

After admitting that all researchers are guessing at the numbers,[30] Ralph Winter points out one factor that makes the disagreements more understandable. He observes the difference between his 24,000 estimate and David Barrett's 8,990 estimate. Then he says,

> It is clear in [Barrett's] table that his listing is almost identical to the number of languages which in his opinion need translations [of the Bible]. Now let's see where that leads us. Wycliffe Bible Translators, for example, go into South Sudan and count how many languages there are into which the Bible must be translated, and presented in printed form, in order to reach everybody in that area. Wycliffe's answer is 50 distinct translations. What does "50" mean in this instance? Does it mean 50 groups of people? Certainly not, if we are speaking of unreached peoples, because in many cases quite alien groups can read the same translation.
>
> How do I know this? Gospel Recordings also goes into South Sudan and counts the number of languages. Their personnel, however, come up with 130. Why? Because they put the gospel out in cassette form, and those cassettes represent a more embarrassingly precise language communication than does the written language. Different authors for different reasons, and different organizations for different purposes, are counting different things.[31]

So we can see that the reference to "tongues" in Revelation 5:9 will not yield a precise definition of people groups. Neither will the other designations for people groups in that verse.

"People" (*laou*) and "nation" (*ethnous*), for example, are virtually synonymous and interchangeable in Genesis 25:23 ("Two *nations* are in your womb and two *peoples*, born of you, shall be divided"). Sometimes Israel as a whole is called a "people", but in Acts 4:27 we read about the "peoples (*laois*) of Israel". Nevertheless, in Revelation 21:3 "peoples" (*laoi*) refers to all the groups and individuals in the new earth. These facts prevent us from forming precise definitions of the people groups missionaries are to reach.

How small is a family?

The fact that "all the families" of the earth will be blessed alerts us to the fact that the groupings that God intends to reach with his gospel may be relatively small. The modern nuclear family is not in view but rather something like a clan. For example, Exodus 6:14–15 shows us the sort of grouping that is probably in mind: "These are the heads of their fathers' houses: the sons of Reuben, the firstborn of Israel: Hanoch, Pallu, Hezron and Carmi; these are the *families* of Reuben. The sons of Simeon: Jemuel, Jamin, Ohad, Jachin, Zohar and Shaul, the son of a Canaanite woman; these are the *families* of Simeon." Thus we see that families are smaller than the tribes of Israel (cf. also 1 Samuel 10:20–21).

But they are not as small as households. The case of Achan in Joshua 7 shows this. When Achan had sinned and was to be found out, Joshua said that there would be a test of all the people to find out who the culprit was.

> In the morning therefore you shall be brought near *by your tribes*; and the tribe which the LORD takes shall come near *by families* (*mišpᵉhot*); and the family which the LORD takes shall come near *by households*; and the household which the LORD takes shall come near *man by man*. (Joshua 7:14)

What this shows is that the "family" of the Old Testament is better thought of as a clan. Its size is between the tribe and the "household".

Thus the missionary task of the New Testament was not only to reach every "people" of the size of Israel, nor only to reach every "tribe" the size of Reuben or Simeon or Judah, but it was also to reach all the clans like those of Hanoch, Pallu, Hezron, Carmi and Achan.

The fact that *ethnē* is used so often in the Old Testament and New Testament to designate the focus of missions should not limit our focus to the larger groupings. The word is flexible enough to provide an inclusive designation for groups of various sizes. In fact, Karl Ludwig Schmidt concludes his study of *ethnos* in the *Theological Dictionary of the New Testament* by contrasting it with *laos*, *glōssa*, and *phulē* like this: "*ethnos* is the most general and therefore the weakest of these terms, having simply an ethnographical sense and denoting the natural cohesion of a people in general."[32] Thus *panta ta ethnē* would be the most suitable term for including the others. Which is in fact what we find in Revelation 22:2. Here *ethnē* refers to all the peoples in the new earth, including the "tongues" and "peoples" and "tribes". So *panta ta ethnē* is probably the simplest way of giving a summary designation not only to the larger, but also the smaller groupings as well.

What do "reached" and "unreached" mean?[33]

If the task of missions is to reach all the unreached people groups of the world, we need some idea of what "reached" means so that the people called to the missionary task of the church will know which people groups to enter and which to leave. Paul must have had some idea of what "reached" meant when he said in Romans 15:23, "I no longer have any room for work in these regions." He must have known what it meant to complete the missionary task, when he said in Romans 15:19, "From Jerusalem as far round as Illyricum I have fulfilled the gospel of Christ." He knew his work was done in that region. That's why he headed for Spain. The 1982 Unreached Peoples Meeting which we referred to earlier defined "unreached" like this: An unreached people group is "a people group within which there is no indigenous community of believing Christians able to evangelize this people group".[34] Thus a group would be reached when mission efforts have established an indigenous church that has the strength and resources to evangelize the rest of the group.

Patrick Johnstone points out that in the strict sense "Reaching has nothing to do with response . . . Reaching is really an indication of the quality and extent of the effort to evangelize a people or region, not of discipling and church planting." But he admits that "because of popular usage, we have to extend [the meaning of] reachedness".[35]

Both the narrow and broader meaning are warranted from Scripture. For example, Mark 16:15 renders the mission mandate, "[Jesus] said to them, 'Go into all the world, and preach the gospel to the whole creation.'"[36] This does not say anything about response. If we only had this word, the missions mandate would be fulfilled if the message were universally proclaimed. Similarly Matthew 24:14 says, "And this gospel of the kingdom will be preached throughout the whole world as a testimony to all the nations. And then the end will come." Again there is no mention of response (cf. Luke 24:47; Acts 1:8). So in this limited sense a people group is reached if the message is proclaimed in it as an understandable testimony.

But this is *not* the only way the missions mandate is expressed in Scripture. Matthew 28:19 says, "Go therefore and make disciples of all nations . . ." Here the mandate clearly includes a response. The missions task is not done until at least some individuals in a people group are becoming disciples.[37] This is also the implication of Revelation 5:9 and 7:9 which portray the final company of the redeemed as coming "from every tribe and tongue and people and nation". If there are converts from all the peoples, then the missions mandate must include making converts, not just doing proclamation.

Most mission leaders define a people group as "reached" when there is an indigenous church able to evangelize the group. The reason for this is that the New Testament clearly teaches that a people must continue to be evangelized once the mission task is complete. For example, when Paul finished his missionary work among the peoples of Ephesus, he nevertheless left Timothy there and told him to "do the work of an evangelist" (2 Timothy 4:5). Paul's specific missionary task was evidently to plant the church which would then be able to go on with the task of evangelism (cf. 1 Corinthians 3:6–10). But the task of evangelism is not the same as missions. Missions is what moved Paul away from the peoples of Asia Minor and Greece (even from those who were still unconverted!), and pressed him toward the unreached peoples of Spain (Romans 15:24, 28).

There is a difficulty with defining the specific task of missions as planting an indigenous church in every people group. The difficulty is that our *Biblical* definition of people groups includes groups that may be so small and so closely related to another group that such a church would be unnecessary. How large was the "family" or clan of Carmi in the tribe of Reuben, or the family of Achan in the tribe of Judah? And are we sure that the "families" in Genesis 12:3 are always so distinct that each must have its own church? When Paul said that his special missionary work was completed from Jerusalem to Illyricum, had he in fact planted a church in every "family" or clan?

These questions show that there will always be some ambiguity in the definition of "reached" and in the aim of missionary work.[38] For some "families" or clans, "reached" may mean that there are converts among them and that the church in an adjacent kindred clan suffices as an effective ministry of worship, fellowship and equipping. The task of missions with regard to such near-kinship "families" may not be to plant a church among each one but to plant a church close enough in culture and language that they can effectively be evangelized. It seems to me that this must have been what Paul had done when he said that he no longer had room for work in that vast territory. Surely there were some "families" or clans that had not yet been touched. He would have said I think that this was the work of the nearby churches.

What this implies is that the dividing line between specifically missionary tasks and the tasks of near-neighbor evangelism is sometimes unclear. This is why the terms "E-1", "E-2", and "E-3" evangelism have been invented. They show that there are not two clearly distinct tasks (domestic evangelism vs. frontier missions), but rather there are gradations of cultural distance from the Christian community. Where that distance becomes so great that we start calling its penetration "missions" is not always clear.[39]

Implications

But that there is a distinct calling on the church to do frontier missionary work among all the remaining unreached people groups is crystal clear from the New Testament. Our question today should be: what persons or agencies in the various churches and denominations should pick up this unique Paul-type mission? It is not the *only* work of the church! "Timothy-type ministries" are important. He was a foreigner working at Ephesus, continuing what Paul began. But Paul had to move on, because he was driven by a special commission[40] and by a grasp of God's worldwide mission purpose revealed in the Old Testament. There is no reason to think that God's purpose has changed today.

Who then is to pick up the mantle of the apostle's unique missionary task to reach more and more peoples? Should not every denomination and church have some vital group that is recruiting, equipping, sending and supporting Paul-type missionaries to more and more unreached peoples? Should there not be in every chuch and denomination a group of peoples (a missions agency or board) who see their special and primary task not merely to win as many individuals to Christ as possible, but to win some individuals (i.e. plant a church) among all the unreached peoples of the earth?

The supremacy of God in the worship of the nations

Now what does the conclusion of this chapter have to do with the supremacy of God? God's great goal in all of history is to uphold and display the glory of his name for the enjoyment of his people from all the nations.[41] The question now is: why does God pursue the goal of displaying his glory by focussing the missionary task on *all the peoples* of the world? How does this missionary aim serve best to achieve God's goal?

The first thing we notice in pondering this question is

how the ultimate goal of God's glory is confirmed in the cluster of texts that focus missionary attention on the people groups of the world. For example, Paul said that his apostleship was given "to bring about the obedience of faith *for the sake of [Christ's] name* among all the nations" (Romans 1:5). Missions is for the glory of Christ. Its goal is to re-establish the supremacy of Christ among the peoples of the world. Similarly in Romans 15:9 Paul says that Christ did his own missionary work and inspired Paul's "in order that the nations *might glorify God* for his mercy". So the goal of Christ's mission and ours is that God might be glorified by the nations as they experience his mercy. Accordingly the consummation of missions is described in Revelation 5:9 as persons from "every tribe, tongue, people and nation" worshipping the Lamb and declaring the infinite worth of his glory. All of this is in accord with the repeated Old Testament calls: "Declare his *glory* among the nations, his *marvelous works* among all the peoples!" (Psalm 96:3). The goal of missions is the glory of God.

Diversity: intended and eternal

Another thing we notice as we ponder this question is that the diversity of the nations has its creation and consummation in the will of God. Its origin was neither accident nor evil.[42] And its future is eternal: the diversity will never be replaced by uniformity. The evidence for this is found in Acts 17:26 and Revelation 21:3.

To the Athenians Paul said, "[God] made from one every nation of men to live on all the face of the earth, having determined allotted periods and the boundaries of their habitation." This means that the origin of peoples is not in spite of, but because of, God's will and plan. He *made* the nations. He set them in their place. And he determines the duration of their existence. The diversity of the nations is God's idea. Therefore for whatever reason he focuses the missionary task on all the nations, it is not a response to an accident of history. It is rooted in the purpose he had when he determined to make the nations in the first place.

God's purpose to have diversity among nations is not a temporary one only for this age. In spite of the resistance of most English versions the standard Greek texts of the New Testament now agree that the original wording of Revelation 21:3 requires the translation: "and I heard a great voice from the throne saying, 'Behold, the dwelling of God is with men, and he will dwell with them and they will be his *peoples*.'" Most versions translate: "They will be his *people*." But what John is saying is that in the new heavens and the new earth the humanity described in Revelation 5:9 will be preserved: persons ransomed by the blood of Christ "from every tribe and tongue and people and nation". This diversity will not disappear in the new heavens and the new earth. God willed it from the beginning. It has a permanent place in his plan.

How diversity magnifies the glory of God

Now, we return to our question: How does God's focus on the diversity of the peoples advance his purpose to be glorified in his creation? As I have tried to reflect Biblically on this question, at least[43] four answers have emerged.

First, there is a beauty and power of praise that comes from unity in diversity that is greater than that which comes from unity alone. Psalm 96:3–4 connects the evangelizing of the peoples and the quality of praise that God deserves. "Declare his glory among the nations, his marvelous works among all the peoples! *For great is the LORD and greatly to be praised. He is to be feared above all gods.*" Notice the word "for". The extraordinary greatness of the praise which the Lord should receive is the ground and impetus of our mission to the nations.

I infer from this that the beauty and power of praise that will come to the Lord from the diversity of the nations are greater than the beauty and power that would come to him if the chorus of the redeemed were culturally uniform. The reason for this can be seen in the analogy of a choir. More depth of beauty is felt from a choir that sings in parts than from a choir that only sings in unison. Unity in diversity is more beautiful and more powerful than the unity of uniformity. This carries over to the untold differences that exist between the peoples of the world. When their diversity unites in worship to God the beauty of their praise will

212

echo the depth and greatness of God's beauty far more exceedingly than if the redeemed were from only a few different people groups.

Second, the fame and greatness and worth of an object of beauty increase in proportion to the diversity of those who recognize its beauty. If a work of art is regarded as great among a small and like-minded group of people, but not by anyone else, the art is probably not truly great. Its qualities are such that it does not appeal to the deep universals in our hearts but only to provincial biases. But if a work of art continues to win more and more admirers not only across cultures but also across decades and centuries, then its greatness is irresistibly manifested.

Thus when Paul says, "Praise the Lord all nations, let all the peoples praise him" (Romans 15:11), he is saying that there is something about God that is so universally praiseworthy and so profoundly beautiful and so comprehensively worthy and so deeply satisfying that God will find passionate admirers in every diverse people group in the world. His true greatness will be manifest in the breadth of the diversity of those who perceive and cherish his beauty. His excellence will be shown to be higher and deeper than the parochial preferences that make us happy most of the time. His appeal will be to the deepest, highest, largest capacities of the human soul. Thus the diversity of the source of admiration will testify to his incomparable glory.

Third, the strength and wisdom and love of a leader are magnified in proportion to the diversity of people he can inspire to follow him with joy. If you can only lead a small, uniform group of people, your leadership qualities are not as great as if you can win a following from a large group of very diverse people.

Paul's understanding of what is happening in his missionary work among the nations is that Christ is demonstrating his greatness in winning obedience from all the peoples of the world: "I will not venture to speak of anything except what *Christ has wrought through me to win obedience from the nations*" (Romans 15:18). It is not Paul's missionary expertise that is being magnified as more and more diverse peoples choose to follow Christ. It is the

213

greatness of Christ. He is showing himself superior to all other leaders.

The last phrase of Psalm 96:3 shows the leadership competition that is going on in world missions. "Declare his glory among the nations ... *He is to be feared above all gods.*" We should declare the glory of God among the nations because in this way he will show his superiority over all other gods that make pretentious claims to lead the peoples. The more diverse the people groups who forsake their gods to follow the true God, the more visible is God's superiority over all his competitors.

Fourth, by focusing on all the people groups of the world, God undercuts ethnocentric pride and puts all peoples back upon his free grace rather than any distinctive of their own. This is what Paul was emphasizing in Acts 17:26 when he said to the proud citizens of Athens, "[God] made from one every nation of men to live on all the face of the earth, having determined allotted periods and the boundaries of their habitation." F. F. Bruce points out that "The Athenians prided themselves on being ... sprung from the soil of their native Attica (a claim reflecting the fact that they belonged to the earliest wave of Greek immigration into the land, so that, unlike later arrivals ... they had lost all memory of their immigration)."[44]

To this boast Paul countered: you and the Barbarians and the Jews and the Romans all came from the same origin. And you came by God's will, not your own; and the time and place of your existence are in God's hand. Every time God expresses his missionary focus on *all* the nations he cuts the nerve of ethnocentric pride. It's a humbling thing to discover that God does not choose our people group because of any distinctives of worth, but rather that we might double our joy in him by being a means of bring all the other groups into the same joy.

Humility is the flip side of giving God all the glory. Humility means revelling in his grace, not our goodness. In pressing us on to all the peoples God is pressing us further into the humblest and deepest experience of his grace, and weaning us more and more from our

214

ingrained pride. In doing this he is preparing for himself a people – from all the peoples – who will be able to worship him with free and white-hot admiration.

Notes

1. I use the word "win" in the sense that Paul does in 1 Corinthians 9:19–22. The use of "save" in verse 22 shows that this is what he has in mind: to be used by God in love and witness to win people over to faith in Christ and so to save them from sin and condemnation.

   (19) For though I am free from all men, I have made myself a slave to all, that I might *win* the more. (20) To the Jews I became as a Jew, in order to *win* Jews; to those under the law I became as one under the law – though not being myself under the law – that I might *win* those under the law. (21) To those outside the law I became as one outside the law – not being without law toward God but under the law of Christ – that I might *win* those outside the law. (22) To the weak I became weak, that I might *win* the weak. I have become all things to all men, that I might by all means save some.

2. The word "nations" in this chapter does not refer to the modern political state as in the "United Nations" or the "nation" of France. We will see that its Biblical meaning has to do with an ethnic group which may or may not have political dimensions.

3. I use the word "evangelize" in the broad New Testament sense of speaking the good news of Christ and his saving work. The speaking is with a view to bringing about faith and establishing the church of Christ (Romans 10:14–15; 15:20), but true evangelizing does not depend on a believing response (Hebrews 4:6). For a remarkably thorough historical survey of the concept see David B. Barrett, *Evangelize! A Historical Survey of the Concept* (Birmingham, Alabama: New Hope, 1987).

4. Ralph Winter, "The New Macedonia: A Revolutionary New Era in Mission Begins," in Ralph Winter and Steven Hawthorne, eds., *Perspectives on the World Christian Movement* (Pasadena: William Carey Library, 1981), p. 302.

5. Ralph Winter, "Unreached Peoples: Recent Developments in the Concept," *Mission Frontiers*, August/September, 1989, p. 18.

6. Ralph Winter, "Unreached Peoples: Recent Developments in the Concept," p. 12.

7. See note 38 below on this difference of perspective and its effects.

8. Harley Schreck and David Barrett, eds., *Unreached Peoples: Clarifying the Task* (Monrovia, California: March, 1987), pp. 6–7.

9. See chapter five for a discussion of what reached and unreached means.

10. Galatians 2:14 appears to be an exception in the English text ("If you, though a Jew, live like *a Gentile* and not like a Jew, how can you compel the Gentiles to live like Jews?"). But the Greek word here is not *ethnos*, but the adverb *ethnikos*, which means to have the life patterns of Gentiles.

11. Following are all the singular uses in the New Testament. Matthew 21:43; 24:7 (= Mark 13:8 = Luke 21:10); Luke 7:5; 23:2 (both references to the Jewish nation); Acts 2:5 ("Jews from every nation"); 7:7; 8:9; 10:22 ("whole nation of the Jews"), 35; 17:26; 24:2, 10, 17; 26:4; 28:19 (the last five references are to the Jewish nation); John 11:48, 50, 51, 52; 18:35 (all in reference to the Jewish nation); Revelation 5:9; 13:7; 14:6; 1 Peter 2:9. Paul never uses the singular.

12. For example, Matthew 6:32; 10:5; 12:21; 20:25; Luke 2:32; 21:24; Acts 9:15; 13:46, 47; 15:7, 14, 23; 18:6; 21:11; 22:21; Romans 3:29; 9:24; 15:9, 10, 11, 12, 16; 16:26; Galatians 2:9; 3:14; 2 Timothy 4:17; Revelation 14:18; 16:19; 19:15 – 20:8; 21:24. When I use the term "Gentile individuals" in this chapter I do not mean to focus undue attention on specific persons. Rather, I mean to speak of non-Jews in a comprehensive way without reference to their ethnic groupings.

13. Following Dibelius, this is suggested by F. F. Bruce, *Commentary on the Book of Acts* (Grand Rapids: Wm. B. Eerdmans Publishing Company, 1954), p. 358. But Lenski is surely right that the very next clause in Acts 17:26 militates against such a translation: "... having determined allotted periods and boundaries of their habitation". This naturally refers, as John Stott also says, to various ethnic groups with "the epochs of their history and the limits of their territory". R. C. H. Lenski, *The Interpretation of the Acts of the Apostles* (Minneapolis: Augsburg Publishing House, 1934), p. 729; John Stott, *The Message of Acts* (Leicester: IVP, 1990), p. 286. The point of the verse is to take the air out of the sails of ethnic pride in Athens. All the other *ethnē* have descended from the same "one" as the Greeks, and not only that, whatever time and territory a people has, it is God's sovereign doing and nothing to boast in. "Both the history and the geography of each nation are ultimately under [God's] control" (Stott).

14. LXX is an abbreviation for the Greek Translation the Old Testament called the Septuagint. It comes from the tradition that the translation was made by 70 (LXX) scholars.

15. My survey was done searching for all case variants of *panta ta ethnē* in the plural. The following texts are references to Greek Old Testament (LXX) verse and chapter divisions which occasionally do not correspond to the Hebrew and English versions. Genesis 18:18; 22:18; 26:4; Exodus 19:5;

23:22, 27; 33:16; Leviticus 20:24, 26; Deuteronomy 2:25; 4:6, 19, 27; 7:6, 7, 14; 10:15; 11:23; 14:2; 26:19; 28:1, 10, 37, 64; 29:23 – 30:1, 3; Joshua 4:24; 23:3, 4, 17, 18; 1 Samuel 8:20; 1 Chronicles 14:17; 18:11; 2 Chronicles 7:20; 32:23; 33:9; Nehemiah 6:16; Esther 3:8; Psalm 9:8; 46:2; 48:2; 58:6, 9; 71:11, 17; 81:8; 85:9; 112:4; 116:1; 117:10; Isaiah 2:2; 14:12, 26; 25:7; 29:8; 34:2; 36:20; 40:15, 17; 43:9; 52:10; 56:7; 61:11; 66:18, 20; Jeremiah 3:17; 9:25; 25:9; 32:13, 15; 33:6; 35:11, 14; 43:2; 51:8; Ezra 25:8; 38:16; 39:21, 23; Daniel 3:2, 7; 7:14; Joel 4:2, 11, 12; Amos 9:12; Obadiah 15, 16; Habukkuk 2:5; Haggai 2:7; Zechariah 7:14; 12:3, 9; 14:2, 16, 18, 19; Malachi 2:9; 3:12.

16. Karl Ludwig Schmidt argues that the *mišpᵉḥot* are "smaller clan-like societies within the main group or nation". (*Theological Dictionary of the New Testament*, Vol. 2, ed. Gerhard Kittel, trans. by Geoffrey Bromiley [Grand Rapids: Wm. B. Eerdmans Publishing Company, 1964], p. 365.)

17. Paul may have chosen to use *panta ta ethnē* because this is how the Greek Old Testament translates the promise of God to Abraham in three of its five occurrences (Genesis 18:18; 22:18; 26:4; but not 12:3 and 28:14 which translate it *pasai hai phulai*). But Paul's words do not correspond exactly with any of these five texts. So he may well have been giving his own composite translation from the Hebrew.

18. The evidence for this would be, for example, the repeated use in the Greek Old Testament of the phrase "houses (or households) of the families" which show that the "family" (*patria*) is a larger grouping than a household. Cf. Exodus 6:17; Numbers 1:44; 3:24; 18:1; 25:14–15; Joshua 22:14; 1 Chronicles 23:11; 24:6; 2 Chronicles 35:5; Ezra 2:59. See below on "How small is a family?"

19. This is a psalm to the king and refers in its final application to Christ the Messiah, as is shown by the use made of verse 7 in Hebrews 1:9.

20. Quoted in Johannes Verkuyl, "The Biblical Foundation of the Worldwide Mission Mandate," in Ralph Winter and Steven Hawthorne, eds., *Perspectives on the World Christian Movement*, p. 44.

21. To these reflections could be added Paul's crucial words in Romans 10:14–15 concerning the necessity of people being sent so that they can preach so that people can hear so that they can believe so that they can call on the Lord so that they can be saved. See the discussion of these verses in chapter four.

22. One can't help but sense that John means for us to see a great reversal of the idolatry so prevalent on the earth, expressed, for example, in Daniel 3:7. Nebuchadnezzar had erected an idol and called everyone to worship it. The words used to

describe the extent of that worship are almost identical to the words John uses in Revelation 5:9 to describe the extent of the true worship of God: "All the *peoples*, *nations*, and *tongues* fell down and worshiped the golden image which King Nebuchadnezzar had set up."

23. Psalm 85:9 LXX. See a discussion of this text earlier in this chapter.

24. The Bible Societies' Greek New Testament (3rd ed.) and the Nestlé-Aland Greek New Testament (26th ed.) choose *laoi* as original. The NRSV reads "peoples", as do the commentaries by Heinrich Kraft, Leon Morris and Robert Mounce.

25. From all the uses of *panta ta ethnē* in the Old Testament that Jesus may be alluding to, at least these relate to the missionary vision of the people of God: Genesis 18:18; 22:18; 26:4; Psalm 48:2; 71:11, 17; 81:8; 85:9; 116:1; Isaiah 2:2; 25:7; 52:10; 56:7; 61:11; 66:18–20 (all references are to the LXX verse and chapter divisions).

26. Similar associations are found in Psalm 2:8; 67:5–7; 98:2–3; Isaiah 52:10; Jeremiah 16:19; Zechariah 9:10. But four different Greek expressions are used in these texts, only one of which (Jeremiah 16:19) is the exact wording of the phrase in Acts 1:8.

27. The Greek Old Testament translates the Hebrew *mišpᵉḥot* (families) with *phulai*, which is translated "tribes" in Revelation 5:9. So it may look like this is not a different category of group. But in fact *phulai* usually translates the Hebrew *šēbeṭ* and the Hebrew *mišpᵉḥot* is usually translated by *suggeneia*. So we should take seriously the difference between *mišpᵉḥot* and "tribe" especially since it is clearly a smaller unit according to Exodus 6:14f.

28. David Barrett, ed. *World Christian Encyclopedia* (Nairobi: Oxford University Press, 1981), p. 110.

29. Patrick Johnstone, *Operation World* (Bucks, England: STL Books and WEC Publications, 1987), p. 32.

30. "At this hour in history it is deplorable that no one can do better than guess ... We are all guessing, we are all pleading for help." Ralph D. Winter, "Unreached Peoples: What, Where, and Why?", in: Patrick Sookhdeo, ed., *New Frontiers in Mission* (Grand Rapids: Baker Book House, 1987), p. 153.

31. Ralph D. Winter, "Unreached Peoples: What, Where, and Why?" p. 154.

32. *Theological Dictionary of the New Testament*, Vol. 2, p. 369.

33. There are two problems that I will deal with only briefly here in a note because they are not part of Biblical revelation and do not seem to have much bearing on the missionary task. One is whether all the peoples will be represented at the throne of God even without missions because infants in each of these peoples have died and presumably will go to heaven

and come to maturity for the praise of God. The other problem is whether all clans and tribes will in fact be represented at the throne of God since many clans and tribes no doubt died out before they were evangelized.

With regard to the first problem I do believe that infants who die will be in the kingdom. I base this on the principle that we are judged according to the knowledge available to us (Romans 1:19–20), and infants have no knowledge available to them since the faculty of knowing is not developed. However, God does not ever mention this or relate it in any way to the missionary enterprise or to the promise that all the families of the earth will be blessed. Rather it appears to be his purpose to be glorified through the conversion of people who recognize his beauty and greatness, and come to love him above all gods. God would not be honored so greatly if the only way he got worshipers from all the nations was by the natural mortality of infants.

With regard to the other problem it may be true that some clans and tribes disappear from history with none of their members being saved. The Bible does not reflect on this issue. We would be speculating beyond the warrant of Scripture if we said that there had to be another way of salvation for such tribes besides the way of hearing and believing the gospel of Jesus. (See the support for this in chapter four.) Rather we would do well to assume, in the absence of specific revelation, that the meaning of the promise and the command concerning the nations is that "all the nations" refer to all those that exist at the consummation of the age. When the end comes there will be no existing people group that is left out of the blessing.

34. Ralph Winter, "Unreached Peoples: Recent Developments in the Concept", p. 12.

35. "What Does Reached Mean? An EMQ Survey", *Evangelical Missions Quarterly*, Vol. 26, No. 3 (July, 1990), p. 316.

36. The KJV translates, "Go ye into all the world, and preach the gospel to *every creature*." But "the whole creation" is more likely. The closest parallel to this Greek expression (*pas tē ktisei*) is found in Romans 8:22, "We know that *the whole creation (pasa hē ktisis)* has been groaning in travail together until now." The words and word order are identical; only the case is different, dative in Mark 16 and nominative in Romans 8. For my purposes here we don't need to settle whether Mark 16:9ff is an early addition to the Gospel of Mark. Verse 15 represents one Biblical way of expressing the great commission.

37. "Make disciples of all nations" might be taken to mean: make the whole nation into disciples. But the wording of verses 19 and 20 points in another direction. The word "nations"

(*ethnē*) is neuter in Greek. But the word for "them" in the following clauses is masculine: "baptizing them (*autous*) in the name of the Father and of the Son and of the Holy Spirit, teaching them (*autous*) to observe all that I commanded you." This suggests that the discipling in view is the winning of individual disciples from the nations, rather than treating the nation as a whole as the object of conversion and discipleship. This was affirmed strongly by Karl Barth who lamented that the interpretation that took *ethnē* in the sense of corporate discipling "once infested missionary thinking and was connected with the painful fantasies of the German Christians. It is worthless." (Karl Barth, "An Exegetical Study of Matthew 28:16–20", in Francis M. DuBose, ed., *Classics of Christian Missions* [Nashville: Broadman Press, 1979], p. 46.)

38. This problem of course does not exist by definition for Ralph Winter and other missiologists who define a people group as "the largest group within which the gospel can spread as a church planting movement without encountering barriers of understanding or acceptance". (Ralph Winter, "Unreached Peoples: Recent Developments in the Concept", p. 12.) In other words, if an unevangelized "family" is culturally near enough to another evangelized "family" that the gospel can move without significant barriers, then by definition the unevangelized family, according to Dr. Winter, is not an "unreached people group". It is simply part of a larger reached group that needs to evangelize its members. The difference between Dr. Winter's approach and mine is that I am simply trying to come to terms with the *Biblical* meaning of "families" in Genesis 12:3 while he is defining people groups in terms of what missionary efforts are needed. The two approaches are not at odds. But the difference may result in my calling a "family" or clan an unreached people group in Biblical terms (one of the *panta ta ethnē* to be discipled) which Dr. Winter however would say is not "unreached" for specifically missionary purposes.

39. *Biblically*, reaching every clan in a region is a missionary task regardless of its cultural nearness to other reached clans. But *missiologically*, this effort may not be seen as part of the missionary task. What is needed perhaps is more refined distinctions in our language. Paul certainly saw *his* missionary work as finished before every clan in Asia was evangelized. Yet if the Great Commission of Matthew 28:19 includes "all the families of the earth" in *panta ta ethnē*, then the missionary task *in that sense* is not complete until all the clans are represented in the kingdom. Practically, it is probably wise to emphasize the Pauline strategy as the essence of missions.

40. "Depart; for I will send you far away to the *ethnē*" (Acts 22:21).

41. I have labored to demonstrate this from Scripture in chapter one, and in *Desiring God* (Leicester: IVP, 1989), pp. 227–238; and *The Pleasures of God* (Portland: Multnomah Press, 1991), pp. 101–122.

42. The story of the Tower of Babel in Genesis 11 does not mean that God disapproves of the diversity of languages in the world. We are *not* told that apart from the tower of Babel God would not have created different languages in the world. Blocking an act of pride (Genesis 11:4) was the occasion when God initiated the diversity of languages in the world. But that does not mean that the diversity of languages was a curse that would need to be reversed in the age to come. In fact the diversity of languages is *reported* in Genesis 10:5, 20, 31 before the tower of Babel is mentioned in Genesis 11. What we learn is that God's plan of a common origin for all peoples on the one hand and his plan for diversified languages on the other hand restrain the pride of man on two sides: diversity restrains the temptation to unite against God (as at Babel) and unified origin restrains the temptation to boast in ethnic uniqueness (as, we will see, in Athens). The miracle and the blessing of "tongues" at Pentecost was not a declaration that in the age of promise the languages of the world would disappear, but rather a declaration that in the age of promise every obstacle to humble, God-glorifying *unity* in faith would be overcome.

43. I omit discussing the real possibility that there are mysterious correlations between the numbers and the purposes of the peoples and the numbers of the saints or the angels. Deuteronomy 32:8 says, "When the Most High gave to the nations their inheritance, when he separated the sons of men, he fixed the bounds of the peoples *according to the number of the sons of Israel*." The Greek Old Testament has the strange rendering: ". . . according to the number of the *angels of God*", while the RSV follows, by translating, ". . . according to the number of the sons of God". Making much of this would be speculation. But it does remind us that God has reasons that are often high and hidden.

44. F. F. Bruce, *Commentary on the Book of Acts* (Leicester: Apollos, 1990), p. 382.

Conclusion

The ultimate goal of God in all of history is to uphold and display his glory for the enjoyment of the redeemed from every tribe and tongue and people and nation. His goal is the gladness of his people because God is most glorified in us when we are most satisfied in him. Delight is a higher tribute than duty. The chief end of God is to glorify God and enjoy his glory for ever. Since his glory is magnified most in the God-centered passions of his joyful people, God's self-exultation and our jubilation are one. The greatest news in all the world is that God's ultimate aim to be glorified and man's aim to be satisfied are not at odds.

Worship

The goal of missions therefore is the gladness of the peoples in the greatness of God. "The LORD reigns; let the earth *rejoice*; let the many coastlands *be glad*!" (Psalm 97:10). "Let the nations *be glad and sing for joy*!" (Psalm 67:4). The missionary command to be happy in God is simply a command for the consummation of praise. Professed praise of God without pleasure in God is hypocrisy.

Therefore worship is the fuel and goal of missions. It's the goal of missions because in missions we aim to bring the nations into the white-hot enjoyment of God's glory. And it's the fuel of missions because you can't commend what you don't cherish. You can't call out, "Let the nations *be glad*!" until you say, "*I rejoice* in the Lord." Missions begins and ends in worship.

Prayer

This means that God is absolutely supreme in missions. He is the beginning and the end. He is also the one who sustains and empowers the whole process. "From him, through him, and to him are all things. To him be glory for

222

ever" (Romans 11:36). God's moment-by-moment sustaining of the Christian movement preserves his supremacy, because the one who gives the power gets the glory. "Let him who serves serve in the strength that God supplies that in everything God may get the glory" (1 Peter 4:11).

That is why God has ordained prayer to have such a crucial place in the mission of the church. The purpose of prayer is to make clear to all the participants in missions that the victory belongs to the Lord. "The horse is made ready for the day of battle, but the victory belongs to the LORD" (Proverbs 21:31). Prayer is God's appointed means of bringing grace to the world and glory to himself. "Call on me in the day of trouble and I will deliver you, and *you shall glorify me*" (Psalm 50:15). "Whatever you ask in my name, I will do it, *that the Father may be glorified in the Son*" (John 14:13).

Prayer puts God in the place of the all-sufficient Benefactor and puts us in the place of needy beneficiaries. So when the mission of the church moves forward by prayer, the supremacy of God is manifest and the needs of Christian missionaries are met. In prayer he is glorified and we are satisfied. "Till now you have asked nothing in my name; ask, and you will receive *that your joy may be full*" (John 16:24). The purpose of prayer is the Father's fame and the saints' fullness.

Suffering

God himself is the fullness we live on and the fountain of life that we commend in missions. He is our treasure. His steadfast love is better than life (Psalm 63:3). Therefore the greatness of his worth is seen most clearly when we are willing to give up our lives for the sake of his love. We measure the worth of a treasure by what we will gladly give up in order to have it.

Suffering alone proves nothing. But suffering accepted because of the "surpassing worth of knowing Christ", and losses embraced "in order to gain Christ" (Philippians 3:8) prove that Christ is supremely valuable. "Blessed are you when men persecute you . . . Rejoice and be glad, for your reward is great in heaven" (Matthew 5:12). The extent of our *sacrifice* coupled with the depth of our *joy* displays the worth we put on the reward of God. Loss and suffering, joyfully accepted for the kingdom of God, show the supremacy of God's glory more clearly in the world than all worship and prayer.

Therefore God ordains that the mission of his church move forward not only by the fuel of worship and in the power of prayer, but at the price of suffering. "If anyone would come after me, let him deny himself and take up his cross and follow me" (Mark 8:34). "A servant is not greater than his master. If they persecuted me, they will persecute you" (John 15:20). "If they have called the master of the house Beelzebul, how much more will they malign those of his household" (Matthew 10:25). "The Son of man must suffer many things" (Mark 8:31). "As the Father has sent me, even so send I you" (John 20:21). "Behold, I send you out as sheep in the midst of wolves" (Matthew 10:16). "I will show him how much he must suffer for the sake of my name" (Acts 9:16).

Is knowing Christ crucial?

Since the price is so high one may well ask, is it really necessary? If the goal of God in history is to uphold and display his glory for the enjoyment of the redeemed, may it not be that he will redeem people without missions? Could people come to praise the true God from hearts of saving faith while still ignorant of Jesus and his saving work? Could nature or other religions lead people into eternal life and joy with God?

The Biblical answer we have seen is No. It is a stunning New Testament truth that since the incarnation of the Son of God all saving faith must henceforth fix on him. This was not always true. Before Christ, the people of Israel focused faith on the promises of God (Romans 4:20). And the nations were allowed to walk in their own ways (Acts 14:16). But those times were called the "times of ignorance". But now since the coming of the Son of God into the world, Christ is made the conscious center of the mission of the church. The aim of missions to "bring about the obedience of faith *for the sake of his name* among all the nations" (Romans 1:5). This is a new thing with the coming of Christ. God's will is to be glorified in his Son by making him the center of all missionary proclamation. The supremacy of God in missions is affirmed Biblically by affirming the supremacy of his Son as the focus of all saving faith.

People or peoples?

Since the eternal destiny of every individual hangs on knowing Christ and embracing him gladly as the highest value of life, is then the task of missions to maximize the number of people redeemed or the number of peoples reached? The Biblical answer is that God's call for missions in Scripture *cannot* be defined merely in terms of crossing cultures to maximize the total number of individuals saved. Rather God's will for missions is that every people group be reached with the testimony of Christ and that a people be called out for his name from all the nations. It may be that this definition of missions will in fact result in the greatest possible number of white-hot worshipers for God's Son. But that remains for God to decide. Our responsibility is to define missions his way and then obey.

The ultimate goal of God in all of history is to uphold and display his glory for the enjoyment of the redeemed *from every tribe and tongue and people and nation.* The beauty of praise that will come to the Lord from the diversity of the nations is greater than the beauty that would come to him if the chorus of the redeemed were culturally uniform or limited. Moreover, there is something about God that is so universally praiseworthy and so profoundly beautiful, and so comprehensively worthy and so deeply satisfying that God will find passionate admirers in every diverse people group in the world. His true greatness will be manifest in the breadth of the diversity of those who perceive and cherish his beauty. The more diverse the people groups who forsake their gods to follow the true God, the more visible is God's superiority over all his competitors.

By focusing on all the people groups of the world God undercuts ethnocentric pride and puts all peoples back upon his free grace rather than any distictive of their own. This humility is the flip side of giving God all the glory. Humility means revelling in his grace not our goodness. In pressing us on to all the peoples God is pressing us further into the humblest and deepest experience of his grace, and weaning us more and more from our ingrained pride. In doing this he is preparing for himself a people – from all the peoples – who will be able to worship him with free and white-hot admiration.

Therefore the church is bound to engage with the Lord of Glory in his cause. It is our unspeakable privilege to be caught up with him in the greatest movement in history – the ingathering of the elect "from all tribes and tongues and peoples and nations" until the full number of the Gentiles come in, and all Israel is saved, and the Son of man descends with power and great glory as King of kings and Lord of lords and the earth is full of the knowledge of his glory as the waters cover the sea for ever and ever. Then the supremacy of Christ will be manifest to all and he will deliver the kingdom to God the Father and God will be all in all.

Afterword
The supremacy of God in going and sending
Tom Steller

Tom Steller is Pastor for Missions and Leadership Development, Bethlehem Baptist Church, Minneapolis, Minnesota.

There is a wonderful passage in the often neglected Epistle of 3 John which sums up the burden of this book beautifully. We want to leave you with its truth ringing in your mind and heart. There are only two ways for us to respond to the truth we have been considering about the supremacy of God in missions. We must either go out for the sake of his Name, or we must send and support such people who do, and do so in a manner worthy of God. Listen to the words of the apostle John who heard the heartbeat of Jesus as he leaned on his breast, and who listened with his own ears to the giving of the Great Commission:

(1) The elder to the beloved Gaius, whom I love in truth. (2) Beloved, I pray that in all respects you may prosper and be in good health, just as your soul prospers. (3) For I was very glad when brethren came and bore witness to your truth, that is, how you are walking in truth. (4) I have no greater joy than this, to hear of my children walking in the truth. (5) Beloved, you are acting faithfully in whatever you accomplish for the brethren, and especially when they are strangers; (6) and they bear witness to your love before the church; *and you will do well to send them on their way in a manner worthy of God. (7) For they went out for the sake of the Name, accepting nothing from the Gentiles. (8) Therefore we ought to support such men, that we may be fellow workers with the truth.*
(NASB)

It is worth noting well what makes a godly old man happy. The apostle John, who refers to himself simply as "the elder", is overjoyed. He has just received word that Gaius, one of his spiritual children, is walking in the truth. There is no greater joy than this!

What evidence compels this old apostle to be convinced that Gaius' soul is prospering? What is the truth in which Gaius is walking? Apparently some itinerant evangelists/ missionaries, whom John knew, had visited Gaius and were loved by him in some special way. They returned to the church of which John was a part and testified that Gaius treated them well, even though they were strangers to him. This so moved John that he wrote Gaius a letter to encourage him for walking in the truth and for acting faithfully. He wanted to urge Gaius to continue all the more. "You will do well to send them on their way in a manner worthy of God."

Gaius was admonished by the apostle to be a sender. This phrase "to send on one's way" occurs nine times in the New Testament and each one occurs in a missionary context.[1] The most descriptive verse is found in Titus 3:13. In this verse Paul writes to Titus, "Diligently help Zenas the lawyer and Apollos on their way so that nothing is lacking for them." From this verse we can learn that sending is something to be done diligently and is all inclusive – "so that *nothing* is lacking for them".

In 3 John this diligence and thoroughness are captured in the phrase "in a manner worthy of God" (v. 6). This elevates the importance of sending as high as can be imagined. It is a commandment of God (notice the "ought" of v. 8). The reason why we must send them in a manner worthy of God is that they go out for the sake of the Name. The Name of God is at stake in how we treat our missionaries. God is glorified when we support them substantially with our prayers, our money, our time, and myriad other practical ways (notice the "whatever" in v. 5). God is not glorified when our missionaries are simply a name on the back of the church bulletin or a line item in the budget.

It is not of secondary importance to be engaged in this ministry of sending. It is a very high calling. It is walking in the truth. It is the manifestation of a healthy and prospering soul. Senders are fellow workers with the truth. To send in a manner worthy of God is to call to excellence in the support of missionaries. It is a direct participation in God's purpose. The cruciality of sending cannot be over-emphasized. Therefore it must not be done in a shoddy manner, but rather in "a manner worthy of God".[2] There is a world of difference between a church "having" a missionary and a church "sending" a missionary. But when we send them in a manner worthy of God, then God is glorified, our souls prosper, and we are fellow workers with the truth. We are in sync with God's heartbeat and his purpose to be glorified among all the peoples.

But just as there is a God-centeredness to sending, there is also a God-centeredness to going. In fact, the two are intimately related. Listen to the apostle John's flow of thought: "You will do well to send them on their way *in a manner worthy of God. For* they went out *for the sake of the Name*, accepting nothing from the Gentiles. *Therefore* we ought to support *such* ones." According to this text only a certain kind of person is to be supported and sent to the mission field (notice the word "such"). Only those who *go out for the sake of the Name* ought to be supported.

Here is perhaps the best definition of "missionary" in the New Testament. A missionary is someone who goes out for the sake of the Name, accepting nothing from the Gentiles. Private material gain must not be the motive. And even genuine humanitarian concern, though crucial, is not the driving motive. Rather the missionary is propelled by a deep love for the Name and glory of God. Like the apostle Paul, the missionary's aim is to "bring about the obedience of faith among all the Gentiles, *for his name's sake*" (Romans 1:5).

The purpose of this book has not been merely to inform you of the supremacy of God in missions. Rather from start to finish we have sought to invite you to become more personally engaged in the cause of missions with a heart-felt, God-centered passion. Our aim has not been to exalt the missionary, but to exalt God and to exalt his mission. The precise nature of your engagement in the cause of missions will be different from that of any other person. Whether you go as a missionary or stay as a sender is a secondary issue. The primary issue is that whatever you do, you do it for the glory of God (1 Corinthians 10:31) and for the advance of his kingdom (Matthew 6:33) and with a view to its consummation which will embrace every tribe and tongue and people and nation (Matthew 24:14; Revelation 7:9).

David Bryant calls one who has this mindset a "world Christian".[3] Not every Christian is called to be a missionary. But every follower of Christ is called to be a world Christian. A world Christian is someone who is so gripped by the glory of God and the glory of his global purpose that he chooses to align himself with God's mission to fill the earth with the knowledge of his glory as the waters cover the sea (Habakkuk 2:14). Everything a world Christian does he does with a view to the hallowing of God's name and the coming of God's kingdom among all the peoples of the earth. The burning prayer of the world Christian is "Let the peoples praise thee, O God. Let all the peoples praise thee" (Psalm 67:3). So whether we are those who send or those who go, let us glory in the supremacy of God in missions and let us link arms together as we join the refrain of old, "Let the nations be glad!"

Notes

1. See especially the uses of *propempō*, in Acts 15:3; Romans 15:24; 1 Corinthians 16:6, 11; 2 Corinthians 1:16; and Titus 3:15.
2. John Stott commenting on v. 6 says, "They are not just to be received when they arrive, but to be so refreshed and provided for (no doubt with supplies of food and money) as to be sent forward in a manner worthy of God ... Such thoughtful sending forth of missionaries on their journey is not only a 'loyal thing' (v. 5, RSV), but a 'beautiful' thing (*kalos poiēseis, you will do well*)." *The Letters of John: An Introduction and Commentary* (Leicester: IVP, 1988), p. 225.
3. David Bryant has helped define and popularize the notion of "world Christian" in his book *In the Gap* (Downers Grove: IVP, 1979).

Index of
Scripture references

237